Michael J. Martin, PhD

JAPANESE MILITARY AND CIVILIAN AWARD DOCUMENTS

1868-1945

Schiffer Publishing Ltd
4880 Lower Valley Road • Atglen, PA 19310

Library of Congress Control Number: 2016944626

Designed by Molly Shields
Type set in Alexander Black/Times New Roman
ISBN: 978-0-7643-5202-7
Printed in Hong Kong

Published by Schiffer Publishing, Ltd.
4880 Lower Valley Road
Atglen, PA 19310
Phone: (610) 593-1777; Fax: (610) 593-2002
E-mail: Info@schifferbooks.com
Web: www.schifferbooks.com

Other Schiffer Books on Related Subjects:
Japanese Military Sake Cups 1894–1945 (978-0-7643-1881-8)
Japanese Generals 1926–1945 (978-0-7643-3754-3)
Japanese Admirals 1926–1945 (978-0-7643-3952-3)

CONTENTS

ACKNOWLEDGMENTS

I want to thank Richard Catalano for his advice, translation, and inspiration for this book. He provided valuable insights and historical information for this book. He actually wrote a couple of small sections of this book; however, he did not want official credit as an author for his work. Furthermore, his work in this field, which is documented on his website, has been outstanding. I thank Richard for his help and friendship during this project.

I want to thank Laura Wellman for her services as my photographer. She used her equipment, bought more equipment, and borrowed other equipment to photograph the material in this book. Laura brought energy to photo shoots that inspired me. I am grateful to have worked with her. If I did not have her services I think the book would have remained a fantasy.

I wish to thank a few more people. Fellow militaria collector Kris Meda provided the initial encouragement to take the leap of faith and submit a book proposal. I am grateful for his friendship. Pieter van Gulik provided invaluable material and historical information which was beyond my means of possessing. Last, Yukari Ura provided many of the translations of my documents and research on topics which are almost impossible to find in English.

Finally, I must thank my wife Christina. I thank her for helping me build my collection over the years and supporting me in crazy projects, like writing a book.

INTRODUCTION:

BASICS OF JAPANESE AWARD DOCUMENTS

I can remember the day that I became addicted to collecting Japanese award documents. It was the fall of 2005, and I was in my first year of graduate school. I had bought an Order of the Rising Sun 8th Class medal from a Japanese dealer on eBay. The medal included the award document that was just a curiosity piece for me. However, when the set came in the mail I quickly lost interest in the medal and became intrigued by the document. I studied the design of the document and marveled at the beautiful detail. I went to the library and checked out a few Japanese dictionaries and started to translate the document from scratch. This was a crazy idea at the time because I had no training in reading Japanese. I vividly remember my excitement at figuring out the date of the document after hours of translations. This one document gave me hours of enjoyment. My obsession with Japanese award documents began at this moment.

The reader should understand why I organized the book like I did. One considered option was to have pictorial reference of every class and variation of documents. This seemed initially logical, yet, I quickly

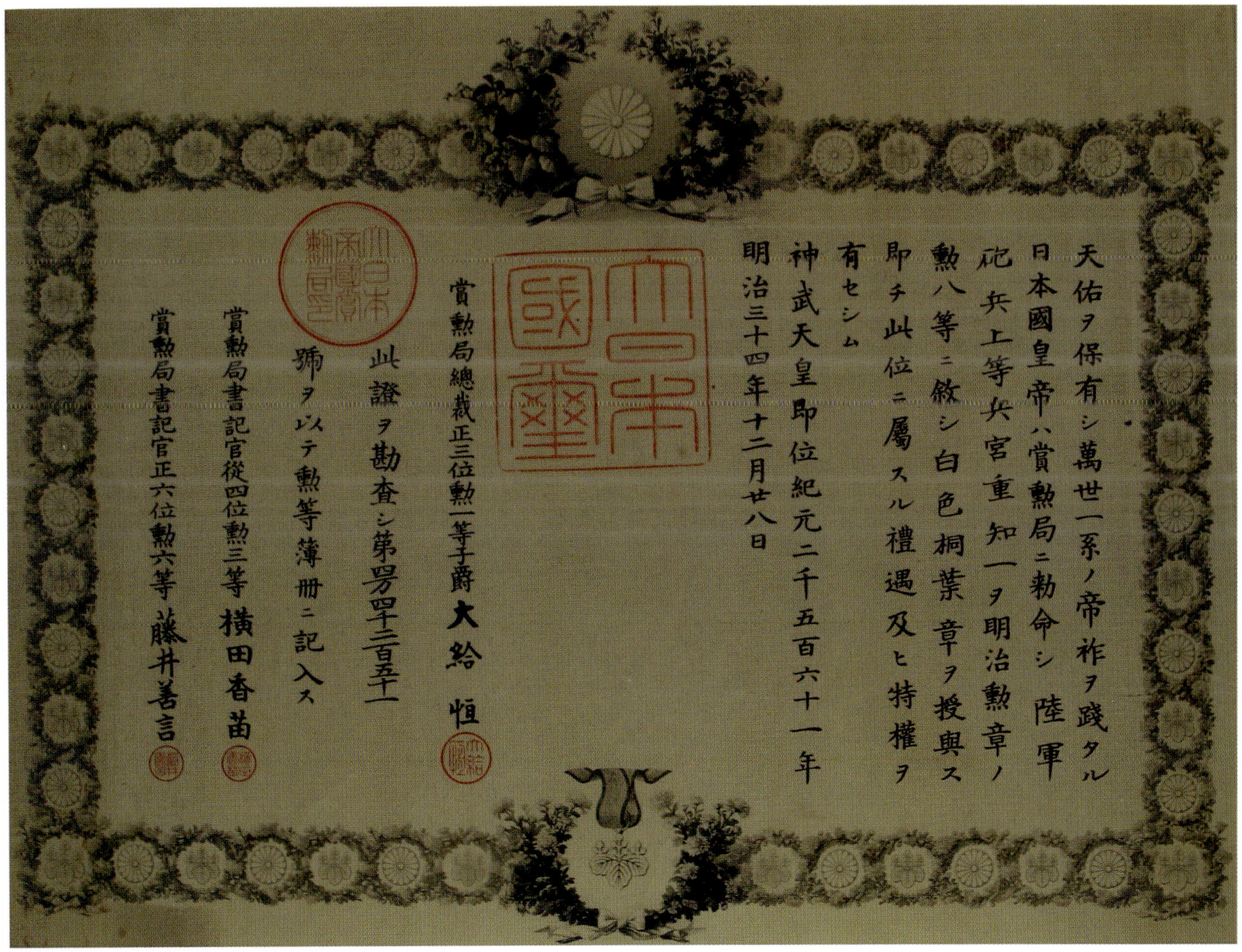
天佑ヲ保有シ萬世一系ノ帝祚ヲ踐タル
日本國皇帝ハ賞勲局ニ勅命シ 陸軍
砲兵上等兵宮重知一ヲ明治勲章ノ
勲八等ニ敍シ白色桐葉章ヲ授與ス
即チ此位ニ屬スル禮遇及ヒ特權ヲ
有セシム
神武天皇即位紀元二千五百六十一年
明治三十四年十二月廿八日
賞勲局總裁正三位勲一等子爵大給 恒
此證ヲ勘査シ第四千三百五十一
號ヲ以テ勲等簿冊ニ記入ス
賞勲局書記官從四位勲三等 横田香苗
賞勲局書記官正六位勲六等 藤井善言

This was the first document I ever owned. It is an Order of the Rising Sun 8th Class from 1901. This version of the Order of the Rising Sun 8th Class features a medal design in black and white. The later version features the medal in color. *Author's Collection*

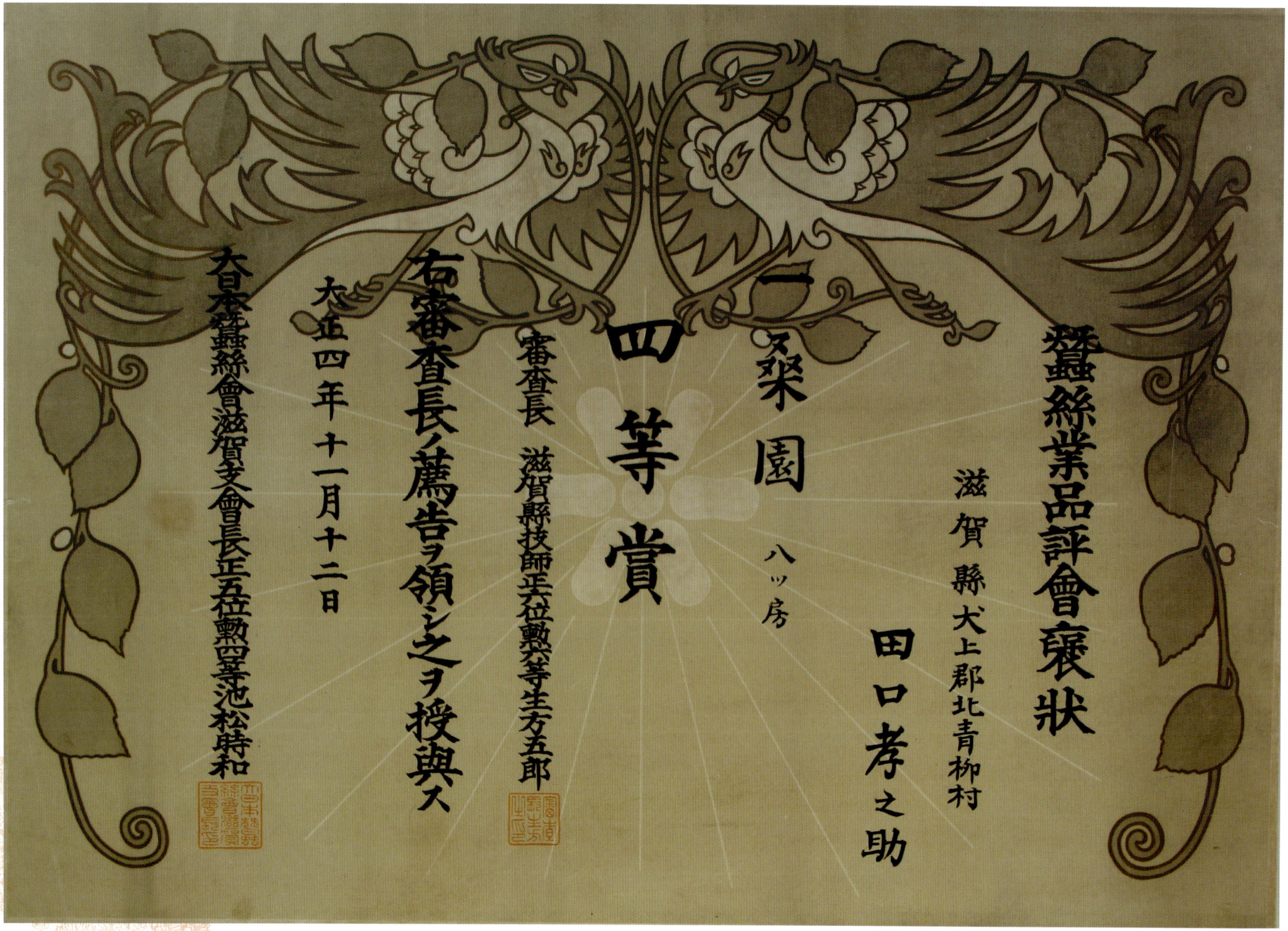

蠶絲業品評會褒狀

滋賀縣犬上郡北青柳村
田口孝之助

一桑園 八ツ房

四等賞

審査長 滋賀縣技師正六位勳六等生方五郎

右審査長ノ薦告ヲ領シ之ヲ授與ス

大正四年十一月十二日

大日本蠶絲會滋賀支會長正五位勳四等池松時和

Opposite: This gorgeous document is for a silkworm fair in 1915. The person had earned fourth place at the event. The competition was in Shiga Prefecture. This highly stylized document features two Ho-O birds facing each other with their tail feathers streaming around the document. These types of documents are fairly inexpensive, yet, quite stunning. *Author's Collection*

realized that this would be nearly impossible to do effectively. I personally did not have access to every order document. For instance, I could not find an Order of the Golden Kite 1st Class to take high quality pictures of. Thus, I avoided this format. I encourage fellow collectors to take on this challenge if they have access to these documents as I do not have the space in this book to include every order and medal document.

I opted to follow a format for this book that focused on the great variety of Japanese award documents and the history behind the documents. I do not claim to provide a complete catalog with pictures of all award documents. This would require volumes of books. I focus on introducing the collector to the field as well as the history.

This book should be viewed as a detailed introduction into the field of collecting Japanese award documents with tools for translating and understanding the documents. I placed our award information in chronological order, starting in the 1870s and ending in 1945, which corresponds to the Japanese Imperial Age. The Japanese government still awards documents that look very similar to the documents in this book, but modern documents are not included herein. The documents I selected are quite varied on purpose. I felt that including a wide selection of military and civilian award documents was necessary in order to completely introduce someone to the field. The challenge in this book is connecting the document to the history of Japan, which I hope I do well. I acknowledge that this book is slanted toward military documents. This stems from an increasing interest worldwide in collecting militaria (the hobby of collecting military items). I tried to include a variety of civilian documents and history in this book, though we recognize that these sections may not be as detailed as the military sections. I hope that the reader understands this context. For most of the documents featured herein, I include a translation of the key parts as well as detailed photographs of the document when feasible. Thus, I will try to highlight the history, beauty, and translation of the documents in this book.

Collecting Japanese award documents has become an afterthought to the possession of the actual award. Considering the popularity of collecting medals and the barriers to collecting documents in the West, this precedence seems logical. The goal of this book is to elevate the prestige of award documents and introduce the hobby to collectors.

There are a couple of significant reasons why collecting Japanese award documents is a rewarding field. A medal collector is sometimes interested in obtaining the award documents to match the medals and orders in their collection. I do not want to downplay this desire of the medal collector; however, I want to focus on the intentions of a document collector. First, the documents are quite beautiful. I argue that Japanese award documents are the most attractive of all the award documents from any major country before World War II. These beaytiful elements come from the intricate detail of the border, the striking look of the characters written vertically, the stunning representation of the award at the bottom of the document, and more. The most beautiful documents are not often the most expensive documents either. The collection shown in this book features some documents costing $5 that rival the attractiveness of $600 documents. This great variety of documents provides an easy entry point for collectors.

Opposite: This is welcome home document for a soldier who fought in the Russo–Japanese War, also called the 1904–05 War. The document is very attractive with a silver border and three flags at the top center. This particular victory celebration document was given by the Miyagi Prefecture Welcoming Association. The traditional Japanese system of eras would call the war Meiji 37–8 Years War because Meiji 37–38 are the years 1904–05. *Author's Collection*

The second reason for collecting Japanese award documents is the history behind the documents. The Japanese seem to have had a great propensity for awarding documents, which offers collectors a chance to collect pieces of history. The military historian can focus on a specific war as each war tended to have a prolific set of documents which were awarded to soldiers and sailors. These military documents include the typical orders and war medals from each conflict as well as promotions, military notebooks, war effort citations, welcome home messages, and wound documents related to the conflict. All of these documents provide individual glimpses and stories of real people involved in a conflict. This book tries to connect the collector pieces of this history, though it is just a brief glimpse. This richness of Japanese history can provide collectors and historians with stories tied to the documents.

People interested in the civilian history can be equally rewarded. Civilian award documents were given out for a variety of reasons and ranged from student diplomas to horse breeding citations to documents recognizing the deeds of firemen. I continually see new variations in documents as well as new occasions for giving the document. The emergence of new documents keeps the hobby fresh.

So, if Japanese award documents have this great appeal, then why is collecting these documents not popular in the West? The first barrier would be access. Unlike militaria from the Third Reich, Western soldiers did not literally take away as many Japanese artifacts, which had a reference to the Imperial Age home as souvenirs. Most of the Japanese award documents on the market today are coming directly from Japan. Internet auction sites like eBay and Yahoo Japan Auctions provide collectors with unprecedented access to these documents. Furthermore, there are dealers who are starting to specialize in providing Westerners access to Japanese militaria. Thus, the barrier of access to Japanese award documents is being removed.

The other barriers are just as significant and will be dealt with in this book. Western collectors can be intimidated by the Japanese characters on the documents. I agree that collecting documents, which you do not have a clue what they were awarded for, seems silly. This book will help the collector learn the basics of reading these documents. Interestingly enough, many of the documents are actually quite simple to decipher, the easiest being documents for orders and medals as well as many military documents. Once you know the basics, translating many of these types of documents takes little time. I provided translations for most of the documents featured in the book. Sometimes the translations are a little rough, especially on the civilian documents, so please keep that in mind if you are working on your own translations. Translating languages is not an exact science; it is an art that is hard to master. Nonetheless, you do not have to be a university trained linguistics expert to understand the basics of many documents. The other barriers to collecting Japanese award documents include storage and display, which will also be dealt with later in this book. The issue of translation needs attention first though.

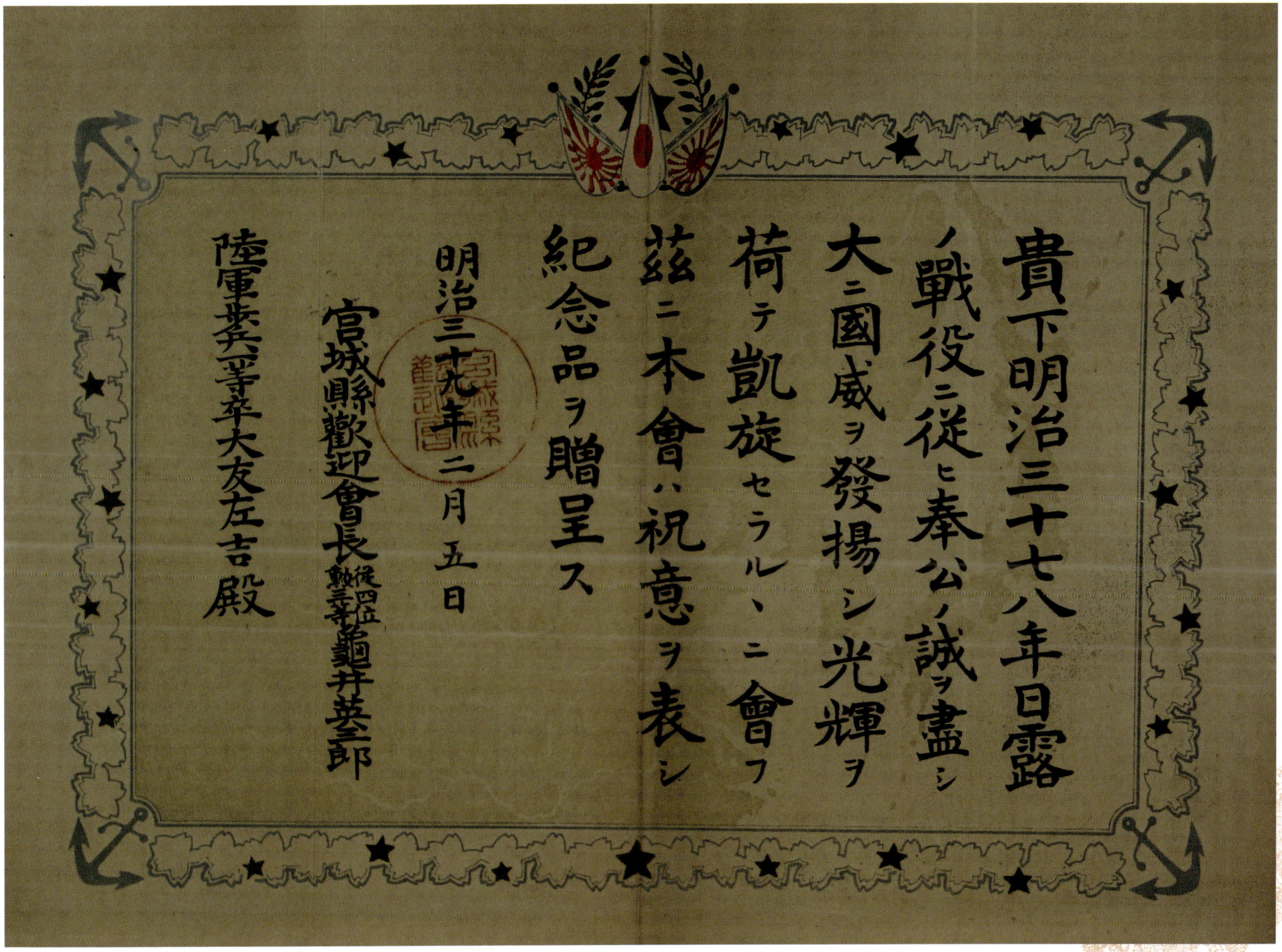

貴下明治三十七八年日露
ノ戰役ニ從ヒ奉公ノ誠ヲ盡シ
大ニ國威ヲ發揚シ光輝ヲ
荷テ凱旋セラル、ニ會フ
茲ニ本會ハ祝意ヲ表シ
紀念品ヲ贈呈ス

明治三十九年二月五日

宮城縣歡迎會長 従四位勲三等 龜井英三郎

陸軍歩兵一等卒大友左吉殿

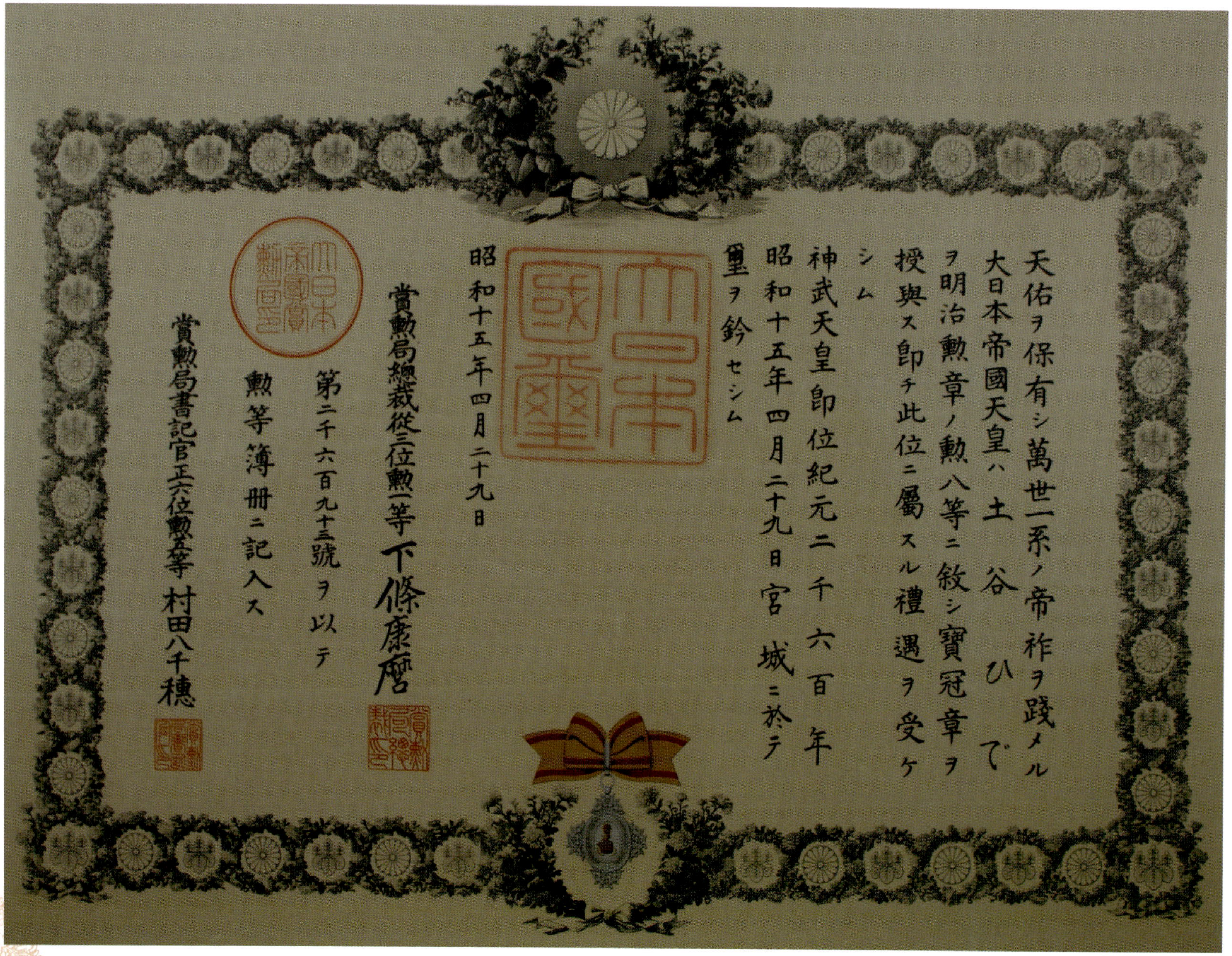

天佑ヲ保有シ萬世一系ノ帝祚ヲ踐メル
大日本帝國天皇ハ 土 谷 ひ で
ヲ明治勳章ノ勳八等ニ敘シ寶冠章ヲ
授與ス卽チ此位ニ屬スル禮遇ヲ受ケ
シム
神武天皇卽位紀元二千六百年
昭和十五年四月二十九日宮城ニ於テ
璽ヲ鈐セシム

大日本國璽

昭和十五年四月二十九日

賞勳局總裁從三位勳一等 下條康麿

大日本帝國賞勳局

第二千六百九十三號ヲ以テ
勳等簿冊ニ記入ス

賞勳局書記官正六位勳五等 村田八千穗

The Order of the Precious Crown 8th Class. This was the only order given just to women. This one is dated 1940. All Order of the Precious Crown Medals and Documents are hard to find, if not rare. They are also beautiful in design. The lower orders of Precious Crown medals were worn as a pin on the breast. Japanese orders were given in eight or seven different classes. The class awarded depended on the person's rank, so an 8th Class order represented the more common folk while the 1st Class order was received by the imperial family or high ranking officials. *Author's Collection*

A QUICK REFERENCE TO READING DOCUMENTS

Generally speaking, most of the larger documents are divided into two parts, the left and right sides. This is easy to determine since the national seal of Japan is usually impressed near the top center and a depiction of the medal is at the bottom center. Most times, the left and right sides are divided by this seal. For most collectors, the important information is on the right side. Please remember, this is the general format for the larger order and medal documents. Other documents can follow different formats; however, the key data translation points listed in this section can carry over to many other documents. Documents are meant to be read from right to left, so let's start on the right.

The information found on the right side is the name and class of the order or medal, the recipient's name, and the date of the award. In addition, the recipient's imperial rank, military rank, and previous earned orders can be found on some documents. The characters around this information basically states (in varying expressions over the years) that the order was given by the Japanese Emperor. The translations of order, war medal, and commemorative medal documents throughout this book will include much of this information.

The left side of larger documents also has the date of the award (on documents after 1911), and it also shows the individual medal number. There will also be the names and stamps of the officials of the Decoration Bureau. These signatures were printed, as were the red stamps.

Depending on the year of the document, the recipient's name can be found in the first or second line. Since these were printed documents with only the individual information being hand-written, it is easy to find the name by holding the document at an angle and seeing the change in ink.

Upon finding the name location, it is important to see if there is any personal information that precedes and then follows the actual name. There are a few points that can be found, and they appear in this order:

1. Deceased
2. Military Rank
3. Imperial Rank
4. Decorated rank
5. Personal name
6. Name of the Award
7. Date
8. Serial Number

Not all of these will appear on each document. Let's briefly look at each one. The reader can refer to the documents featured in the previous and next few pages for the possible placement of each data point. The data points are listed by number in the photographs to help the reader learn how to translate. We provide a variety of examples to help in this process:

1. Deceased: When a deceased soldier was given a posthumous award (故), the documents were all dated to the day of his death.

2. Military Rank: If the person was in the military, then their military rank would be listed on all commemorative and war medal documents. The practice of recording the military rank of the recipient on all order documents stopped sometime before 1918. This includes documents for the Order of the Golden Kite as it was a military award. If a rank was recorded, it would start with either army (陸軍) or navy (海軍) and then the rank. For example an army infantryman who was a private 1st class would be listed as 陸軍一等兵. Likewise, a navy ensign would be 海軍少尉. Please note that the branches of army (e.g., cavalry, infantry, engineers, etc.) will have a special character in the middle of the person's military rank. For example, an army infantryman (歩兵) would have this designation listed in the middle of the rank so that it would read service, branch, and then rank (陸軍歩兵一等兵). The characters for the different branches are listed in the appendices.

3. Imperial Rank: Imperial rank is sometimes referred to as noble or court rank. This was a fairly complicated system that showed one's standing in society. Generally speaking, there are sixteen ranks in eight classes, junior (従位) and senior rank (正位) being in each class. One could have a junior 8th Rank (the lowest—従八位) or a senior 8th Rank (one rank higher—正八位); the lower the number, the higher the rank. Not everyone possessed this kind of rank, so this is often missing.

4. Decorated Rank: This rank showed any previous orders received. There are two kinds of this rank, one set of characters for the Order of the Rising Sun, Sacred Treasure, and Precious Crown awards (勲等) and a different set of characters for the Order of the Golden Kite (功級–thus, Order of the Golden Kite 7th Class would read as 功七級). The bundling of three orders together with one set of characters can be frustrating for collectors. If you see a document for a Japanese male who earned an order of merit in the 6th Class (勲六等) you cannot tell if it was an Order of the Rising Sun or Order of the Sacred Treasure. Japanese women were only eligible to earn the Order of the Sacred Treasure and Precious Crown. Once you can memorize those Kanji (Chinese characters which are used in Japan), they are easy to spot. Again, as with the imperial rank, these are sometimes missing.

5. Personal Name: The family name comes first, from one to three Kanji in most cases, and then the personal name, with the same number of Kanji.

6. Name of the Award: The names of the orders and medals are listed in two different places depending on the award. The name of the order will be listed after the name of the person who earned the document. The name of the war or commemorative medal will be listed on the far right at the start of the documents. Because there are a wide variety of orders, medals, and other awards, which could have been awarded, we chose to provide a detailed list of these translated names in the appendices.

7. Date: The date of the bestowal of the document will be listed in a variety of places. The reader needs to become familiar with the dating system used in Imperial Japan, which relies on the name of the emperor to identify the year. The appendices will provide translations and a guide to help with dates.

8. Serial Number: The serial number of the order and medal is listed on the right side. The numbering for the orders appears to have been reset sometime right before the end of World War II or just afterwards. These numbers refer to the entry in the official registry rolls of the orders.

The following documents are a variety of the most common larger documents as well as a couple of smaller documents. These are for novice collectors to study and compare. If someone can master where to find these most important pieces of information then they are well on their way to understanding how to read Japanese award documents.

Opposite: An early period version of the order document, Order of the Rising Sun 6th Class from 1878, highlighted with key characters for translating. *Author's Collection*

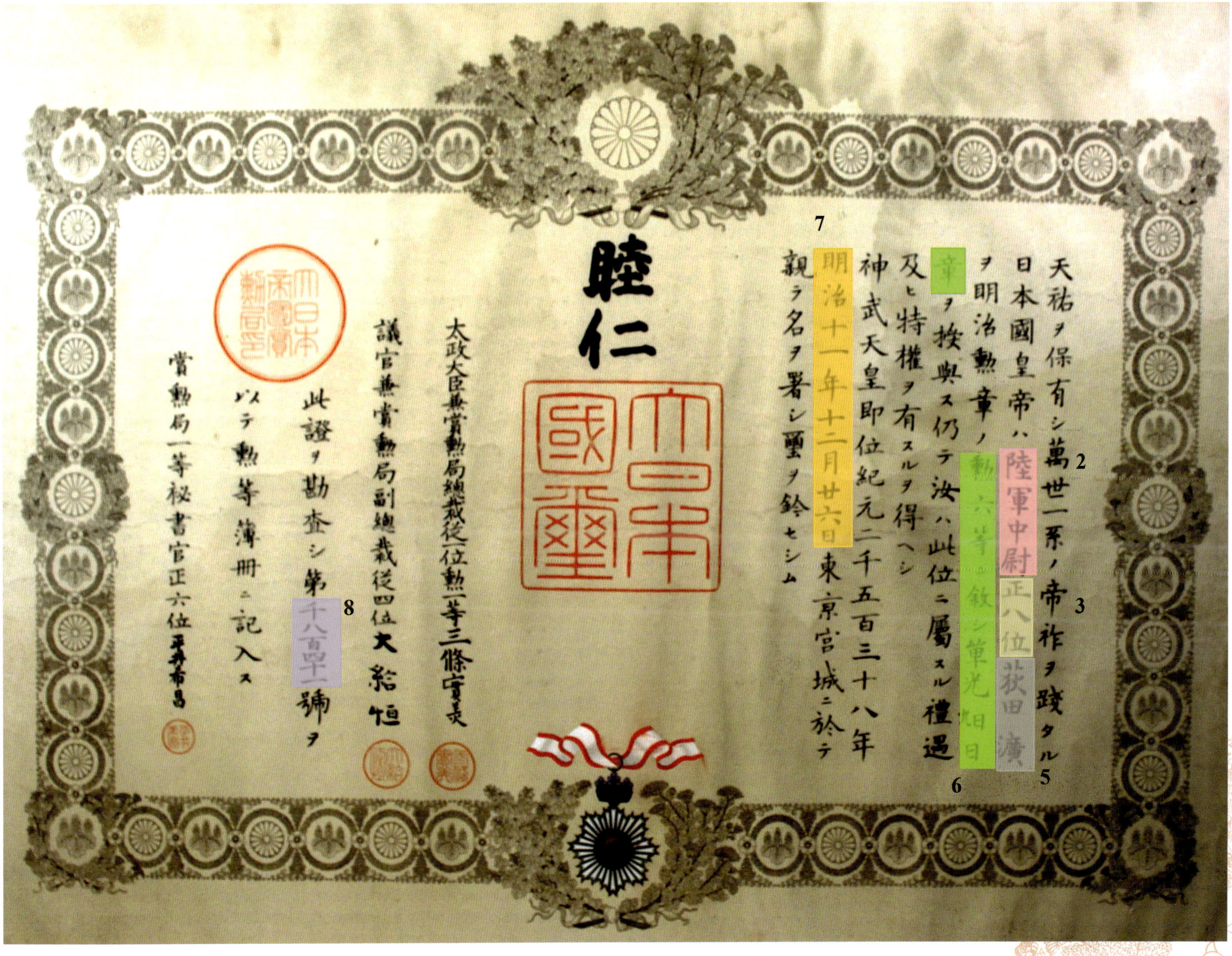
天祐ヲ保有シ萬世一系ノ帝祚ヲ踐タル
日本國皇帝ハ陸軍中尉正八位荻田濱
ヲ明治勳章ノ勳六等ニ敍シ單光旭日
章ヲ授與ス仍テ汝ハ此位ニ屬スル禮遇
及ヒ特權ヲ有スルヲ得ヘシ
神武天皇即位紀元二千五百三十八年
明治十一年十二月廿六日東京宮城ニ於テ
親ラ名ヲ署シ璽ヲ鈐セシム
睦仁
大日本國璽
太政大臣兼賞勳局總裁從一位勳一等三條實美
議官兼賞勳局副總裁從四位大給恒
此證ヲ勘査シ第千八百四十二號ヲ
以テ勳等簿冊ニ記入ス
賞勳局一等秘書官正六位平井希昌
大日本賞勳局
2
3
5
6
7
8

The center of the larger documents will have the national stamp of Japan in red, and at the bottom often a representation of the medal or ornate design. Some higher class awards will also have the emperor's signature above the national stamp. The section on the left of the stamp includes the information and signatures of two or three officials related to the document. The officials' title, ranks, previous awards, and their signature and personal stamp are included in a column.

Although the many rows of text on any Japanese award document can be daunting for someone who cannot read Japanese, remembering the positions of the most important information and then having a translation key (see appendices) can help solve many translation issues and add a lot of pleasure to collecting award documents.

The documents for Japanese war and commemorative medals are fairly similar to that of the documents of the four different Japanese orders. The differences are fairly important, though. The first difference is that the military rank of the recipient is always recorded. The way the name, rank, and rankings are written is the same as on the orders. When no rank is written, you can be certain it was given to a civilian. A related difference is that the name is always isolated in the second line, not integrated in the main text as on the order citations. This makes identifying the name easy. Differences between the war and commemorative

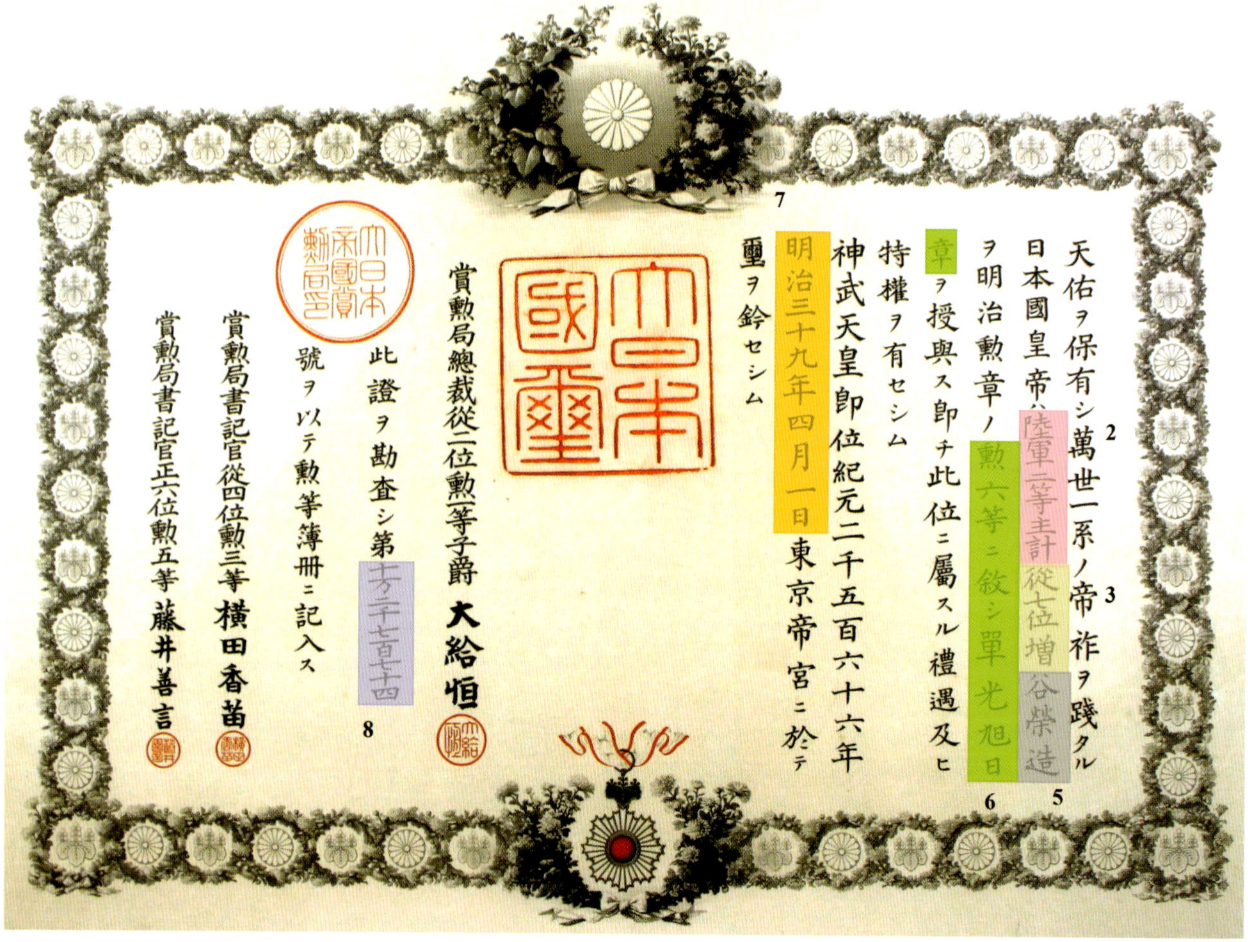
天佑ヲ保有シ萬世一系ノ帝祚ヲ踐タル
日本國皇帝ハ陸軍三等主計従七位増谷榮造
ヲ明治勲章ノ勲六等ニ叙シ単光旭日
章ヲ授與ス即チ此位ニ屬スル禮遇及ヒ
特權ヲ有セシム
神武天皇即位紀元二千五百六十六年
明治三十九年四月一日東京帝宮ニ於テ
璽ヲ鈐セシム
大日本國璽
賞勲局總裁従二位勲一等子爵 大給恒
此證ヲ勘査シ第十万二千七百七十四
號ヲ以テ勲等簿冊ニ記入ス
賞勲局書記官従四位勲三等 横田香苗
賞勲局書記官正六位勲五等 藤井善言

A mid-period version of the order document, Order of the Rising Sun 6th Class from 1906 (with flared ribbon), highlighted with key characters for translating. *Author's Collection*

Opposite: A late period version of the order document, Order of the Rising Sun 6th Class from 1937 (with straight ribbon), highlighted with key characters for translating. *Author's Collection*

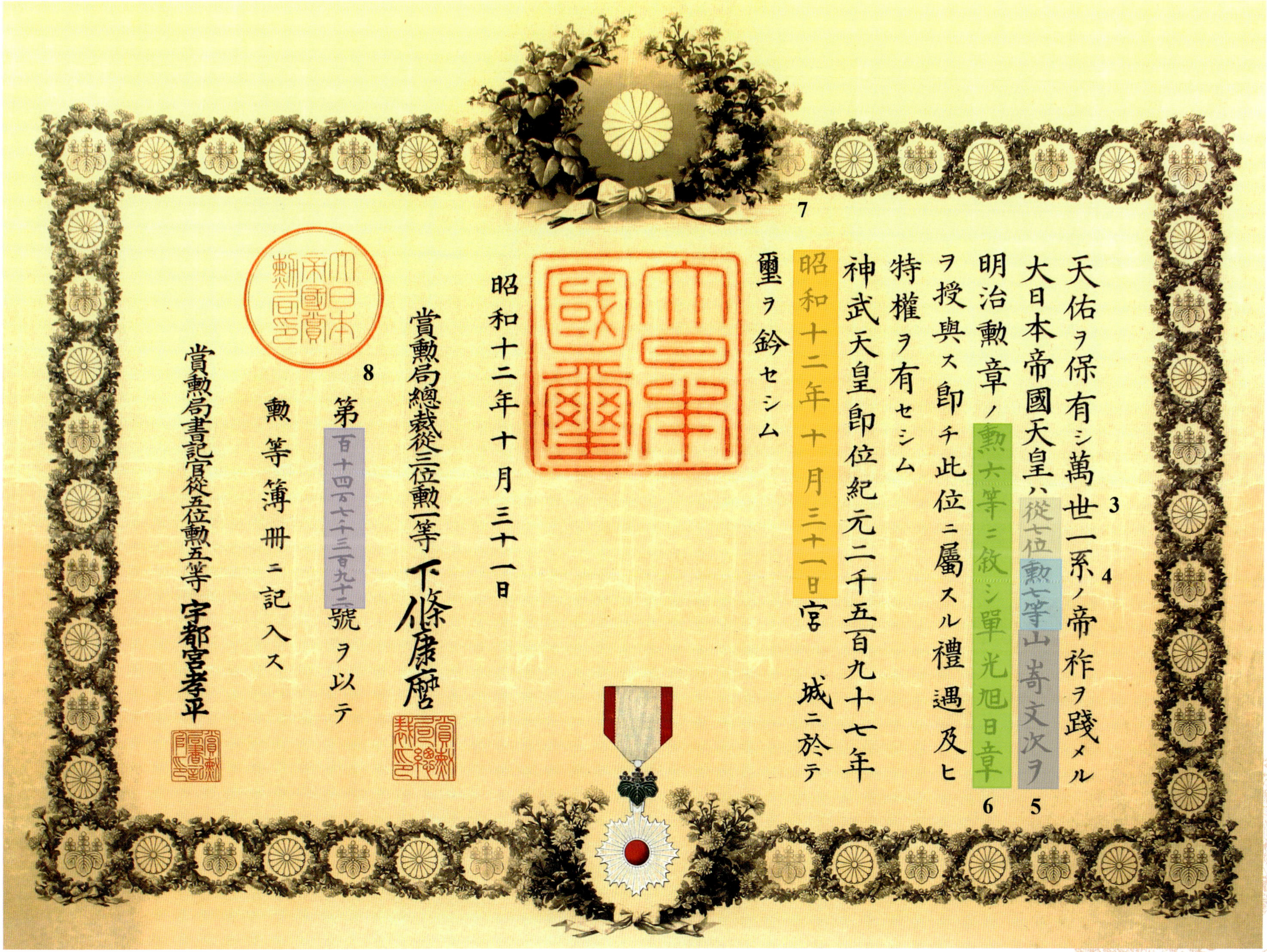

天佑ヲ保有シ萬世一系ノ帝祚ヲ踐メル
大日本帝國天皇ハ從七位勳七等山嵜文次ヲ
明治勳章ノ勳六等ニ敍シ單光旭日章
ヲ授與ス卽チ此位ニ屬スル禮遇及ヒ
特權ヲ有セシム
神武天皇卽位紀元二千五百九十七年
昭和十二年十月三十一日宮城ニ於テ
璽ヲ鈐セシム

大日本國璽

昭和十二年十月三十一日
賞勳局總裁從三位勳一等 下條康麿

第百十四万七千三百九十二號ヲ以テ
勳等簿冊ニ記入ス
賞勳局書記官從五位勳五等 宇都宮孝平

medal documents seem to be mostly stylistic. Border designs vary, and of the twelve commemorative medals, only four (the 1920 War Victory Medal, the 1920 National Census Medal, 1930 Korean Census Medal, and the 1940 National Foundation Medal) have a drawing of the medal. The other ten are blank in that area. All of the war medal documents show the medal.

The above information can enhance your enjoyment of reading and collecting documents. They contain quite a lot of information, so they are excellent ways to deepen the pleasure of collecting while learning.

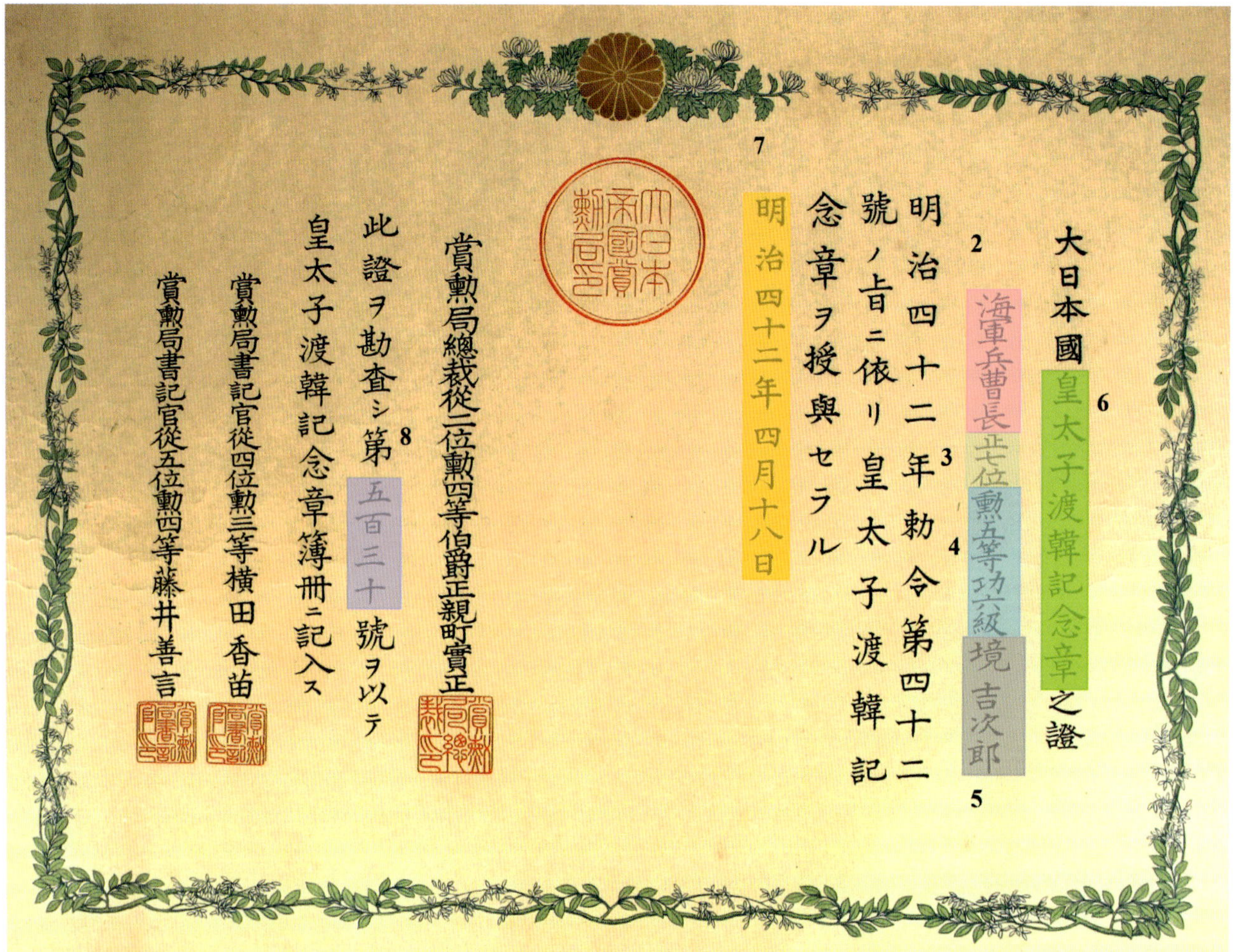
大日本國皇太子渡韓記念章之證

海軍兵曹長正七位勲五等功六級 境吉次郎

明治四十二年勅令第四十二號ノ旨ニ依リ皇太子渡韓記念章ヲ授與セラル

明治四十二年四月十八日

賞勲局總裁従二位勲四等伯爵正親町實正

此證ヲ勘査シ第五百三十號ヲ以テ皇太子渡韓記念章簿冊ニ記入ス

賞勲局書記官従四位勲三等横田香苗

賞勲局書記官従五位勲四等藤井善言

A commemorative medal document, Crown Prince's Voyage to Korea from 1909, highlighted with key characters for translating. *Author's Collection*

Opposite: A war medal document, 1904–05 War, or Russo-Japanese War, from 1906, highlighted with key characters for translating. *Author's Collection*

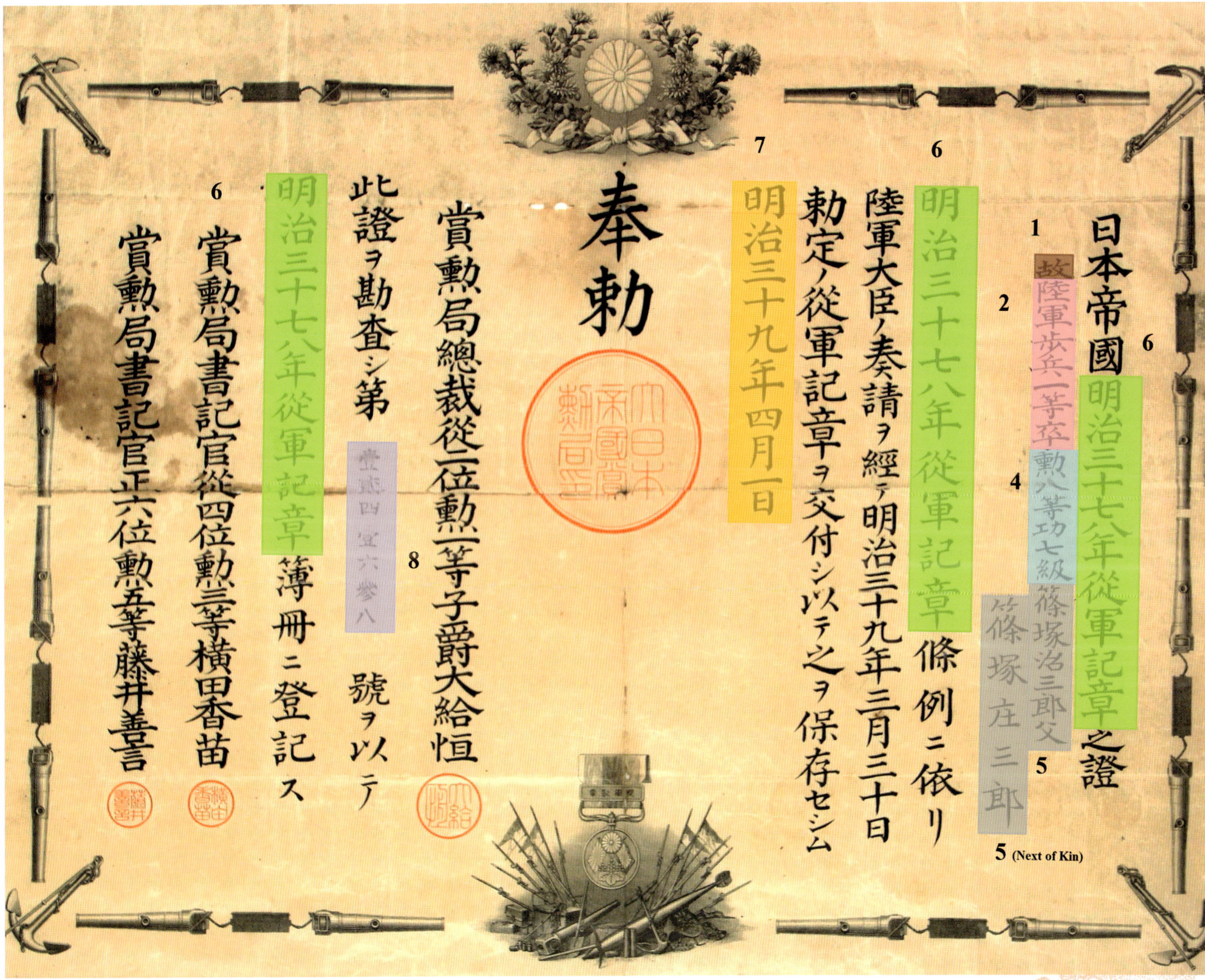

7 6 1 2 4 5 6

日本帝國 故 陸軍歩兵一等卒 勲八等功七級 篠塚治三郎父 篠塚庄三郎 明治三十七八年從軍記章之證

明治三十七八年從軍記章條例ニ依リ
陸軍大臣ノ奏請ヲ經テ明治三十九年三月三十日
勅定ノ從軍記章ヲ交付シ以テ之ヲ保存セシム

明治三十九年四月一日

奉勅

賞勲局總裁從二位勲一等子爵大給恒

此證ヲ勘査シ第壹貳四空六參八號ヲ以テ
明治三十七八年從軍記章簿冊ニ登記ス

賞勲局書記官從四位勲三等横田香苗

賞勲局書記官正六位勲五等藤井善言

6 8 5 (Next of Kin)

支那事變從軍記章之證

陸軍騎兵中佐從五位勳四等藤村作三

支那事變從軍記章

令ノ旨ニ依リ

從軍記章ヲ授與セラル

昭和十三年十月十二日

賞勳局總裁從三位勳一等下條康麿

第六万五千四百十九號ヲ以テ支那事變

從軍記章簿冊ニ記入ス

賞勳局書記官從五位勳五等宇都宮孝平

A war medal document, China Incident from 1938, highlighted with key characters for translating. *Author's Collection*

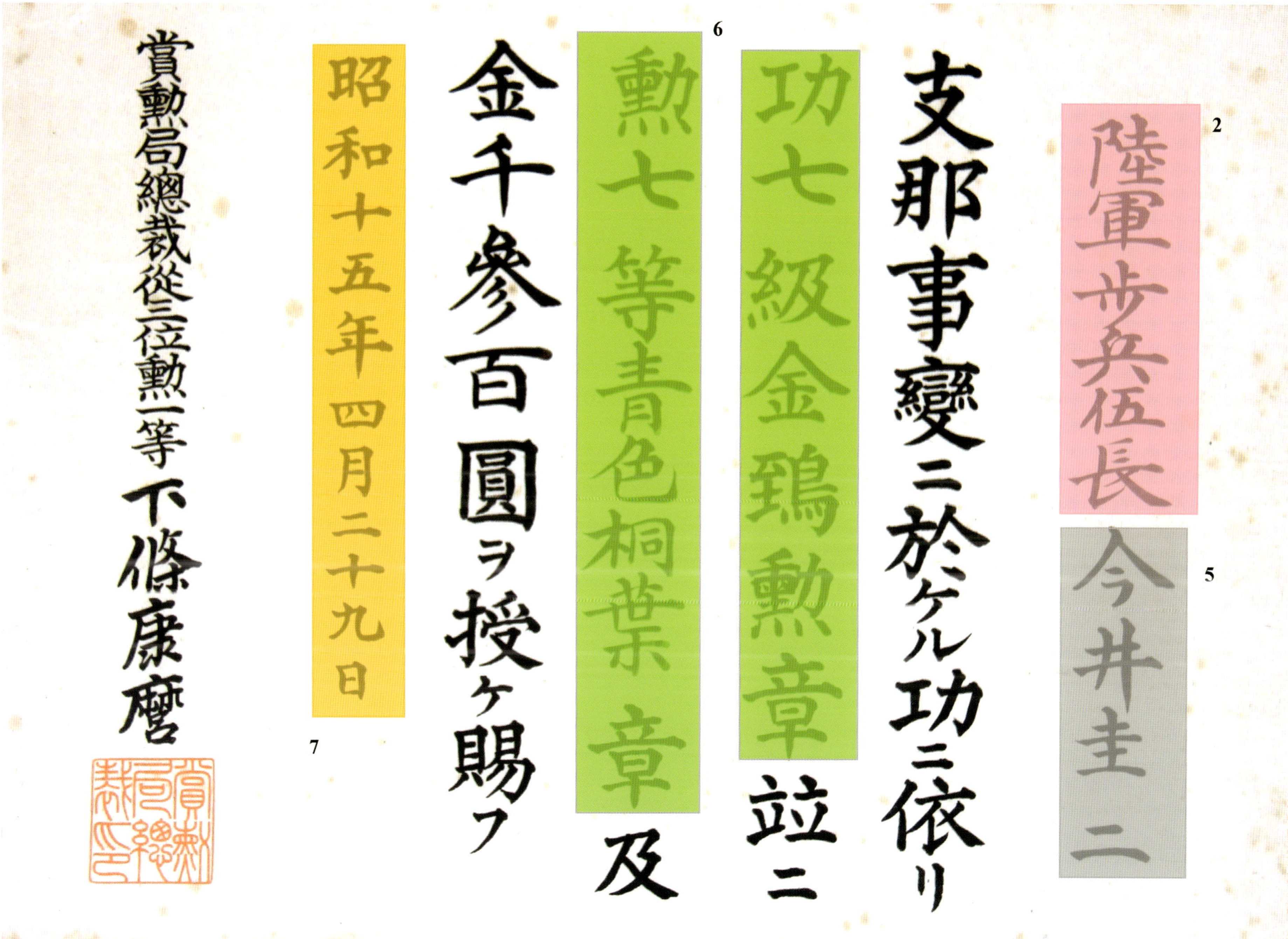
陸軍歩兵伍長
今井圭二
支那事變ニ於ケル功ニ依リ
功七級金鵄勳章竝ニ
勳七等青色桐葉章及
金千參百圓ヲ授ケ賜フ
昭和十五年四月二十九日
賞勳局總裁從三位勳一等下條康麿

A small version of an award document, given for Order of the Golden Kite 7th Class and Order of the Rising Sun 7th Class during the China Incident in 1940, highlighted with key characters for translating. *Author's Collection*

1 MEIJI RESTORATION:

BIRTH OF THE EMPIRE (1868–1894)

The transformation of Japan from a small feudal state on the edge of Asia into a regional power has been described as one of the greatest transformations in the modern era. While documents from this twenty-five-year time period are harder to find, the events represented by these documents are critical to an accurate portrayal of the historical development of Japan. The economic and social changes within the Meiji Restoration set the groundwork for military victories and the creation of an empire at the start of the twentieth century.

This painting depicts a delegation from the United States visiting Japanese officials. The years following Matthew Perry's forcing the Japanese to sign a trade treaty with the United States were chaotic for the Japan government. The subsequent reign of Emperor Meiji would be just as transformative. Many historians regard the Meiji Restoration as one of the greatest social transformations of a society in the modern age. Japan would emerge from this time period reborn and ready to enter the power struggle in Asia. *Author's Collection*

The End of the Shogunate Reign and Establishment of Imperial Rule

The events which brought an end of the Shogunate reign are linked to the colonization of Eastern Asia and the Pacific region by Western nations. Japanese leaders, who were usually part of the samurai class, had cultivated a policy of isolation from Western powers for hundreds of years. The increased activity of Western navies in East Asian waters and the Opium Wars in China brought home the fact that eventually Japan would have to deal with the Western nations. A debate ensued on how to deal with Westerners. Many samurai favored defending the homeland from invasion while some preferred trade. The breakthrough came in 1854 when American Commodore Matthew Perry forced a trade deal between the United States and Japan. After a few minor incidents with Western nations many Japanese leaders came to realize that Japan was not ready to fight Western powers that had a significant technological edge. They decided to slowly open the county and adopt certain Western technologies that could strengthen their military and eventually allow them to throw the Westerners out of Japan.[1]

The political situation in Japan was quite complicated in the time before Emperor Meiji. The country was ruled by the shogun of the Tokugawa shogunate. The emperor of Japan, who at this time was Emperor Kōmei, had religious and political power as well as being the symbolic leader of Japan. The Shogun had military power and used this power to be the de facto leader of Japan. This particular arrangement was in place for over 200 years. The appearance of Westerners spurred political and domestic unrest, as well as violence and war between the numerous domains (regions of Japan). A growing group of daimyo, domain leaders, supported the idea of restoring Imperial rule in Japan and eliminating the role of the Shogun. This idea came to a reality with the defeat of Shogun supporters during the middle of the Boshin Wars in 1868–69. Prince Mutsuhito, who had become Emperor Meiji in 1867 after his father died, became the leader of Japan. This backwater Asian nation was set to undergo one of the greatest social and economic revolutions in modern history.[2]

This is Emperor Meiji posing in his Western military uniform. He was at the center of many of the Western reforms, which were critical to the transformation of Japan during his reign. Many of these actions alienated traditional Japanese military leaders and politicians. This included stripping the samurai of many of their privileges. Despite these early conflicts, Emperor Meiji was a beloved emperor. *Author's Collection*

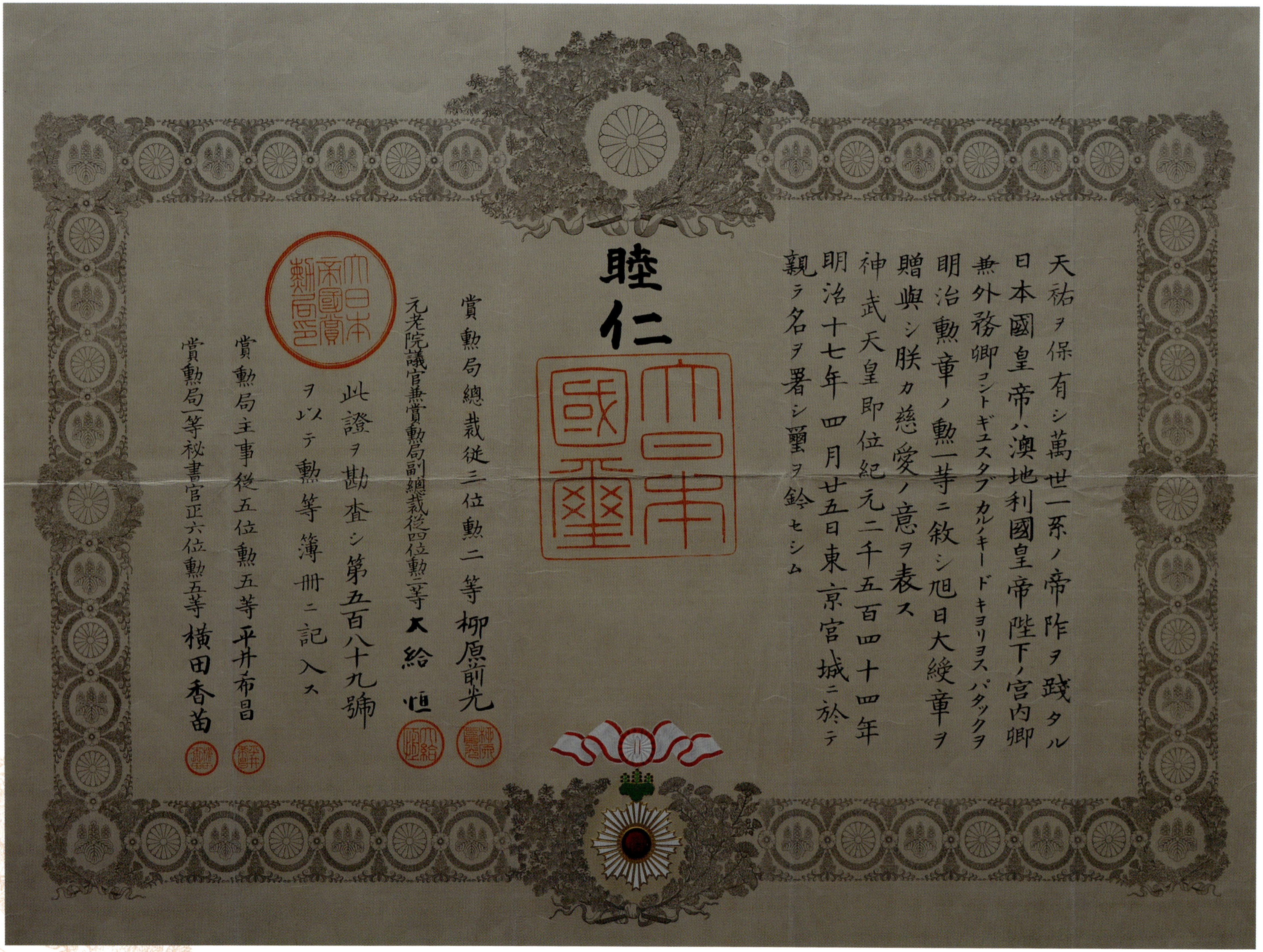
天祐ヲ保有シ萬世一系ノ帝祚ヲ踐タル
日本國皇帝ハ澳地利國皇帝陛下ノ宮内卿
兼外務卿コントギユスタフカルノキードキヨリヨスパタックヲ
明治勲章ノ勲一等ニ敘シ旭日大綬章ヲ
贈與シ朕カ慈愛ノ意ヲ表ス
神武天皇即位紀元二千五百四十四年
明治十七年四月廿五日東京宮城ニ於テ
親ラ名ヲ署シ璽ヲ鈐セシム

睦仁

賞勲局總裁従三位勲二等 柳原前光
元老院議官兼賞勲局副總裁従四位勲二等 大給恒

此證ヲ勘査シ第五百八十九號
ヲ以テ勲等簿冊ニ記入ス

賞勲局主事従五位勲五等 平井希昌
賞勲局一等秘書官正六位勲五等 横田香苗

Opposite: Translation of Order of the Rising Sun 1st Class, right side only: "Through the honor of the immortal Emperor, the Empire of Japan bestows this award. Count Gustav Kalnoky von Korospatak. Order of the Rising Sun 1st Class. Imperial Year 2544 [1884]. Meiji 17 [1884], April 25. Tokyo Imperial Shrine."
Courtesy of an Anonymous Collector

The document pictured on the previous page is a very rare piece. It is an award document for an Order of the Rising Sun 1st Class from 1884 given to Count Gustav Kalnoky von Korospatak who was the Minister of Foreign Affairs of the Empire of Austria-Hungary in 1884. Orders in the first class were some of the highest awards given. The Order of the Rising Sun was the first order instituted in 1875. The early documents looked quite different than their later version. They were also a little larger on average. The newer version was introduced sometime around 1890, around the same time as the institution of the Orders of the Sacred Treasure and Golden Kite. These aforementioned orders were never featured on the older order pattern. The document also features the signature of Emperor Meiji. The emperor signed many of these early documents, even documents for orders as low as the 6th class. He soon restricted his signature to higher class documents as more and more orders were bestowed. 1st class documents were reserved for highest ranking nobles and military men of Japan. High end orders were also given to high ranking dignitaries from around the world, which is a tradition that continues in many countries.

The role the Emperor Meiji had during the Meiji Restoration is debatable. Mutsuhito (the given name of Emperor Meiji) was just a teenager when his father, Emperor Komei, died in January of 1867. Mutsuhito began his reign in February and by November he was in danger of being deposed. The transition from shogun reign to imperial reign started a conflict between opposing clans called the Boshin War in 1868. The samurai representing the old military shogun-controlled system were severely defeated and the war was over four months later. With the old military system out of the way, the Meiji Restoration could initiate changes that included providing universal elementary education for boys and girls and doing away with the four-tiered class structure. The young Emperor Meiji was surrounded by brilliant and capable politicians and organizers who designed and implemented the restoration. It would be unfair to suggest that he had no role in the restoration. Emperor Meiji made decisions on critical matters and intervened on critical issues, such as the decision not to invade Korea in the early 1870s. He also made tours around Japan to galvanize public support. The mythology that grew around Emperor Meiji was his lasting legacy. He became the face of a growing economic and military

This is a stunning view of the Order of the Rising Sun 1st Class medal. The medal is surrounded by a floral motif that was standard in early Rising Sun documents (before 1890).
Courtesy of an Anonymous Collector

powerhouse. Emperor Meiji was not viewed as a living god like his grandson during World War II; yet, the success of the Meiji Restoration would ensure that Emperor Meiji's legacy would last through history.[3]

The Japanese government faced numerous issues at the start of the Meiji reign. The first move was one of the most drastic. The system of domains ruled by daimyos was abolished. Some daimyos were given titles and roles in provincial government; however, this move to reorganize Japan took it out of the feudal age in just a few years. The central government also slowly replaced the samurai and shogun bureaucracy with a central bureaucracy that worked under the emperor. The biggest change came in 1876 when the hereditary privileges of the samurai class were abolished. Many of the samurai were receiving stipends for just being samurai. Their military skills of swordsmanship and archery had little use in the new Japan. The central government encouraged systems of meritocracy, which gave power to the most capable rather than those of a particular class. Naturally, some of the samurai resisted this change.[4]

The chrysanthemum watermark was found on these older documents and on many more to come. *Author's Collection*

The border of the older Order of the Rising Sun Documents features alternating imperial chrysanthemums and paulownia flowers. This document border style would be replaced around 1890. I have not seen either Order of the Sacred Treasure or Golden Kite with this border style as it predates these orders.
Courtesy of an Anonymous Collector

The top center design features flowers around the imperial chrysanthemum seal, which would become a standard style for many documents. Below the document is the signature of Emperor Meiji. Almost any order document which was in the 1st Class would feature the emperor's signature. Emperor Meiji signed many lower class orders in the early years as well. This includes 6th Class Orders of the Rising Sun. He slowly relegated his signature to higher ranking documents as the number of documents being awarded increased dramatically. One could imagine the honor of earning a document with the emperor's signature. *Courtesy of an Anonymous Collector*

Creation of a Modern Military

The creation of a modern military was not an easy undertaking, but, it was extremely important for the security and meritocracy of Japan. The featured document shown here was for an early member of the Imperial Guard. Documents from this prestigious military unit are hard to find. This document also illustrates how commoners in Japan could obtain rank and leadership in the Meiji Japanese military. The Imperial Guard was founded in 1867 and was made up of former samurai and retainers. The unit would soon grow to a full division with conscripted Japanese. The idea of conscription was a dangerous idea to the old military elite of samurai. When the idea was first discussed in 1869, a group of samurai assassinated a political leader who advocated for conscription. The samurai viewed themselves as the military of Japan and feared arming and training commoners. The first Japanese national army in 1871 was comprised of samurai from a variety of daimyos. However, Japanese government leaders believed that the Western practice of mass conscription was the most effective way of building loyalty to the emperor for all Japanese. The system of conscription was started in 1873. The first few years of conscription was meet with resistance from the populace. The Satsuma Rebellion of 1877 created a military urgency with the general public, but led to an acceptance of conscription in the military.[5]

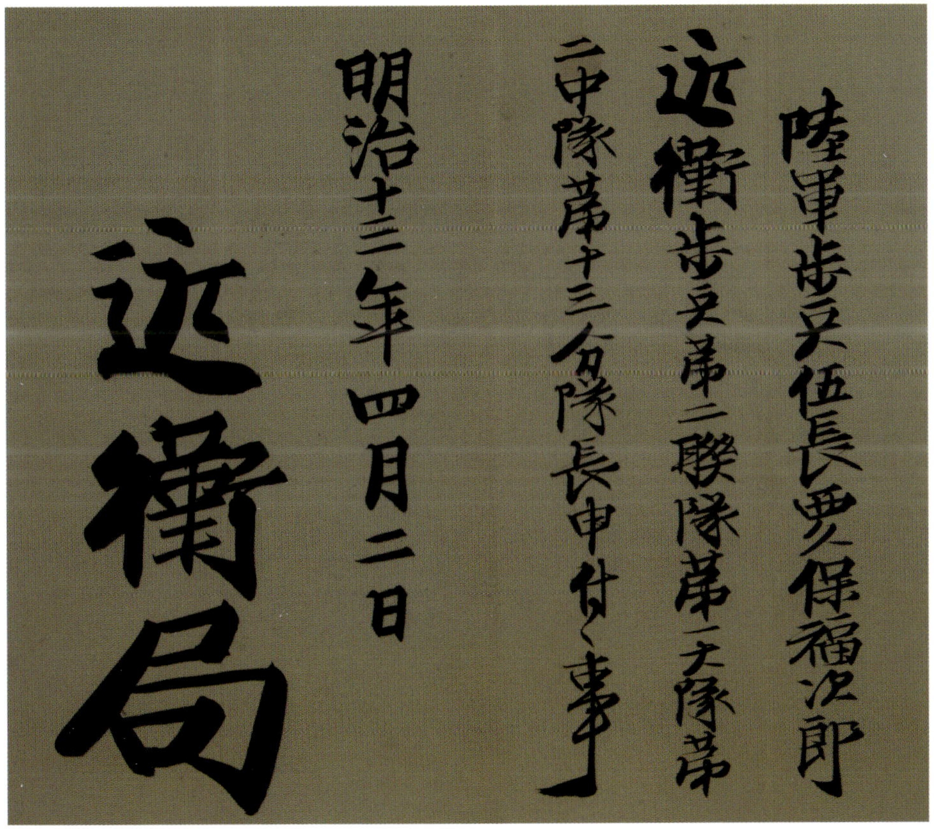

陸軍歩兵伍長西久保福次郎
近衛歩兵第二聯隊第一大隊第
二中隊第十三分隊長申付ク事
明治十三年四月二日
近衛局

Translation of Military Assignment document from the Imperial Guards: "Army Infantry Corporal Nishikubo Fukujirō. You have been assigned to lead the 13th Squad, 2nd Company, 1st Battalion, 2nd Infantry Regiment, Imperial Guard. Meiji 13 [1880]. Imperial Guard Bureau." *Author's collection*

This is the rare watermark for the Japanese Imperial Guard. The characters translate as Imperial Guard Bureau. *Author's collection*

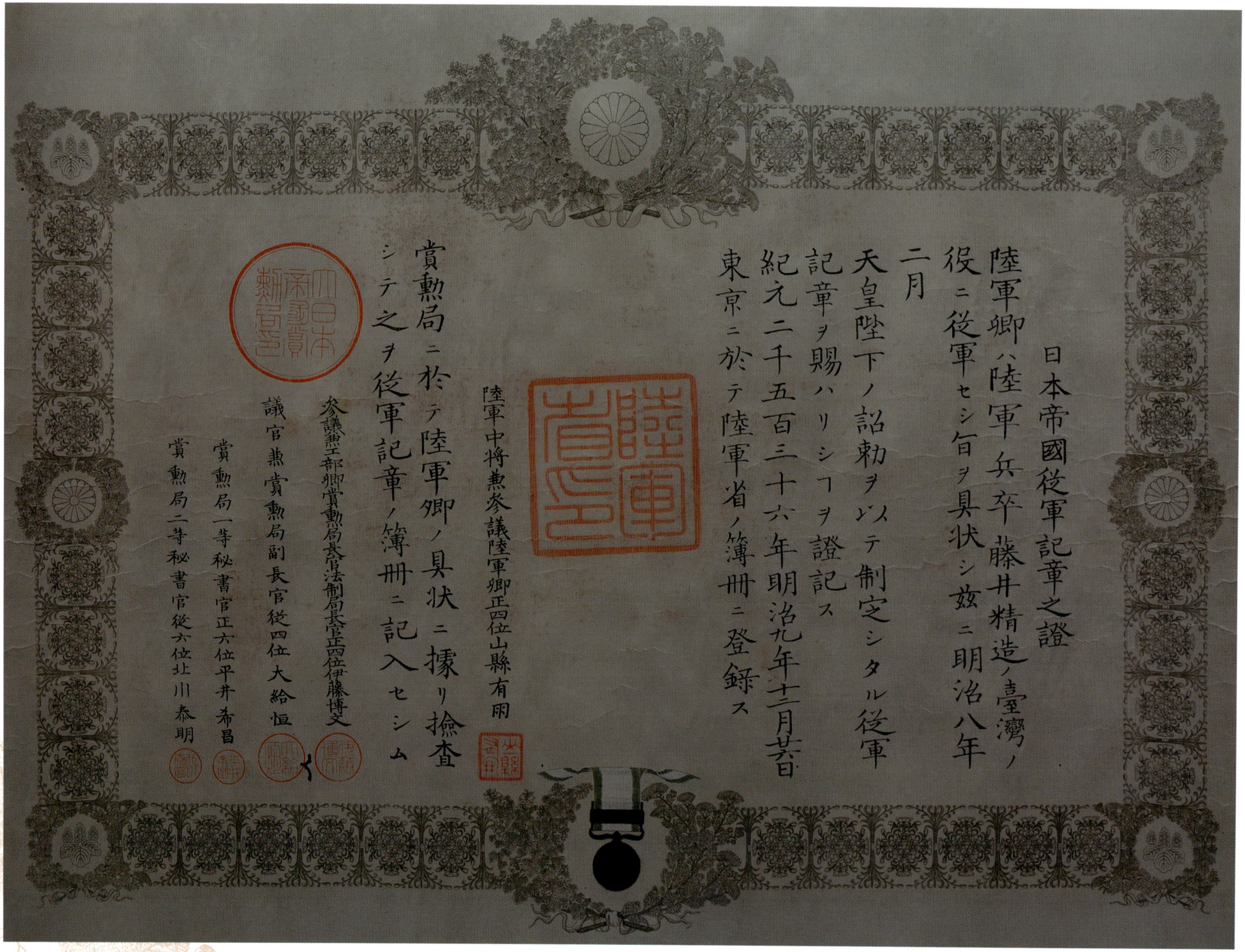
日本帝國從軍記章之證
陸軍卿ハ陸軍兵卒藤井精造ノ臺灣ノ
役ニ從軍セシ旨ヲ具狀シ茲ニ明治八年
二月
天皇陛下ノ詔勅ヲ以テ制定シタル從軍
記章ヲ賜ハリシコヲ證記ス
紀元二千五百三十六年明治九年十二月廿
東京ニ於テ陸軍省ノ簿冊ニ登錄ス
陸軍中將兼參議陸軍卿正四位山縣有朋
賞勳局ニ於テ陸軍卿ノ具狀ニ據リ撿査
シテ之ヲ從軍記章ノ簿冊ニ記入セシム
參議兼工部卿賞勳局長官法制局長官正四位伊藤博文
議官兼賞勳局副長官從四位大給恒
賞勳局一等秘書官正六位平井希昌
賞勳局二等秘書官從六位北川泰明

Opposite: Translation of 1874 War Medal, right side only: "Record of Awarding the Imperial Japan Dispatch Medal. Army Private Fujii Seizou receives this medal as a reward for his dispatch to Taiwan in Meiji 8 [1875] February. Based upon the rescript of His Imperial Majesty, this is a record of the awarding of the Dispatch Medal. Imperial Year 2536, Meiji 9 [1876] December 26 at the Imperial Palace. To be recorded in the Army Ministry rolls." *Courtesy of an Anonymous Collector*

The 1874 War Medal was awarded for an event which resembled more of an expedition than a war. The whole event was quite unusual; yet, it set a pattern for Japanese expansion. In 1871 several dozen sailors from Okinawa were killed after being shipwrecked on Formosa (now called Taiwan). Formosa was controlled by the Qing Chinese government though this control was weak. Okinawa was part of the Ryūkyū Islands, and the Japanese government claimed sovereignty of these islands. The islands were also claimed by China. The Japanese government did not act immediately. They actually had intentions to invade Korea. This idea was put on hold in 1873 for a variety of reasons. However, the government leaders decided that an expedition to Formosa in 1874 could help solidify their claims in the Ryūkyū Islands and position Japan as a power in Asia. The Japanese government sent several thousand samurai to Formosa on a punitive mission. The expedition had little actual military action, though many samurai died from disease. The Chinese government paid the Japanese government an indemnity, and the Japanese left the island by late 1874. The expedition gave Japan complete control of the Ryūkyū Islands, which were annexed and converted into the Okinawa Prefecture by the end of the decade.[6]

The newly formed conscription army was put to the test in 1877 when a large group of samurai rose up in armed rebellion against the new government. The Satsuma Rebellion was a pivotal test for the new military and imperial government. The samurai class had slowly lost their feudal rights. In 1876, they had lost the right to carry swords and then they lost their stipends. Many of the samurai were unhappy with these developments. Open rebellion emerged in the Satsuma Domain in January 1877. The rebellion was relegated to just the southern island of Kyushu. The rebellion required the Japanese government to use the entirety of their new conscripted army, 40,000 troops. The samurai were soundly defeated by the peasant conscripted army in September 1877. The end of the rebellion signified the end of any organized resistance to the Meiji government and the Meiji Restoration.[7]

The first war medal document mimicked the design of early order documents. The medal would be featured in the center around a floral wreath. Later war medal documents would feature the war medal surrounded by various implements of battle. The document was awarded in 1876 and is extremely rare. *Courtesy of an Anonymous Collector*

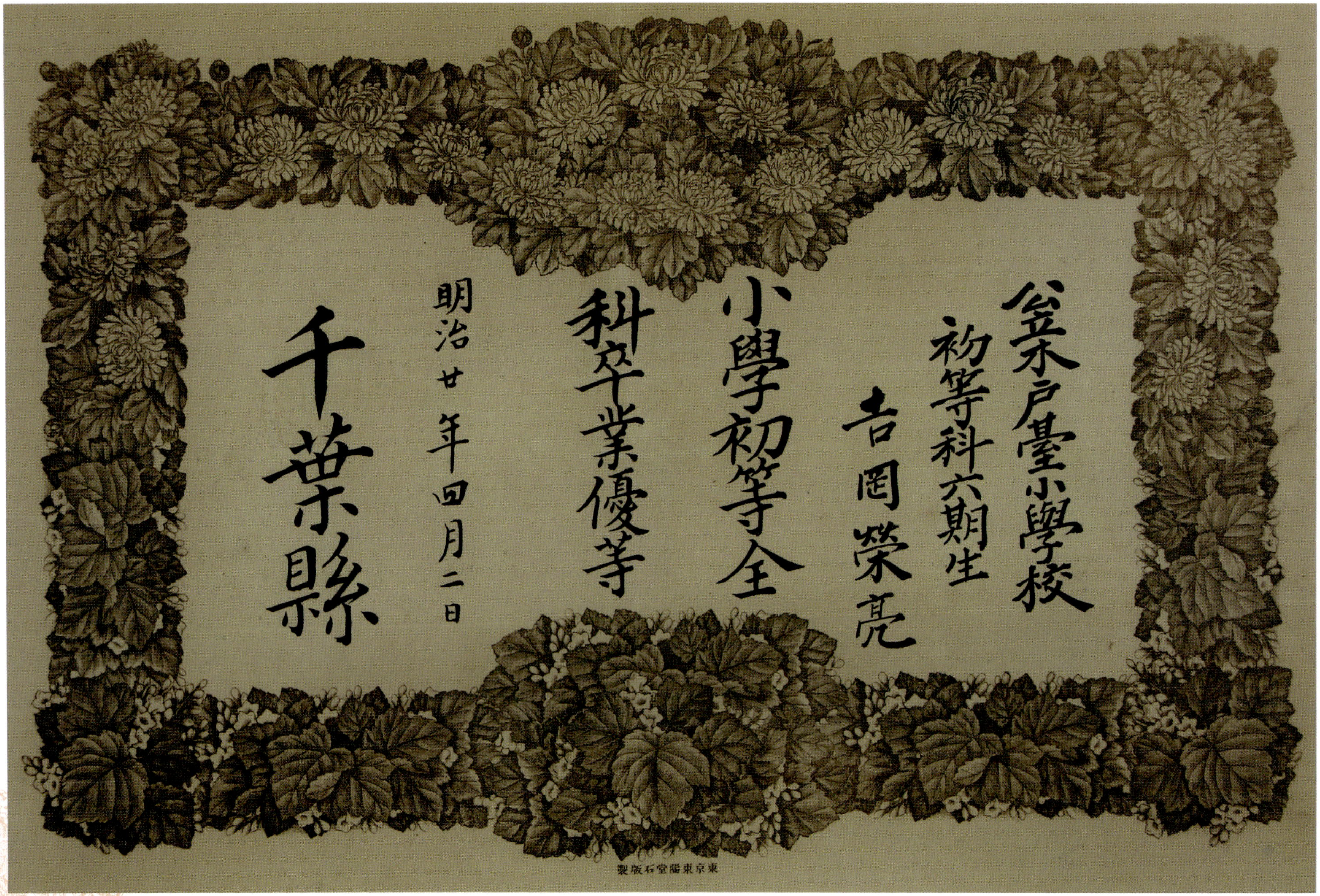
粂戸臺小學校
初等科六期生
吉岡榮亮
小學初等全
科卒業優等
明治廿年四月二日
千葉縣
東京東陽堂石版製

Opposite: Translation of elementary school graduation document: "Public Kidodai Elementary School. Elementary course, 6th Class, Yoshioka Eisuke. [You have completed] all the courses in elementary course [and] graduated with excellent grades. Meiji 10 [1877], April 2. Chiba Prefecture."
Author's collection

Japan's Liberal Reforms

The Japanese government announced their program for compulsory education in 1872. The move was bold and followed the ideals of other Western nations. The new system was met with stiff resistance in some areas. Around 10% of all of the schools were torched during riots in the first few years of the program. Attendance rate of youth also stood low, between 25–50%. However, the program laid down a precedent that every individual in Japan deserves an education. Public acceptance of compulsory education as well as military conscription was eventually tied to the popular concept of serving the emperor. It became the duty of a Japanese citizen to participate in these public institutions to fulfill their duty to the emperor. This ideal became stronger as the Japanese Empire became stronger and larger. Attendance for both girls and boys had reached over 90% in 1905. The creation of a modern education system, including universities, reinforced meritocracy in Japan.

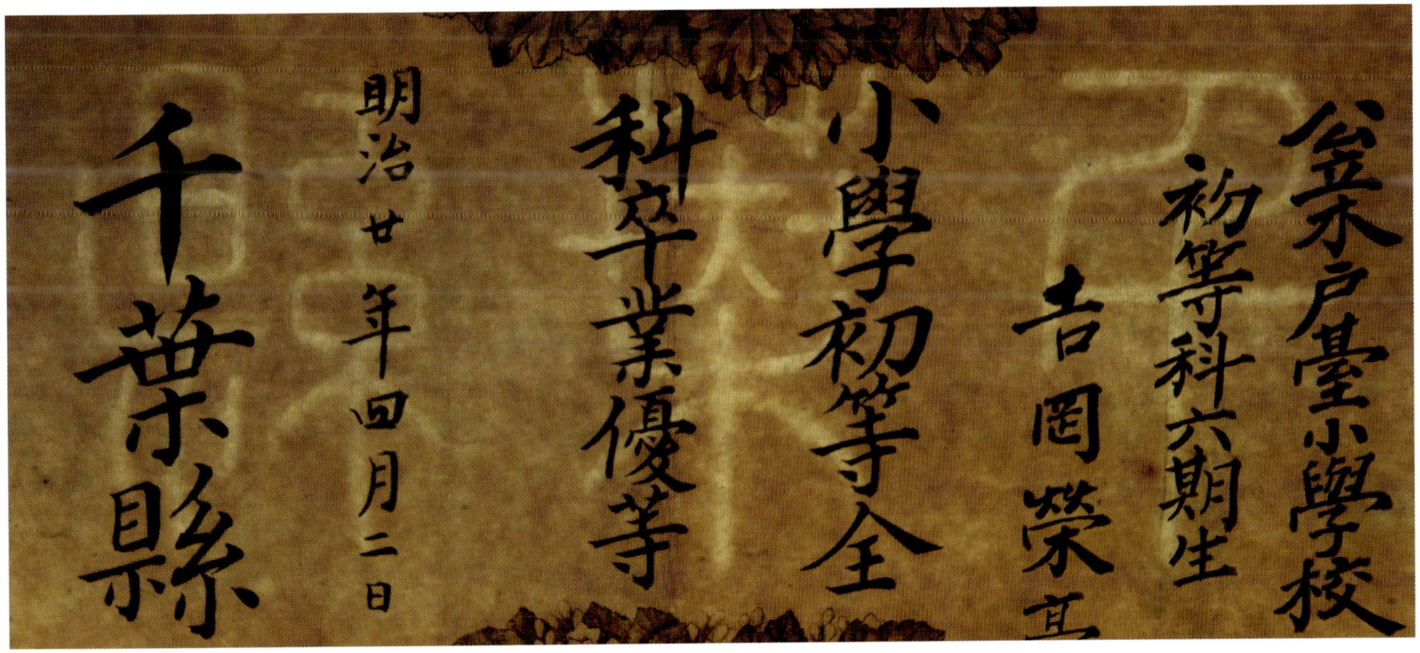

The watermark reads "Chiba Prefecture."
Author's collection

Opposite: Translation of award certificate for rice cultivation: "Award certificate. Osaka Prefecture, Settsu Koku, Shimashimo County, Kasuga Village. Morita Kiuemon. Rice, 4th award. This [award] is granted [to you] based on assessment. Meiji 13 [1880], December 11." *Author's collection*

Agricultural production was critical for the early Japanese economy. The government collected up to 80% of their revenue from agriculture in the early days of the Meiji reign. Japanese farmers were encouraged to increase their production and competitions were a feature of this initiative. They would closely resemble county fairs in the United States. Documents like the featured rice award document testify to the importance that the Japanese government placed on increased agricultural production. The money crop in Japan became silk. Silk production increased from 2.3 million pounds to 10.2 million pounds from 1868 and 1893. This commodity accounted for 42% of Japanese export revenues during this time. The increased productivity in the agricultural sector was critical to Japan during this era. The population of Japan increased dramatically through the Meiji era. Japanese farmers had to increase productivity to feed this growing population. The geography of Japan, of which about three-fourths is unsuitable for agricultural use, dictated that Japanese farmers would have to increase efficiency rather than cultivate more land. The theme of Japan having to maximize their natural resources to meet the needs of their growing population and modern economy would be repeated continually throughout the imperial age.[8]

The industrial revolution of Japan was slow to start in the new Japanese Empire. The new, modern state of Japan also required a new national tax code. The Japanese government was actually quite broke at the start of the restoration. Industrial production exploded by the 1880s. From 1880 to 1900, manufacturing output rose 5% annually, which outpaced the global average and even that of the United States. The Japanese government realized that a stable and prosperous nation required a strong economy. The new tax system instituted in Japan was revolutionary. Taxes under the shogunate were collected through the village rather than the individual. The new system levied taxes on property owners at a rate of 3% on the assessed value of the property. The creation of taxes meant that the infrastructure of Japan had to be developed. Telegraph lines, railroads, and roads were built. A postal service was instituted. Even the idea of time changed as the average Japanese now needed to pay attention to the exact time of day because of the newly developed infrastructure. The lasting legacies of all of these economic and social changes were monumental. Japan was no longer a provincial and feudal country. Japan was ready to enter the world stage as a growing power.[9]

This locomotive was part of the imperial train, Benkei-gō. The locomotive took part in the Great Imperial Visits made to Hokkaidō from 1872 and 1885. The development of an advanced rail system was critical for Japan during their industrial revolution. This locomotive was also used in the American Civil War. *Author's collection*

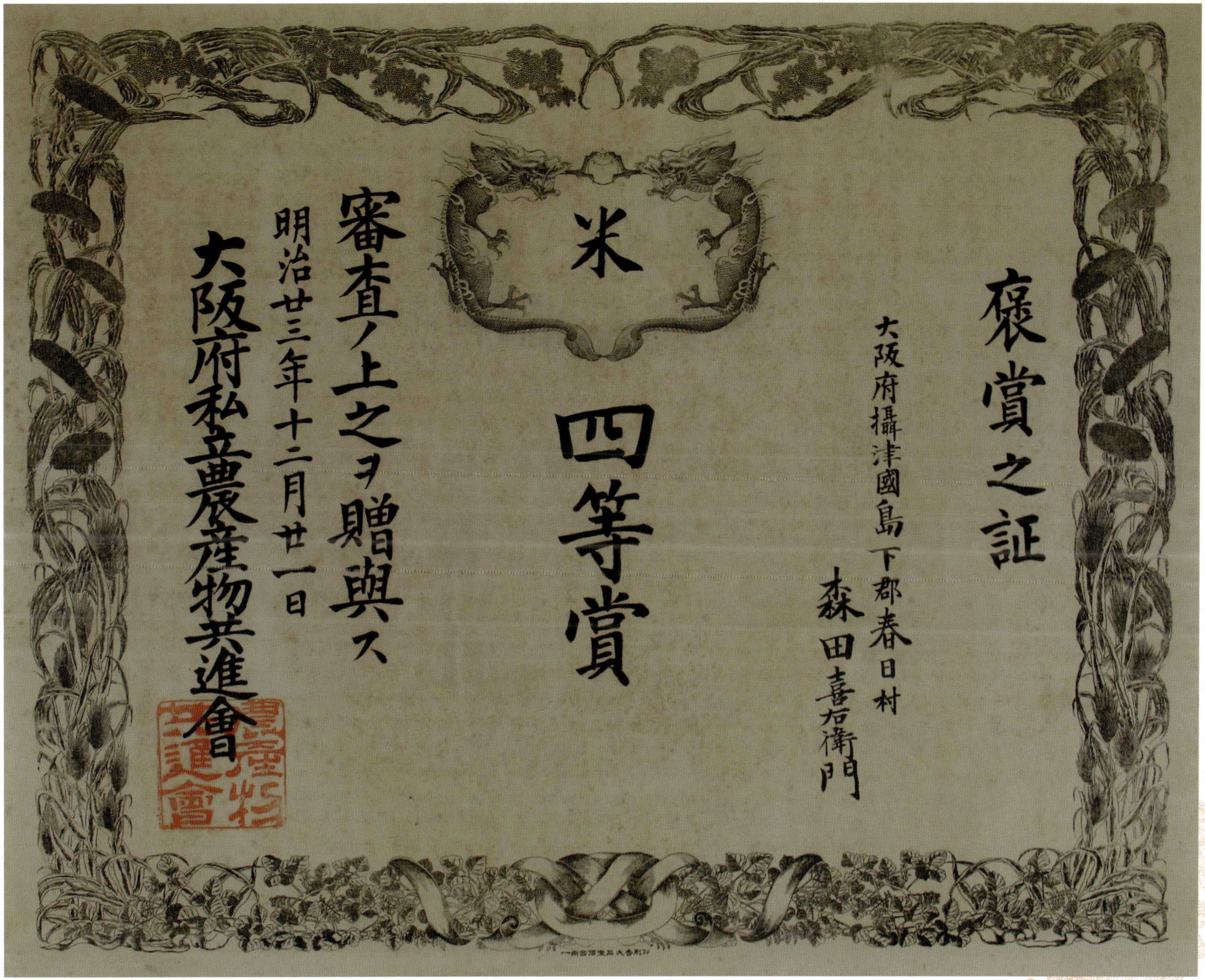
褒賞之証

大阪府攝津國島下郡春日村

森田喜右衛門

米

四等賞

審査ノ上之ヲ贈與ス

明治廿三年十二月廿一日

大阪府私立農產物共進會

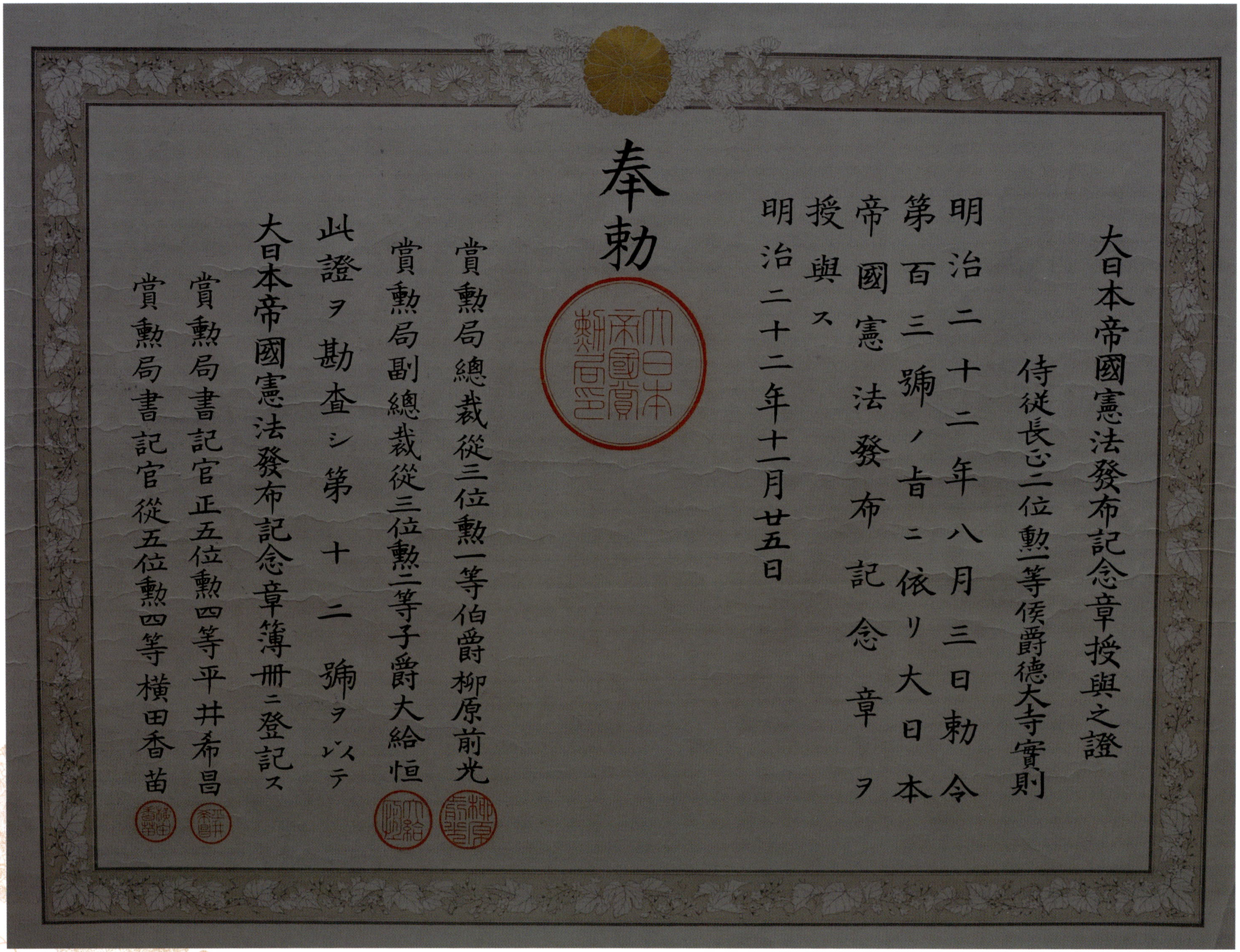

大日本帝國憲法發布記念章授與之證

侍從長正二位勲一等侯爵德大寺實則

明治二十二年八月三日勅令第百三號ノ旨ニ依リ大日本帝國憲法發布記念章ヲ授與ス

明治二十二年十一月廿五日

奉勅

賞勲局總裁從三位勲一等伯爵柳原前光

賞勲局副總裁從三位勲二等子爵大給恒

此證ヲ勘査シ第十二號ヲ以テ大日本帝國憲法發布記念章簿冊ニ登記ス

賞勲局書記官正五位勲四等平井希昌

賞勲局書記官從五位勲四等横田香苗

Opposite: Translation of Imperial Constitution Promulgation Commemorative Medal, right side only: "Record of Awarding that Imperial Constitution Promulgation Commemorative Medal. Imperial Attendant Head, 2nd Senior Court Rank, Order of Merit 1st Class, Sanetsune Tokudaiji. On Meiji 22 [1889], October 3rd by Order of the Japanese Government, the Imperial Constitution Promulgation Commemorative Medal is established by imperial edict 103. Meiji 22 [1889], November 25th." *Courtesy of an Anonymous Collector*

Creation of the Imperial Constitution and Imperial Diet

The document featured opposite was awarded to Marquis Sanetsune Tokudaiji, Minister of the Imperial Household and Keeper of the Imperial Seals. He came from an old Kuge family from Kyoto. Marquis Tokudaiji was an extremely high ranking official which his high rank and order testifies to. Documents to people as famous as Marquis Tokudaiji are quite rare. The document also tells the story of Japan's Imperial Constitution. The growing Japanese Empire faced a dilemma as to how the political system of Japan would be organized. Enthusiasm for a constitution and representative governmental body grew through the 1870s and 1880s. The unstable nature of Japanese politics during this era made progress slow. The drafting of the constitution began in secret in 1886. The politicians drafting the constitution studied European constitutions for guidance. The role of emperor in the government would resemble a European constitution of the era. The Japanese constitution, promulgated in 1889, did much to solidify the power of the government and gave limited freedoms to the average Japanese. Two different legislative bodies were created—the House of Representatives and House of Peers. The House of Representatives was elected by the Japanese citizenry. The voting population of Japan was quite limited initially. In fact, only 1% of the Japanese population (only men) had paid enough taxes to actually become eligible to vote in the first election. The House of Peers was comprised of the nobility of Japan and resembled the House of Lords in Britain. The House of Peers was designed to protect the legislative body from populace reforms. The constitution also ensured that the emperor retained some power as he could permanently veto any law proposed by the Diet. The military also had to answer to the emperor. While the new Japanese constitution did not give the average Japanese as many freedoms as their Western contemporaries, the constitution paved the way for the modern Japanese political system.[10]

The top center of the constitution document features the chrysanthemum Imperial seal in gold. This document is very hard to find. This particular document is numbered twelve. *Courtesy of an Anonymous Collector*

The border of the document features leaves and branches inside a light brown border. *Courtesy of an Anonymous Collector*

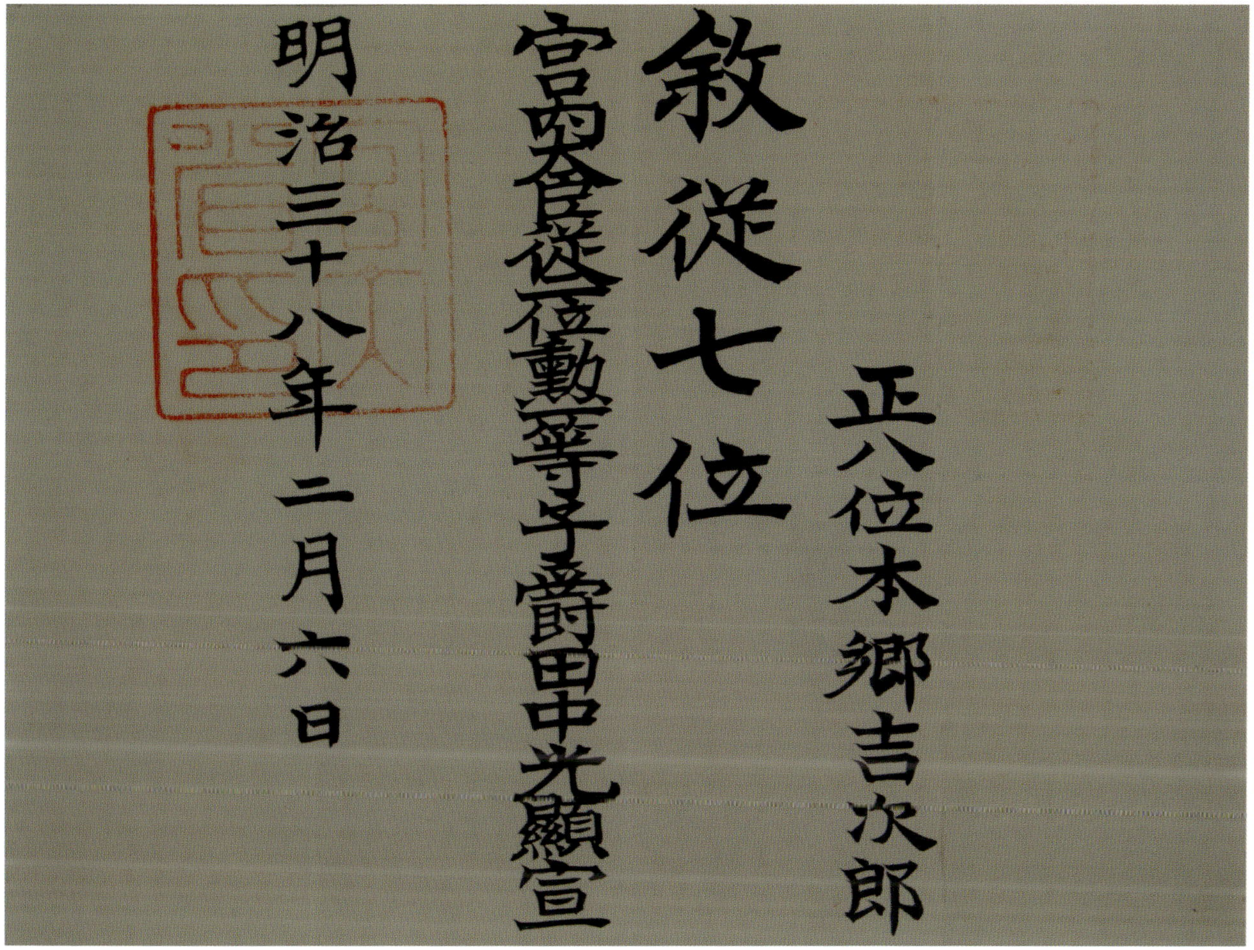
正八位本郷吉次郎
敍從七位
宮内大臣從二位勲一等子爵田中光顯宣
明治三十八年二月六日

Japan had a long history of social ranks. These ranks originated over millennia ago. The number of ranks had been as high as forty-eight; however, by 1887 the number of ranks had been reduced to sixteen. The ranks were divided into two categories: junior and senior. Someone who had a social rank of junior 7th outranked someone in the senior 8th class while that person outranked the person who is in the junior 7th class. These ranks were important because they helped delineate your positon in society. For example, a non-commissioned officer would have a lower social class (i.e., junior 7th class) as compared to a captain (i.e., senior 7th class). Even the class of an order someone could receive would be dictated by their social rank. People usually rose in social rank by advancing in their careers, whether civilian or military.

Translations of Junior 7th Rank promotion document: "Honjou Kijirou, holder of the Senior 8th Court Rank, is hereby promoted to the Junior 7th Court Rank. [By authority of] Imperial Household Minister Viscount Tanaka Mitsuaki, Holder of the Junior 2nd Court Rank and the 1st Class Decoration. Meiji 38 [105] February 6." *Author's collection*

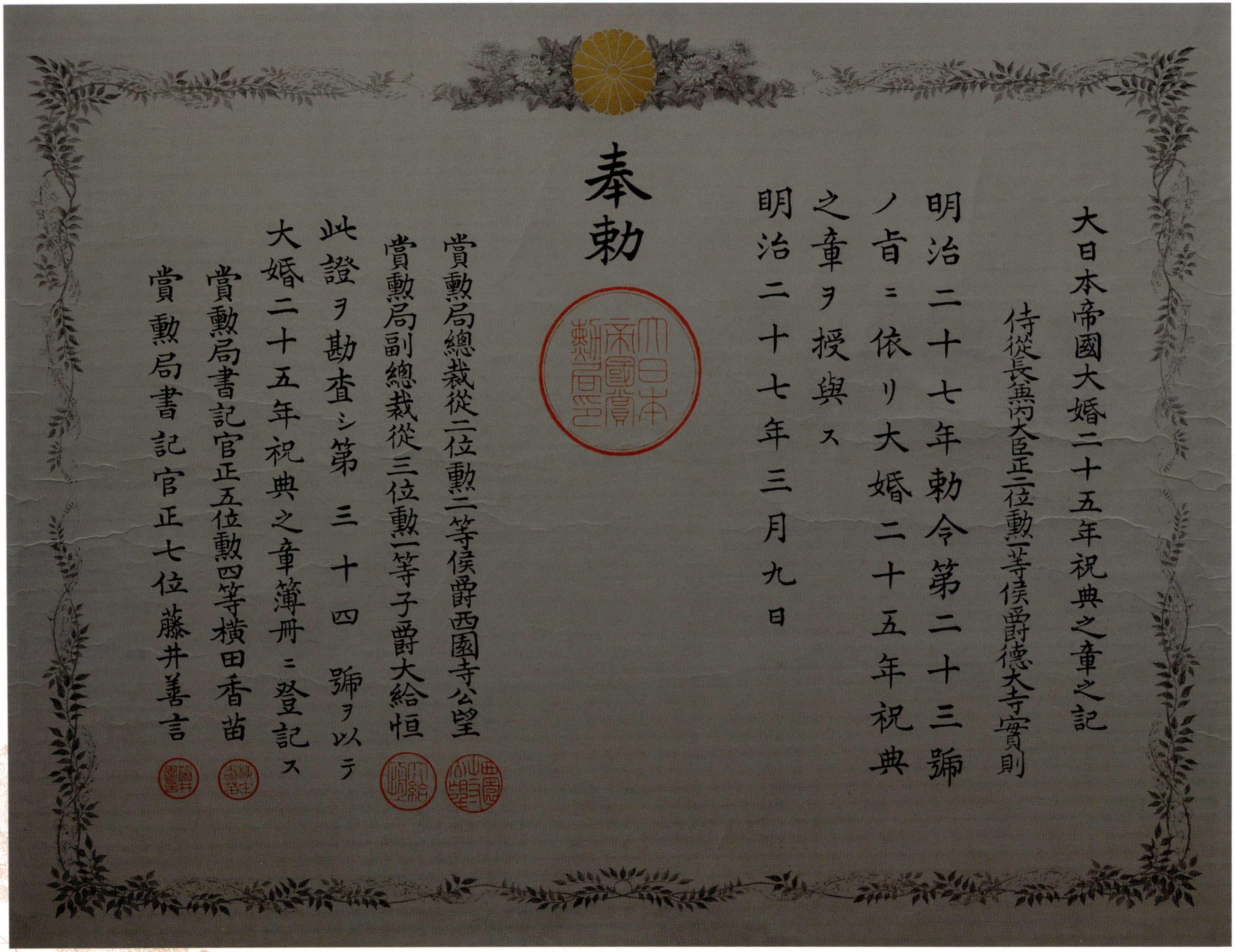

大日本帝國大婚二十五年祝典之章之記

侍從長兼内大臣正二位勲一等侯爵德大寺實則

明治二十七年勅令第二十三號ノ旨ニ依リ大婚二十五年祝典之章ヲ授與ス

明治二十七年三月九日

奉勅

賞勲局總裁從二位勲二等侯爵西園寺公望

賞勲局副總裁從三位勲一等子爵大給恒

此證ヲ勘査シ第三十四號ヲ以テ大婚二十五年祝典之章簿冊ニ登記ス

賞勲局書記官正五位勲四等横田香苗

賞勲局書記官正七位藤井善言

Opposite: Translation of 25th Wedding Anniversary Commemorative Medal document, right side only: "Record of Awarding that 25th Wedding Anniversary Commemorative Medal. Imperial Attendant Head, Senior 2nd Imperial Rank, Order of Merit 1st Class, Sanetsune Tokudaiji. In Meiji 27 [1894], the 25th Wedding Anniversary Commemorative Medal is established by Imperial Edict 23. Meiji 27 [1894], March 9th." *Courtesy of an Anonymous Collector*

This document is the 25th Wedding Anniversary Commemorative Medal celebrating the marriage of Emperor Meiji and Empress Shōken. It is a rare document only given to those associated with the celebration. This document was given to Marquis Sanetsune Tokudaiji who also received the previously featured Imperial Constitution Commemorative Medal document. The end of the first twenty-five years of the Meiji rule was worth celebrating. Japan had emerged from the feudal shogun era as a regional Asian power. The newly instituted social systems were increasing Japanese productivity to levels equal to Western nations. However, Japan was not viewed as an equal player on the world stage. Japan lacked the military victories in battle and colonial territories. Japanese military leaders, most being former samurai, had not lost their willingness for war. They turned to their attention towards Korea and northern China for territory that would bring them to war with China and then Russia.

The top center of the 25th Wedding Anniversary Commemorative Medal document features the golden chrysanthemum imperial seal. This document is rare with this one being numbered 314. The award was quite exclusive to high ranking officials who attended the imperial wedding anniversary celebrations. The two characters below the seal translates to "awarded to." *Courtesy of an Anonymous Collector*

The border of this document is comprised of leaves and flowers in a very simple design. *Courtesy of an Anonymous Collector*

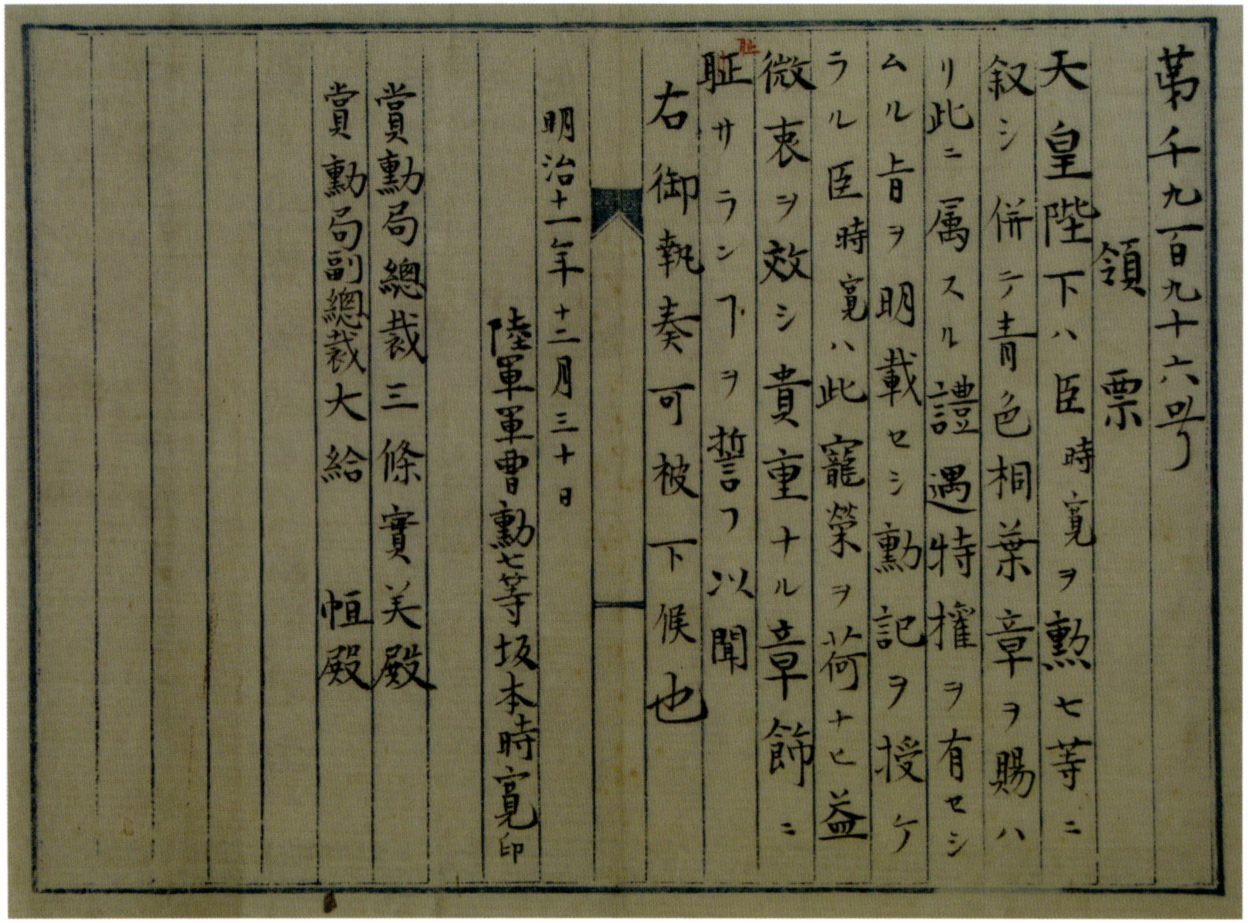

第千九百九十六号
領票
天皇陛下ハ臣時寛ヲ勲七等ニ
叙シ併テ青色桐葉章ヲ賜ハ
リ此ニ属スル禮遇特権ヲ有セシ
ムル旨ヲ明載セシ勲記ヲ授ケ
ラル臣時寛ハ此寵榮ヲ荷ナヒ益
微衷ヲ效シ貴重ナル章飾ニ
耻サランヿヲ誓フ以聞
右御執奏可被下候也
明治十一年十二月三十日
陸軍軍曹勲七等坂本時寛 印
賞勲局總裁三條實美殿
賞勲局副總裁大給恒殿

Translation of issuance document for an Order of the Rising Sun 7th Class, right side only: "Issuance number 1996. Receiving Slip. The Emperor ranked his subject Tokihiro (pronunciation of first name is unknown) the Green Paulownia Leaves Badge Seventh Order of Merit (7th Class Order of the Rising Sun), and granted [to him] an award which states that [he] owns prerequisites that come with merit. Tokihiro, the Emperor's subject, humbly says to the Emperor that he, being responsible for proposing with his favor, vows to be true to the precocious decoration with his utmost sincerity. [I humbly] request that you pass the right message on to the Emperor. Meiji 11 [1878], December 30. Army Sergeant, Order of Merit 7th Class, Sakamoto Tokihiro." *Author's collection*

Chapter 1 Endnotes

1. A. Gordon, *A Modern History of Japan: From Tokugawa Times to the Present* (New York: Oxford Press, 2009), 50.
2. A. Gordon, *A Modern History of Japan: From Tokugawa Times to the Present* (New York: Oxford Press, 2009), 57–59.
3. D. Keene, *Emperor of Japan: Meiji and His World, 1852–1912* (New York: Columbia University Press, 2002), ix-xiii.
4. A. Gordon, *A Modern History of Japan: From Tokugawa Times to the Present* (New York: Oxford Press, 2009), 62–65.
5. A. Gordon, *A Modern History of Japan: From Tokugawa Times to the Present* (New York: Oxford Press, 2009), 66–67.
6. A. Gordon, *A Modern History of Japan: From Tokugawa Times to the Present* (New York: Oxford Press, 2009), 74–75.
7. W. G. Beasley, *The Modern History of Japan* (New York: Praeger, 1974), 117–119.
8. A. Gordon, *A Modern History of Japan: From Tokugawa Times to the Present* (New York: Oxford Press, 2009), 93–95.
9. A. Gordon, *A Modern History of Japan: From Tokugawa Times to the Present* (New York: Oxford Press, 2009), 70, 95.
10. A. Gordon, *A Modern History of Japan: From Tokugawa Times to the Present* (New York: Oxford Press, 2009), 91–92.

2 JAPAN'S EARLY MILITARY VICTORIES:
CREATING THE EMPIRE (1894–1910)

Japan had emerged from the Meiji Restoration free from Western dominance, yet its power was not solidified. Japan wanted to establish itself as a legitimate power in the region. This situation would require a display of military dominance and a colony. The eyes of Japan's leaders turned to their neighbors to the West and joined the fray for control of still nominally independent Korea. To conquer Korea, Japan would be obliged to go to war against China and Russia.

This iconic painting shows Adm. Tōgō on his flagship *Mikasa* before the Battle of Tsushima during the Russo–Japanese War. The war and particularly this naval battle catapulted Japan on to the world stage as a military power. *Author's Collection*

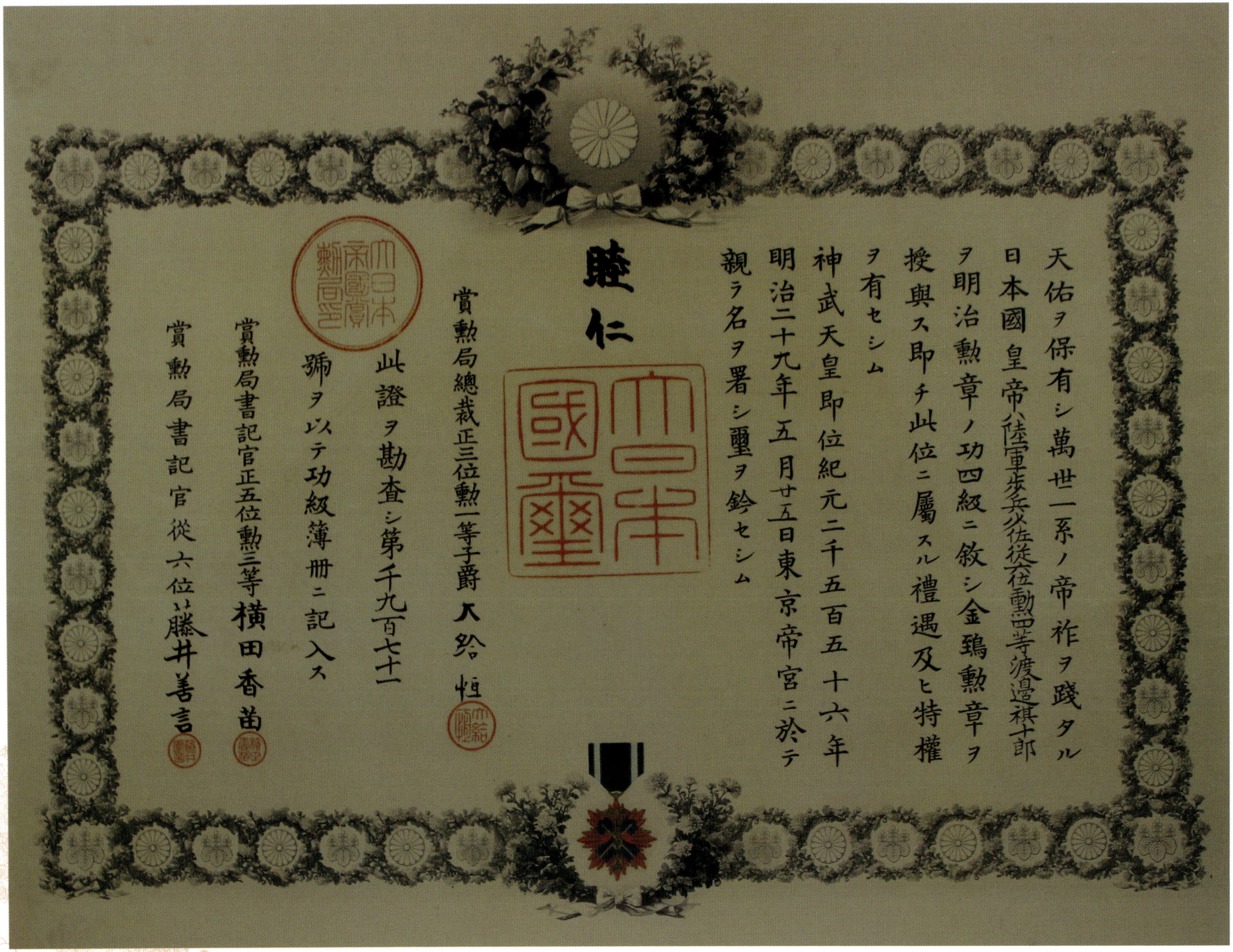

天佑ヲ保有シ萬世一系ノ帝祚ヲ践タル
日本國皇帝ハ陸軍歩兵少佐従六位勲四等渡邉祺十郎
ヲ明治勲章ノ功四級ニ敍シ金鵄勲章ヲ
授與ス即チ此位ニ屬スル禮遇及ヒ特權
ヲ有セシム
神武天皇即位紀元二千五百五十六年
明治二十九年五月廿五日東京帝宮ニ於テ
親ラ名ヲ署シ璽ヲ鈐セシム

睦仁

賞勲局總裁正三位勲一等子爵大給恒

此證ヲ勘査シ第千九百七十一
號ヲ以テ功級簿冊ニ記入ス

賞勲局書記官正五位勲三等横田香苗

賞勲局書記官従六位藤井善言

Opposite: Translation of Order of the Golden Kite 4th Class document, right side only: "Through the honor of the immortal Emperor, the Empire of Japan bestows this award. Army Infantry Major, Junior 6th Rank, Order of Merit 4th Class, Watanabe Kijuro. Order of the Golden Kite 4th Class medal. Imperial Year 2556 [1896]. Meiji 29 [1896], May 25, Tokyo Imperial Shrine." *Author's Collection*

First Sino–Japanese War

The Order of the Golden Kite was instituted in 1890 to recognize actions in battle. The order could be given to anyone, but the class of the order was given according to the military rank of the recipient. In other words, enlisted men would receive the lower grades while high-end officers would receive the highest grades. Japan would have its first opportunity to bestow the order during the First Sino–Japanese War of 1894–1895. The Order of the Golden Kite pictured at the start of this section was a 4th class version given to Watanabe Kijuro, who was an army major. His actions during the First Sino–Japanese War earned him one of the first Golden Kite awards given within Japan. Emperor Meiji himself signed this document. This document is only one of forty-nine Order of the Golden Kite 4th class awards signed during his reign. One could imagine Maj. Kijuro in command of a battalion during the Battle of P'yônyang. His soldiers might have been part of the surprise northern flanking maneuver used when crossing the Taedong River. Maj. Kijuro would have commanded his troops to remain hidden as they moved into position until the appropriate time when they launched the assault. The Chinese had failed to protect against this possible move by the Japanese and were facing the Japanese towards the south, which was under assault. This action cut the Chinese defenses off from retreat and led to the rout and capture of the P'yônyang. The war that Kijuro fought in was the first in series of conflicts that would help establish Japan as an empire.

The new version with order of documents, which started at or just before 1890, still featured the medal in the bottom center of the document, just as the older version had done. The medal is surrounded by a motif of chrysanthemums. The Order of the Golden Kite 4th Class can be tricky to distinguish from early Golden Kite documents. The only difference between the 4th and 5th Class is that the 4th Class has gold highlights around the rays. The 4th Class medal was eventually given a rosette to make distinguishing between the two medals easier. *Author's collection*

Japan's war against China, specifically the Qing Chinese Empire, had its roots in the Korean peninsula. For the past twenty years the relationship between Korea, China, and Japan had been precarious. Korea bounced back and forth between Chinese and Japanese spheres of influence. The situation could easily be described as a proxy war between China and Japan. A peasant rebellion in Korea was the spark that ignited the war. In early June 1894, the Korean government called on the Chinese empire to assist with troops. A few days later, Japan also sent troops into Korea as they felt obliged to do so under a convention that had been signed a decade before. Korea had asked Japan to refrain from sending troops. Yet, Japanese troops made landings near Seoul and continued to build up troops in the area. The Japanese troops remained in Korea through June and into July even after the rebellion was quashed. The Japanese government decided to pressure Korea into making sweeping reforms with the intention of provoking China into a war. The Korean government did not comply with these demands from the Japanese and insisted that the Japanese troops leave. China also began to send more of their troops into Korea. The situation came to a head on July 23, when Japanese troops stormed the Korean royal palace and installed a pro-Japanese government. Japan now was set to expel the Chinese troops from Korea.[1]

The strategy of the Japanese was straightforward. The navy would seize control of the Yellow Sea. One army would march north through Korea to expel the Chinese and then into Manchuria. A second army would land on the Liaodong Peninsula and take Port Arthur before meeting the other army. Once these two armies secured a route from Manchuria to Peking in northern China, a Japanese force would take the naval base of Weihaiwei in the Chinese Province of Shandong on the China Sea. This naval movement would secure a victory over the Chinese navy and reduce their ability to counterattack. Japan's plan required naval success as they had to ferry troops and supplies during the duration of the war. Japan was able to mobilize

The new version of the order documents featured bolder designs. This is the center motif that features the imperial crest surrounded by a wreath of kiri leaves and chrysanthemum flowers. *Author's Collection*

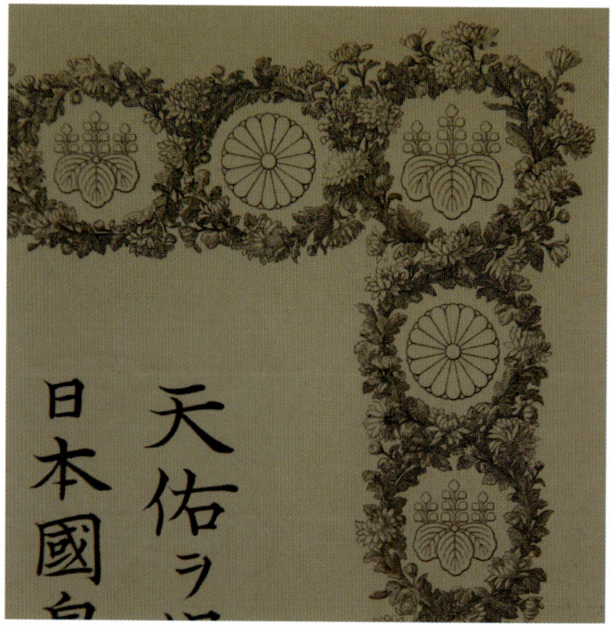

The border of a newer version of the order documents features the same basic border design of alternating imperial mums and paulownia leaves. The new version is still used today. *Author's Collection*

over 100,000 troops quickly. These troops were better trained and equipped than their Chinese opponents.[2]

The strategy of the Chinese naval and land encounters was more cautious and defensive than that of the Japanese. Their decisions gave the Japanese the initiative in the initial phases of the war. The sea and land battles began on July 24–25, 1894. A naval engagement was fought near Feng Island south of Incheon and Seoul, which saw Japan neutralize part of the Chinese Navy and secured the western Korean coast.[3] Three days later, the Japanese victory at the Battle of Sônghwan near Asan opened the route to Seoul, which Japan secured on August 5.[4]

The next and last defended line in Korea was near P'yônyang. The Chinese held the advantage of terrain and had time to dig defensive positions. The Japanese had to march through unfavorable terrain in central Korea, which took over a month. However, the Japanese were better trained and had more competent generals. The advantages of the Chinese position at P'yônyang were neutralized by incompetent commanders and bad logistics. The Japanese attacked the city from three sides starting on September 15, 1894. The Chinese made the fatal blunder of not attacking the Japanese as they crossed the Taedong River. The losses for the Japanese were quite small compared to the Chinese. The defeat became a retreat that lasted for 100 miles to the Yalu River.[5] The defensive line at the Yalu River, which represented the natural boundary between Korea and Manchuria, was quickly compromised. Also, the naval battle at Yalu River on September 17 was a decisive victory of Japan. The Chinese Navy lost a majority of their ships engaged in the battle, which shattered their navy's morale. The Japanese Army overcame the Chinese defensive line on the Yalu River on October 25–26. The Chinese marched their forces towards the provincial capital of Mukden in the heart of Manchuria. Japan had other intentions as they began landing troops on the Liaodong Peninsula with the goal of taking Port Arthur.[6]

The Battle of Port Arthur played out much like previous battles, and the city fell after a two-day battle on November 21, 1894.[7] The Japanese then moved through Manchuria despite the oncoming winter. The Chinese fought numerous defensive engagements, but could not stem the tide of the Japanese offensive. Japan also sought to secure the significant naval port of Weihaiwei on the tip of the Shandong Peninsula in eastern China. This action was designed to open a second front to approach Peking and destroy the rest of the Chinese Navy, which was harbored in Weihaiwei. These operations were concluded successfully with few casualties for the Japanese on February 12, 1895. Japanese forces fighting in Manchuria reached the border with China by early March. The gates to Peking were now wide open and China began to sue for peace.[8]

This drawing comes from the campaign in Weihaiwei in March 1895. This particular battle, the Battle of Yinkou, included fierce street fighting, which is pictured in the drawing. *Author's Collection*

The First Sino–Japanese War was also felt on the home front. The Red Cross Association of Japan, whose main goal was to provide care for wounded and captured soldiers and to help the families of soldiers, could trace its history to the early days of the Meiji Restoration in 1877. The Japanese Red Cross was credited as operating with the highest of standards during the First Sino–Japanese War. It had the most modern technologies and services during the conflict, which helped save many lives.[9] The group purchased much of this new equipment and funded its operations through donations. This was one of the few ways that civilians could be involved with the war. A variety of ways existed for people to be involved with the Red Cross, including various levels of memberships.

The First Sino–Japanese War also brought hardships to families on the Japanese home front as soldiers were away from home for an extended period of time, became permanently wounded, or were killed while in service. The Japanese government tried to respond to these issues, usually in the form of monetary settlements. The small document for family payment assistance was given on behalf of Nishikubo Fukujiro. Other award documents show how Fukujiro was an infantry sergeant and had served in the Imperial Guard. He also had apparently served in some capacity during the First Sino–Japanese War. Interestingly, this family assistance payment came in 1897, two years after the war ended. The fundraising efforts for veterans and their families was a nationwide effort in Japan during the

日本赤十字社

茲ニ
東野太右衛門氏
本社忠愛ノ主旨ニ協同セラルヽヲ以テ社則ニ照ラシ締盟シテ正社員ニ列ス

明治廿七年十月七日

日本赤十字社總裁
大勲位彰仁親王

日本赤十字社長
正三位勲一等子爵佐野常民

Opposite: Translation for Membership Award document from the Japan Red Cross, right side only: "For loyal duty to the society, Higashino Tauemon is recognized as a Full Member." The document is dated March 31, 1895. *Author's Collection*

war. Their successful efforts accompanied a rise of nationalism in Japan. For the first time, many Japanese actually felt like citizens; and war contributions were their way to make a difference.[10]

Ending the war with China was not an easy task, although China was eager to end the war. They feared a march on Peking; however, Japan had involvement by Western powers in the negotiations. The Treaty of Shimonoseki was signed on April 17, 1895, after much intrigue, which included an assassination attempt on a Chinese diplomat, and the Japanese occupation of the Pescadores Islands and Formosa (modern-day Taiwan). The treaty was quite favorable to Japan. Japan would receive Formosa, part of the Liaodong Peninsula, which included Port Arthur, and several Chinese ports that would open them for increased trade. Furthermore, China would have to pay war indemnities. Korea would remain independent, but Japan's influence over Korea was no longer in doubt.[11]

The ink on the treaty was barely dry when the Western powers stepped forward and demanded some changes to the treaty. By November 1895, Russia, Germany, and France had convinced Japan to cede back part of the territory awarded by the Treaty of Shimonoseki. The biggest change was the loss of the Liaodong Peninsula back to the Chinese. Russia wanted the access to the China Sea and started to build a railroad through China connecting Port Harbor through Russia. This move would set the stage for the Russo-Japanese War ten short years later. In the short run, the Western powers and Japan were able to capitalize on the defeat of China and strengthen their own interests. Their heavy-handed involvement in China would lead to the Boxer Rebellion.[12]

Boxer Rebellion

The Japanese Government recognized the Boxer Rebellion with a War Medal. This document was titled the 1900 War Medal and given to military people and civilians who participated in the Boxer Rebellion. War medal documents recognized the service of veterans. They did not necessarily list the particular battle a soldier may have fought in. However, the limited actions involved in the Boxer Rebellion provides collectors with a clear picture of what a recipient might have experienced in this conflict. This document is also rather rare considering the low numbers of participants in this conflict. The Boxer Rebellion War Medal document featured was given to Sakai Kichijiro. The document is numbered 25,070. The Boxer Rebellion was a brief conflict, yet the combatants displayed tremendous acts of bravery. For instance, the Japanese had taken the lead in destroying the Chinese defense positions at Tientsin. They laid explosive charges at a gate in the city's wall while under heavy Chinese fire. As they retreated to safety, the line was cut by Chinese fire. A Japanese lieutenant named Inawe bravely went back in the line of fire and lit the charge with a match. The explosion blew up the gate and killed Lt. Inawe.[13] This type of heroic and selfless act during the Boxer Rebellion earned the Japanese respect from the Europeans fighting alongside them.

The events that led to the Boxer Rebellion were rooted in Chinese resentment of the spreading of Christianity by Westerners. The Boxers derived their name from

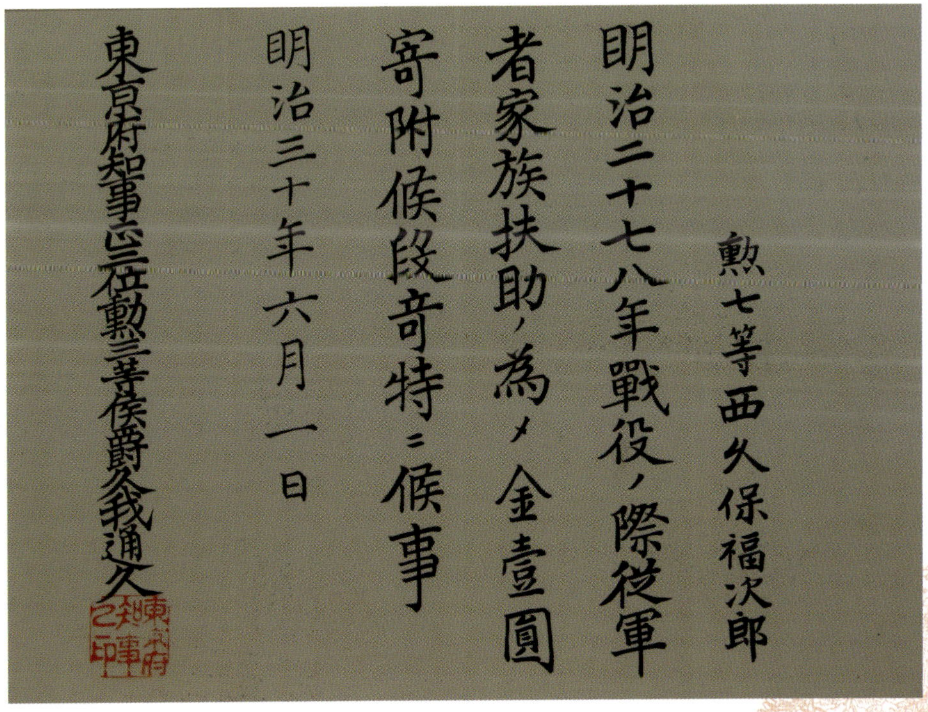
勲七等西久保福次郎
明治二十七八年戰役ノ際從軍
者家族扶助ノ爲メ金壹圓
寄附候段奇特ニ候事
明治三十年六月一日
東京府知事正四位勲三等侯爵久我通久
東京府知事之印

Translation from family pay for assistance with this document for 1894–95 War: "Order of Merit 7th Class, Nishikubo Fukujito. For services during the Meiji 27–8 [1894–95] war. This refers to Family Assistance Payment. Meiji 30 (1897), June 1." *Author's Collection*

日本帝國明治三十三年從軍記章之證

海軍上等兵曹從七位勲六等境 吉次郎

明治三十三年從軍記章條例ニ依リ
海軍大臣ノ奏請ヲ經テ明治三十五年四月十九日
勅定ノ從軍記章ヲ授與ス
明治三十五年五月十日

奉勅

賞勲局總裁正三位勲一等子爵大給恒

此證ヲ勘查シ第二万五千七十號ヲ以テ
明治三十三年從軍記章簿冊ニ登記ス

賞勲局書記官從四位勲三等横田香苗

賞勲局書記官正六位勲六等藤井善言

Opposite: Translation of 1900 War Medal document, right side only: "Record of Awarding the 1900 War Dispatch Medal. Navy Chief Petty Officer, Junior 7th Rank, Order of Merit 6th Class, Sakai Kichijiro. Given the 1900 War Dispatch Medal by order of the Ministry of the Army, this medal having been established by Imperial edict on Meiji 34 [1901], March 29th. Meiji 35 [1902], May 10th." *Author's Collection*

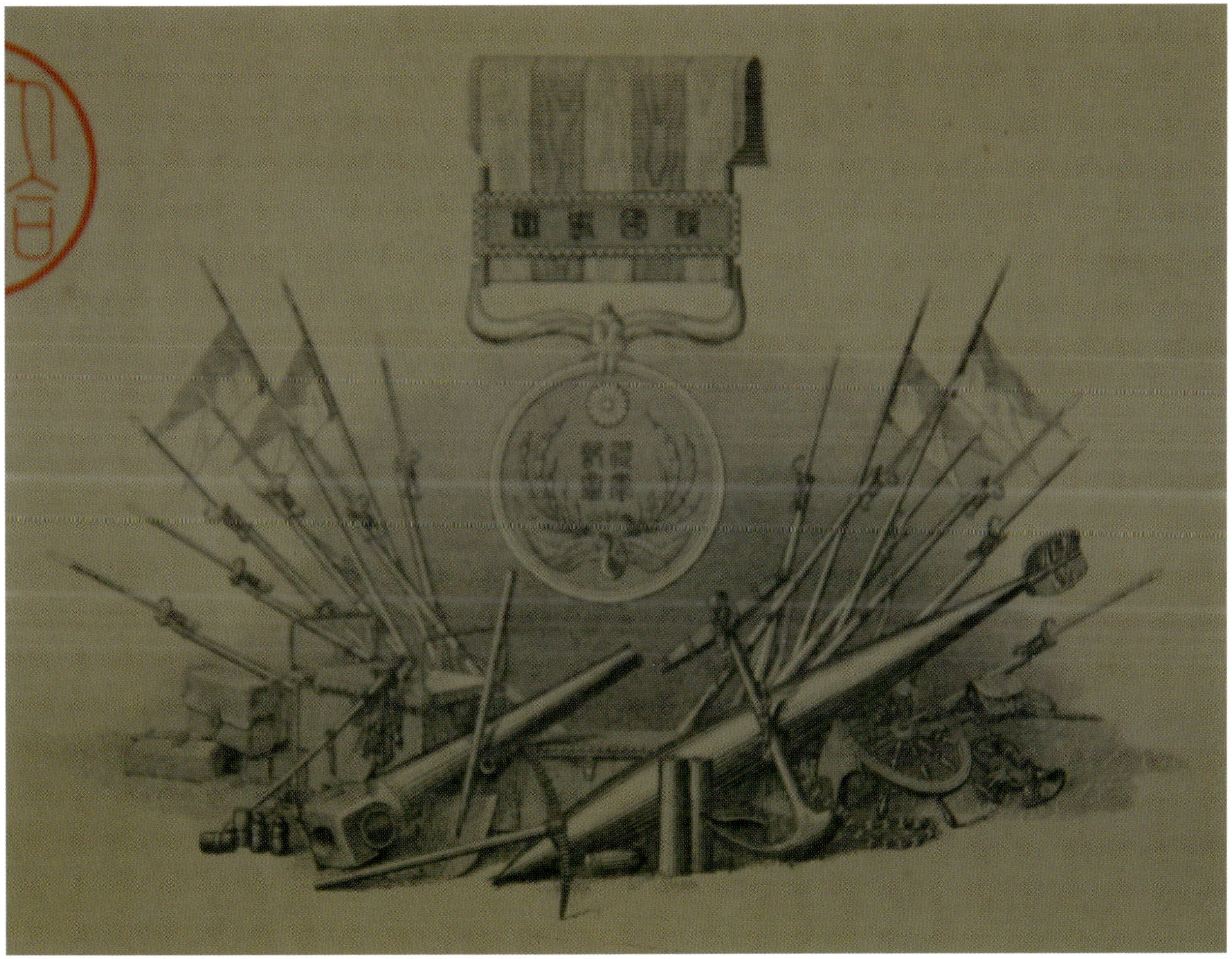

The center design of the 1900 War Medal document featuring the medal. The front of the 1900 War Medal is pictured with various implements of battle spread out below it. This design would be used for the first five different war medal documents. *Author's Collection*

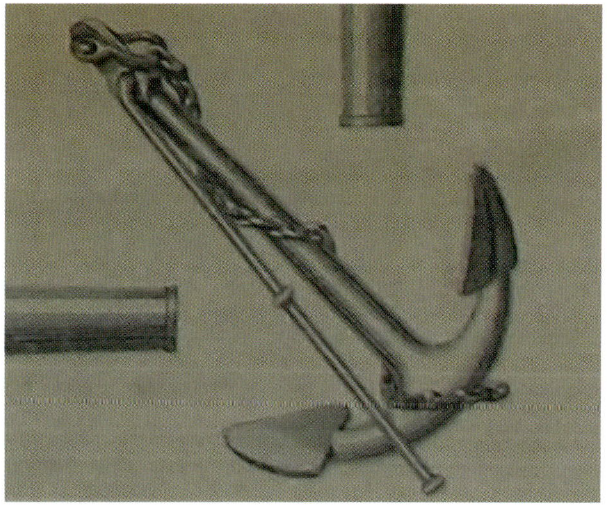

The corner of design of cannons facing an anchor would also be used through the 1914–1920 War Medal Document. *Author's Collection*

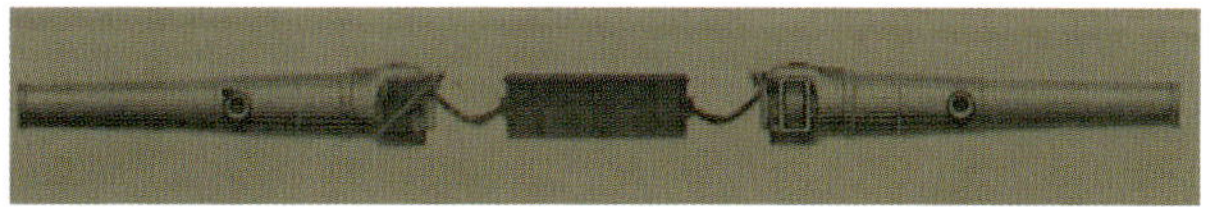

The border of block and cannons was used for all war medal documents from 1894 through 1920. *Author's Collection*

The top of the document features the imperial mum crest and chrysanthemum with branches. This design was used on all of the war documents and eventually a World War I Victory Medal Document. *Author's Collection*

the Righteous and Harmonious Fists secret society, which began in Shandong Province in northern China. They had been growing in strength and popularity from 1898–1900. The Chinese reaction to the Boxers was complicated. China had been weakened by their loss to Japan, and the Boxers represented a real internal threat. The Chinese Empress Dowager ordered her troops not to interfere with them.[14] The situation boiled over by May 1900, as the Boxers began to attack railroads and telegraph lines in the Northern Province of Chihli (now referred as Hebei). After an initial clash with the Boxers, the government troops began to work with them. These developments were not unnoticed by Westerners in Peking. They realized that the Chinese government was likely to side with the Boxers and they began to call on their representative governments to send troops to protect Westerners. The response was quick as Russian, British, French, American, Italian, and Japanese troops landed on the coast near Tientsin, eighty-five miles from Peking. The Westerners and Christian Chinese nearby began to flee to Peking seeking protection. The rebellion became a war as the Chinese government felt compelled to support the Boxers for fear of internal revolution. They declared war on the Western nations on June 17, 1900.[15]

Japan joined the United Kingdom, France, United States, Russia, Germany, Austria-Hungary, and Italy in the war against the Boxers. They were the only non-Western nation to dispatch troops, which signified a Japanese rise to power in Asia. They also provided the most men. The Japanese soldiers participated in storming the besieged city of Tienstin. The taking of this city was a product of Japanese tactics and bravery. Gen.Fukushima Yasumasa planned a night assault that would attack the gates of the walled city. However, he specifically did not attack two city gates. He predicted that the Chinese would fight to the death if surrounded but would also flee if they had the option. An explosive charge was placed on the south gate by Japanese engineers, but the fuse was cut by Chinese bullets. A Japanese lieutenant named Inawe (his story was recounted earlier) rushed towards the wall under fire and used a match to light the fuse; he was killed by the subsequent explosion. Gen. Yasumasa's plan went as he had predicted, and the Chinese retreated from the city.[16]

The combat would last through mid-August 1900. Japan would also be involved in the siege of Peking, which relieved the besieged Westerners. The conflict demonstrated the professional nature of the Japanese military and the bravery of Japanese soldiers. The aftermath of the conflict would find China in an even weaker position. Events in Manchuria would prove to be more pivotal for Japan, however. The Russians used the war with China as a pretext to invade and occupy Port Arthur on the Liaodong peninsula and Manchuria.[17]

Russo–Japanese War

Wars in the twentieth century increasingly became total wars, which required the whole populace to fight. The Women's Patriotic Association was a group that found an important role on the home front during conflicts. The nucleus of this group was formed in 1901 by wives of influential Japanese men.[18] The group was formed as a social organization to help with a variety of social issues. This group was not just a wartime woman's organization. Thus, their document could be given during peacetime or wartime. During wartime, the Women's Patriotic Association worked in a variety of capacities, including seeing soldiers off to war and helping with family hardships.

The war with Russia from 1904–1905 required a commitment at home and on the battlefront, which was unique for Japan. The roots of this conflict actually stretch back to before the First Sino–Japanese War; however, the events right after the conflict set the stage for war a decade later. The Western nations forced Japan to return key areas to China. Meanwhile, Germany built a fortified port at Tsingtao, and Russia made claims on Port Arthur on the Liaodong Peninsula. The Japanese viewed these actions as provocative. The issue of Korea also remained contentious as Russia sought to fill the void of power left by China in Korea. It is interesting to note that the territory igniting this conflict did not belong to Japan or Russia.

A photograph of Japanese Marines who took part in the Seymour Expedition, which was a multi-national force sent to protect Westerners in Peking (now called Beijing) from the Boxers. *Author's Collection*

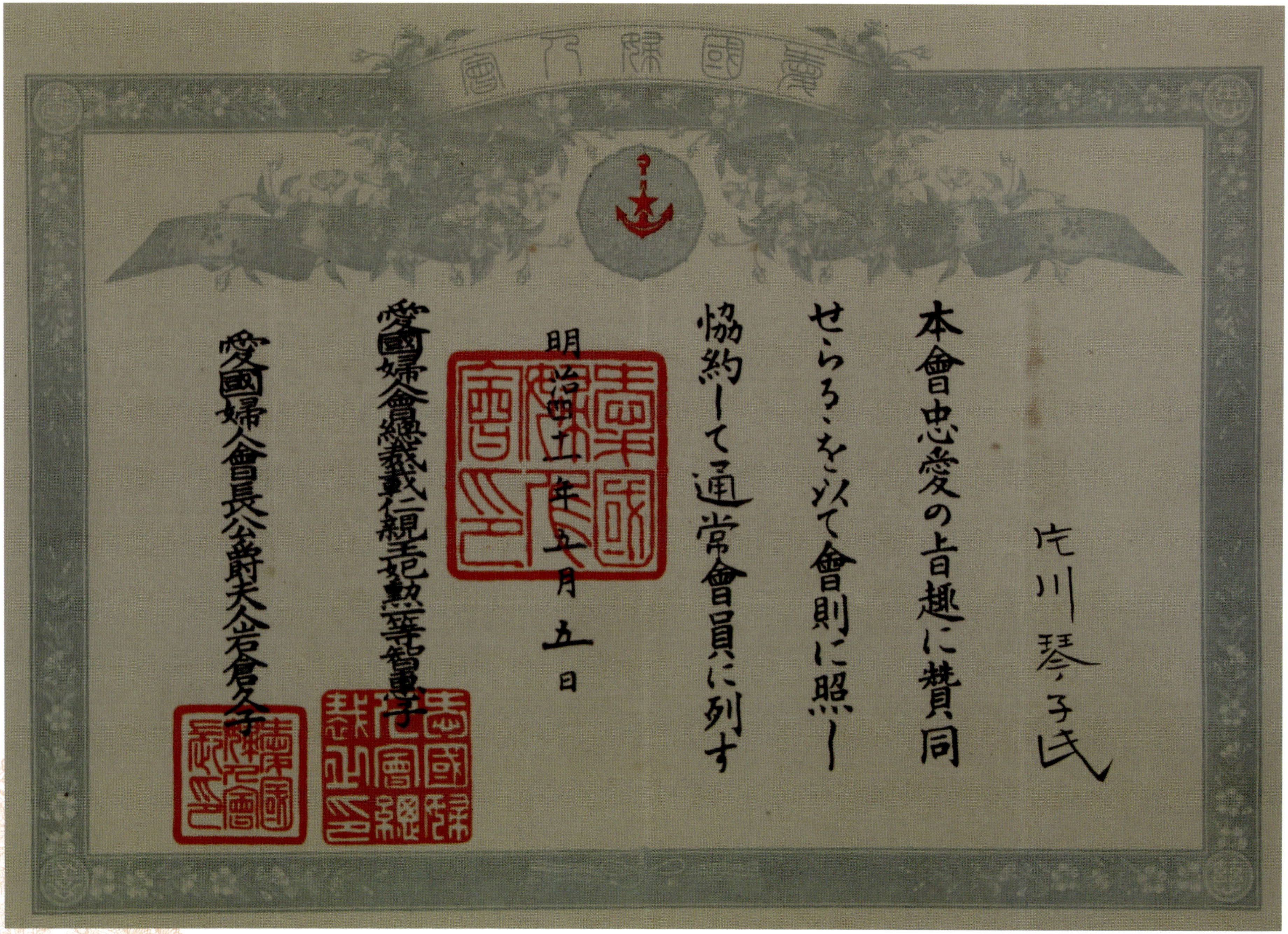

愛國婦人會

片川琴子氏

本會忠愛の旨趣に賛同
せらるゝを以て會則に照し
協約して通常會員に列す

明治四十一年五月五日

愛國婦人會總裁載仁親王妃勲一等智惠子

愛國婦人會長公爵夫人岩倉久子

Translation of Woman's Patriotic Association Membership document, right side only: "Hinotogawa Kotoko is hereby granted regular membership for upholding society regulations and for supporting the aim of the committee loyalty. Meiji 41 [1908] May 5." *Author's Collection*

Japan had sought to ease tensions by asking Russia to sign an agreement in early 1904 stating that Manchuria was outside both of their spheres of influence. Russia balked at this agreement, and Japan felt obliged to take action by declaring war on February 10, 1904.[19]

The two belligerents were quite unequal on paper as Russia could field an enormous army. A closer examination, though, highlights the distinct advantages the Japanese had over the Russians. The Japanese had a better trained military, a more modern navy, and more competent officers. Russian troops and supplies had to travel on the arduous Siberian railroad, and the majority of the Russian Navy would have to travel from European Russia to the North China Sea.[20] Japan put their naval plans into action even before the declaration of war. Naval supremacy in the Yellow Sea was important. Japan launched an attack on the Russian fleet at Port Arthur, which resulted in a draw for both sides with no ships sunk. The naval battles around Port Arthur would continue throughout the spring.[21]

The naval stalemate at Port Arthur meant that the Japanese could begin their troop landings in Korea and begin to march north. The Japanese were able to move their troops into the combat areas much faster. The Russians, who had chosen the Yalu River, could only bring around 20,000 infantry and cavalry to this defensive line of 170 miles. The Japanese had around 42,500 troops. The Japanese river crossings and attacks were quite successful. They outmaneuvered the Russians over a few days and forced the Russians to retreat. The casualties were not extreme, but the outcome of the battle was quite significant. The Russians retreated in haste to Liaoyang in the north. They did not choose to protect their garrison at Port Arthur on the Liaodong Peninsula. This faulty decision allowed the Japanese to move against the port on their terms. More significantly, the defeat of the Russians at the Yalu River smashed the perceptions of European invincibility.[22]

The next move by the Japanese was to cut off, besiege, and capture Port Arthur. The Russians wanted to keep Port Arthur and undertook an audacious action to support the harbor: They would sail their Baltic Fleet half-way around the world to engage the Japanese. The Russian's strategic plan would take a long time to happen while the Japanese's plan to besiege Port Arthur was enacted almost immediately. Japanese troops began landing on the Liaodong Peninsula on May 5. They set up a besieging line facing south to Port Arthur and a defensive line facing north towards Manchuria since the Russians still had significant numbers of troops in Mukden. The Russians were compelled to break the siege by attacking the south from the north, but the Japanese defeated the Russian attacking force in mid-June at the Battle of Telissu, which secured the Japanese plans to besiege Port Arthur and sent the Russians reeling north again.[23]

There were a couple of different documents a participant could have been awarded for military conflict. One of the most common and detailed documents were the small award documents, like the one pictured on page 52. They were given in conjunction with the full documents and provided additional information, including possible monetary awards for service or prizes for medals. These small documents could also include a listing of multiple awards. For instance, this small award document was for actions during the Russo–Japanese War and included the Rising Sun 8th Class. The document was awarded in 1906 to Army Infantry Pvt. 1st Class Ueno Taichi. Pvt. Taichi was to receive 200 yen as a prize. He was one of thousands of Japanese who received citations and awards for bravery and service during this bloody war.

The Japanese had secured Port Arthur and negated any immediate danger. Next, they set upon neutralizing the danger of the Russians in Manchuria. The Russian army was in retreat by mid-June as three different Japanese armies advanced north towards Mukden in central Manchuria. Meanwhile the Russian Fleet, trapped at Port Arthur, felt the pressure to break out of the Japanese naval blockade and link up with their fleet at Vladivostok. They chose to attempt the breakout on August 10. The naval engagement that ensued was a draw throughout much of the day until the Russian Navy was dealt a decisive blow. The Russian flagship, *Tsarevitch,* was hit on the bridge, killing the Russian admiral in command of the fleet. The Russians returned to Port Arthur humiliated and destined not to try another engagement.[24]

As the Japanese marched north in Manchuria towards Mukden, a large-scale battle was taking place at Laioyang on August 25. The Russians had superiority in numbers, and the town of Laioyang had three defense rings around the city. However, the morale of the Russian troops was low after the retreat north, and their defensive positions were not ideal. Moreover, Japanese spies had reliable intelligence on the main defense line running outside the city. The Japanese attacks were met with strong Russian artillery fire, which caused many casualties. The Battle of Laioyang lasted until September 5, when the Russians finally retreated north towards Mukden with the bulk of their 200,000 troops. The Russians had caused over 23,000 Japanese casualties during the battle, but the retreat marked another defeat for the Russians. The Japanese celebrations at home were somewhat muted by the tremendous amount of casualties.[25]

The action now turned back to the siege and assault of Port Arthur by the Japanese. The attack began in late July as the Japanese started to take out the Russian defenses one at a time. These positions were well-defended and each fortified position cost the Japanese dearly. In many ways, the Siege of Port Arthur resembled the battles of the First World War with high causalities and the use of defensive wire and deadly artillery. The Japanese military suffered nearly 60,000 casualties, which was twice that of the Russians. However, the siege of the port had left the Russian military and civilians with dwindling supplies and food. The Russians also realized that help was not coming to Port Arthur any time soon, so they surrendered on January 2, 1905.[26]

The journal pictured on the next few pages is an army soldier's passbook, called a *Techo* in Japan. This specific Techo was from a soldier who served in the 1904–05 War. The soldier, Tanaka Shinsuke, had reached the rank of sergeant in Japan's army as an engineer. Sgt. Tanaka Shinsuke belonged to the 9th Division, 9th Battalion, and 3rd Company. He fought in the significant Battle of Mukden in 1905. His Techo provides a rich description of his service, including his entry that indicated he had earned the 1904–05 War Medal, Order of the Rising Sun 8th Class, and Order of the Golden Kite 7th Class. For those willing to take the challenge of translating Techos, they can provide a wealth of information.

The continuous defeats of Russia on the battlefield contributed to the social unrest and subsequent failed revolution in Russia starting in 1905. Additionally, the social turmoil in Russia eroded the fighting capabilities of the Russian military even more. The Japanese continued to push north from Laioyang to Mukden. By late January 1905, the Russians had enforced their positions at Mukden with up to 300,000 troops while the Japanese only had around 200,000. The Japanese were actually feeling the strain of war as the country was running short of troops after a year of fierce fighting. The Japanese, however, would once again utilize deception and flanking movements. Japan deployed a force on the eastern side of the battlefield in view of the Russians. The Russians took the bait and reinforced this side with no awareness of the bulk of the Japanese forces on the left. The lack of accurate military intelligence cost the Russians dearly still again. The Japanese movements on both flanks were successful in slowly enveloping the Russians around Mukden

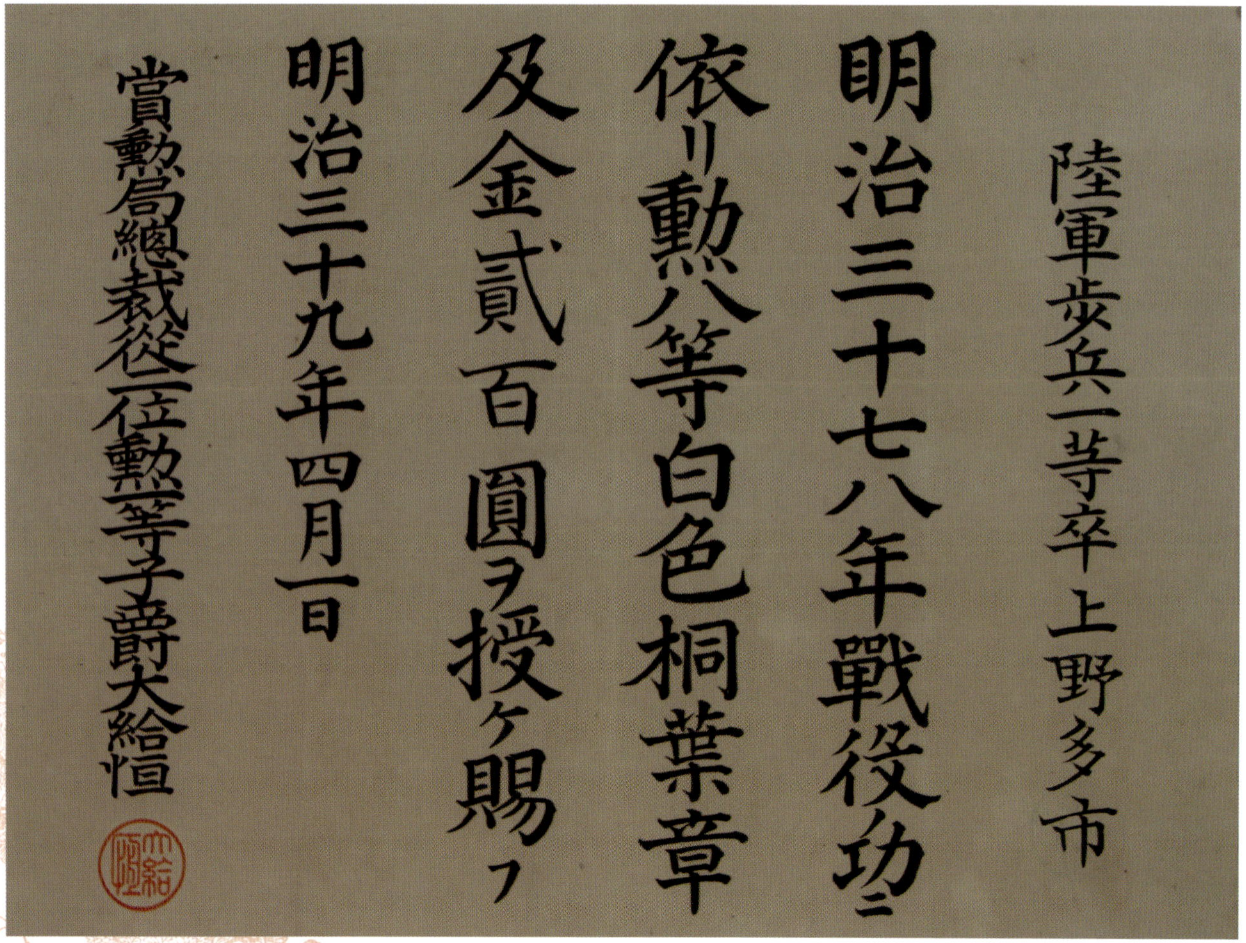

陸軍歩兵一等卒上野多市
明治三十七八年戰役功ニ
依リ勲八等白色桐葉章
及金貳百圓ヲ授ケ賜フ
明治三十九年四月一日
賞勲局總裁従一位勲一等子爵大給恒

Translation for a small award document from Russo–Japanese War, right side only: "Army Infantry First Class Private Ueno Taichi. For Brave War Service during the Meiji 37-8 [1904–05] War, the named person has received the 8th Class Rising Sun as well as a cash award of 200 yen. Meiji 39 [1906], April 1." *Author's Collection*

Opposite left: Cover of army engineer Tanaka Shinsuke's soldier passbook from the Russo–Japanese War. The cover is heavily worn and gold lettering is almost gone. *Author's Collection*

Opposite right: A partial translation of army engineer Tanaka Shinsuke's passbook (personal information page) from the Russo–Japanese War includes the following information: Army Engineer Tanaka Shinsuke reached the rank of Sergeant and served in the 9th Division of the 9th Battalion with the 3rd Company. He was born on September 1, 1881, in Fukui prefecture. *Author's Collection*

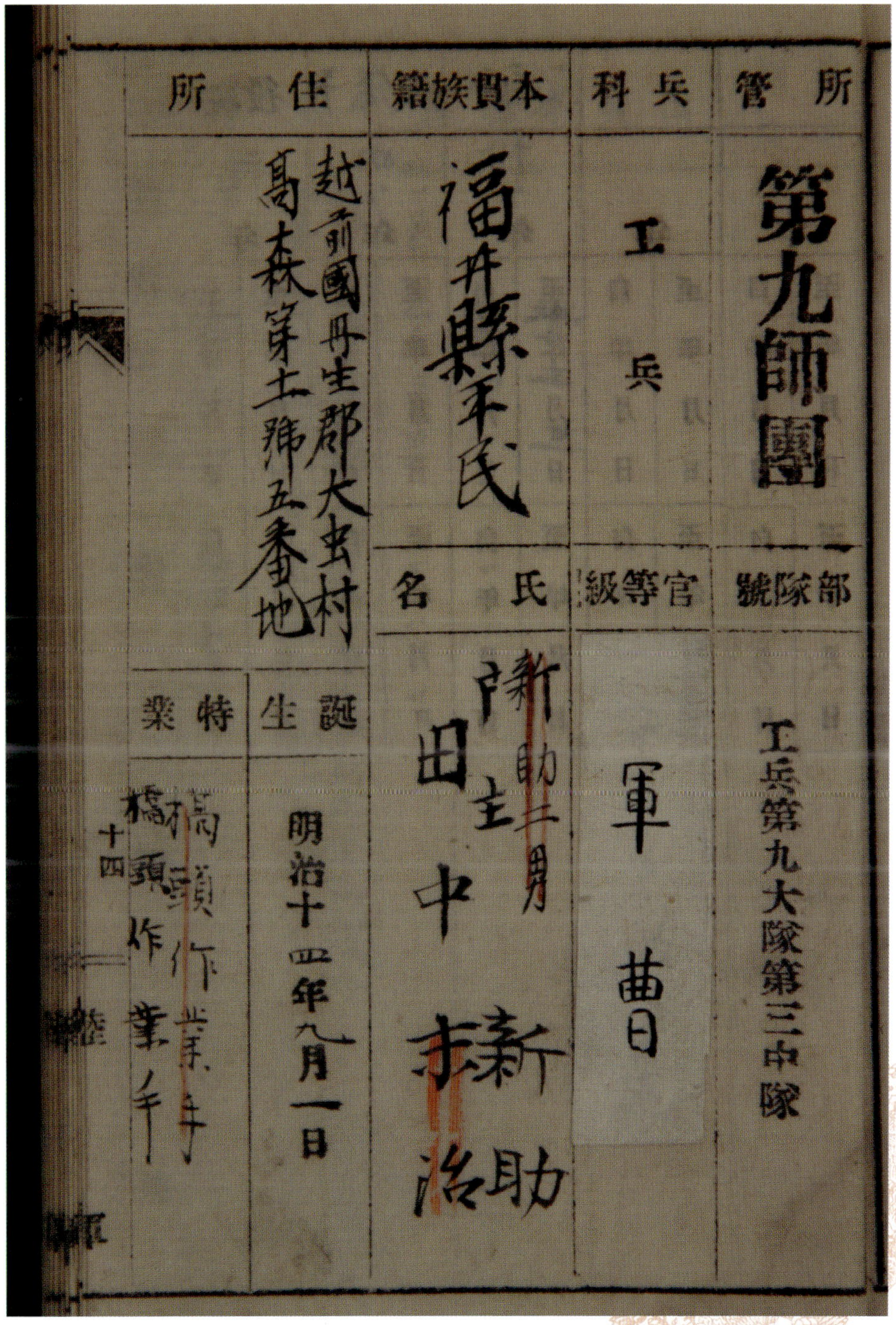

所管	兵科	本貫族籍	住所
第九師團	工兵	福井縣平民	越前國丹生郡大虫村高森[illegible]番地

部隊號	官等級	氏名	誕生	特業
工兵第九大隊第三中隊	軍曹	田中新助	明治十四年八月一日	橋頭作業手

十四 一等

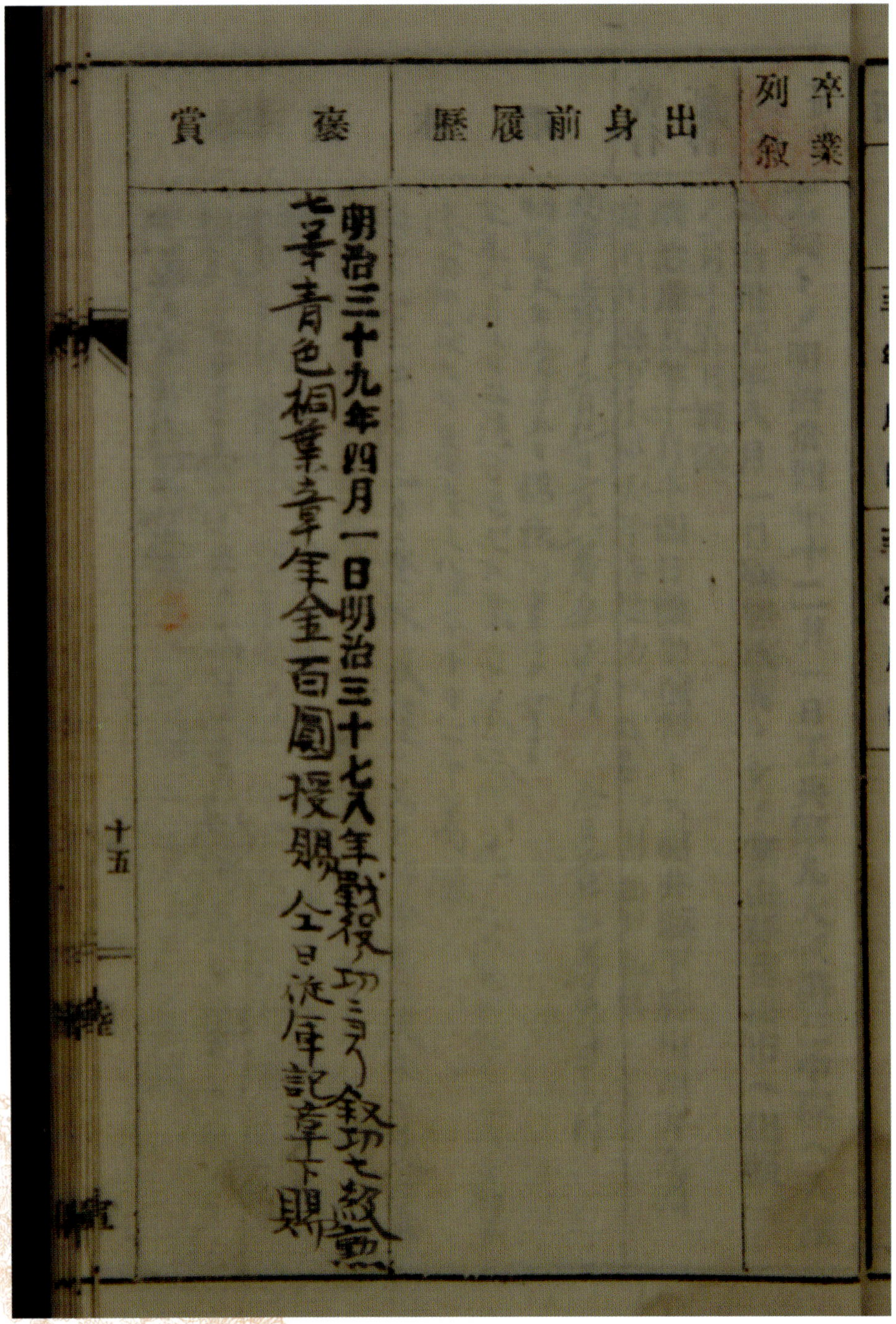

卒業列叙

出身前履歴

褒賞

明治三十九年四月一日明治三十七八年戦役ノ功ニ依リ叙功七級勲七等青色桐葉章年金百圓授賜 仝日従軍記章下賜

十五

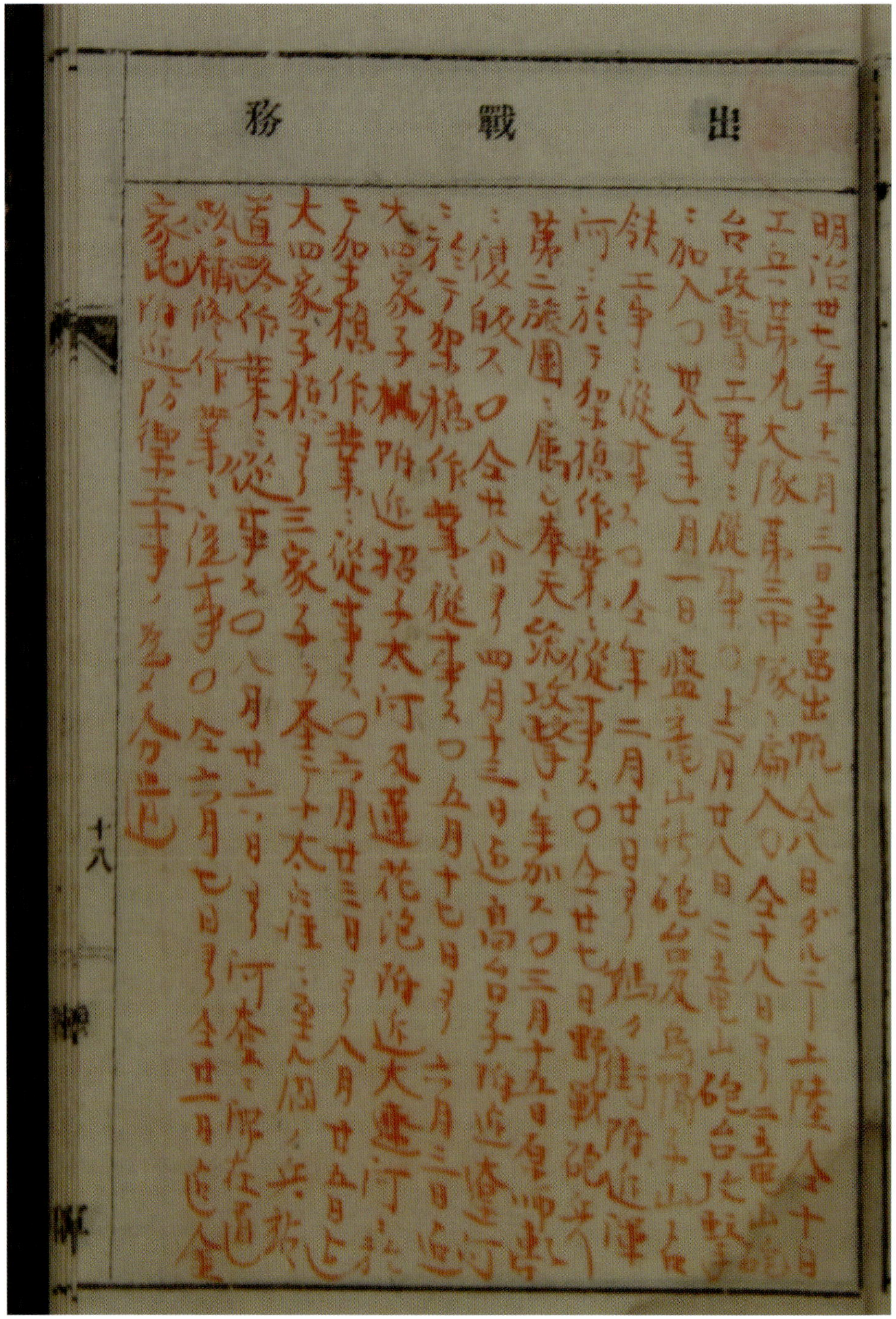

出戰務

十八

Opposite left: Army engineer Tanaka Shinsuke earned some impressive awards during the Russo–Japanese War. A partial translation of his passbook (education and awards page) includes the following information: On April 1, 1906, soldier earned 1904–05 War Medal, Order of the Golden Kite 7th Class, and Order of the Rising Sun 7th Class with 100 yen award. *Author's Collection*

Opposite right: Army engineer Tanaka Shinsuke passbook's service record pages are quite detailed. This is just one of five pages from his military career, which spanned from 1901–1915. The collectors would be most interested in this page, which records part of his service from the Russo–Japanese War. The entry includes his involvement in the attack on Mukden as part of Field Artillery of the 2nd Brigade on February 27, 1905. *Author's Collection*

from March 2–7. The causalities on the Japanese side were high as they pushed relentlessly on the Russians. The Russians suffered casualties as well, but the steady success of the Japanese forces on the flanks crushed the morale of the Russians. By March 9, the Russian commander, Gen. Kuropatkin, ordered a retreat north even deeper into Manchuria. The largest land battle since the Napoleonic age was quite bloody with Russians suffering 90,000 causalities while the Japanese suffered 76,000. The Battle of Mukden was the last land battle of the war.[27]

The defining action in the Russo–Japanese War was the Battle of Tsushima between the Japanese and Russian navies. As mentioned earlier, the Russian navy stationed in European waters made the almost unbelievable journey half-way around the world to the Far East. The journey was made by forty-two ships that embarked in October 1904. The journey would prove to be a logistical nightmare as the Russians had to stop at numerous ports for supplies and maintenance. The Japanese knew of the Russian movements, and Adm. Tōgō used this time wisely to refit and prepare. The Russians finally entered hostile waters by May of 1905 as they sailed towards Vladivostok. Admiral Tōgō correctly guessed that the Russians would take the shortest route to this port through the Straits of Tsushima between Japan and Korea. The two fleets would meet at this point on May 27. The Japanese fielded nearly ninety ships while the Russians could only bring about forty ships to the battle. The two fleets were sailing in-line towards each other. Tōgō decided to conduct the highly dangerous maneuver, called crossing the "T". This terminology means that he turned his fleet across the face of the Russian column. This move would put his ships at an initial disadvantage as they turned one-by-one across the path of the Russian fleet. However, Russian Adm. Rozhestvensky did not take advantage of this situation quickly enough, and the lead Japanese ship made the turn to a highly superior position to fire. As more and more Japanese ships made the turn and crossed the "T," they were able to train all of their guns on the Russians while the Russians could only reply with their forward guns. The Russians lost four valuable battleships and the battle's initiative. The Japanese continued the battle into the night, and the next day they destroyed the Russian fleet almost to a ship. The victory at Tsushima sealed the Japanese victory in the war and established Adm. Tōgō's reputation as one of the greatest naval commanders in modern history.[28]

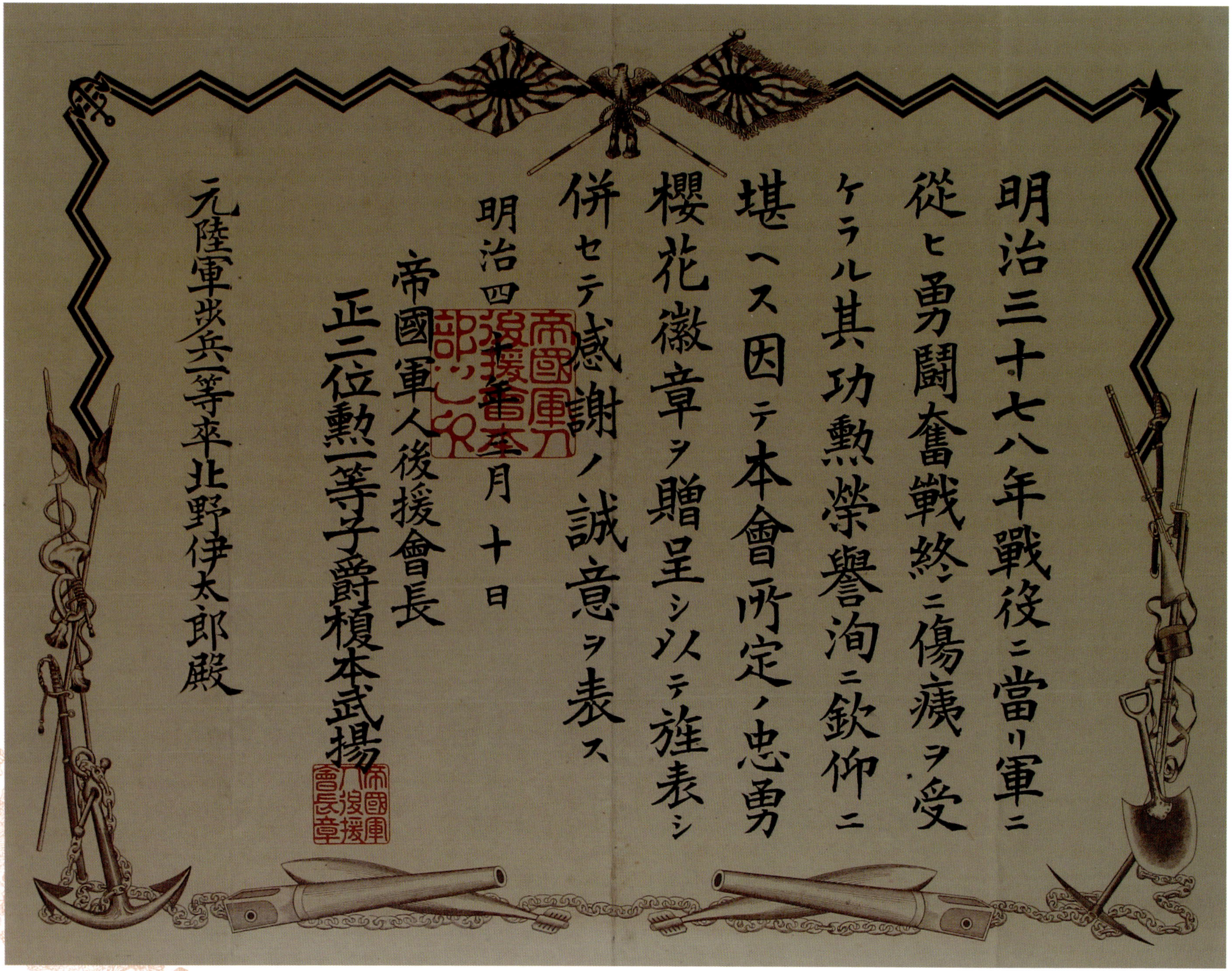

明治三十七八年戰役ニ當リ軍ニ
従ヒ勇鬪奮戰終ニ傷痍ヲ受
ケラル其功勲榮譽洵ニ欽仰ニ
堪ヘス因テ本會所定ノ忠勇
櫻花徽章ヲ贈呈シ以テ旌表シ
併セテ感謝ノ誠意ヲ表ス

明治四十[illegible]年[illegible]月十日

帝國軍人後援會長
正二位勲一等子爵榎本武揚

帝國軍人後援會本部之印

帝國軍人後援會長章

元陸軍歩兵一等卒北野伊太郎殿

Opposite: Translation of Cherry Blossom Badge document from the Imperial Soldier Relief Association, right side only: "You joined the army for the Meiji 37–8 [1904–05] War, fought courageously, and were wounded. Your achievement and gloriousness are highly venerated. Therefore, you are granted the Courageous Cherry Blossom Badge designated by the Association, with which we express our admiration and sincere gratitude. Meiji 40 (1907) March 10." *Author's Collection*

The featured document is for bravery during the Russo–Japanese War. It was awarded by the Imperial Soldier Relief Association. The organization was founded just after the First Sino–Japanese War. The purpose of the group was to promote support for the military as well as the spirit of volunteering. In order to achieve this goal, the group tried to support bereaved families, give consolation, which could include money, and reward military men for any good deeds. For instance, a family could receive up to 200 yen in assistance per year. The Imperial Soldier Relief Association was disbanded in 1938. The document was given in 1907 to ex-army infantryman first class soldier Kitano Itaro.[29]

The naval battle at Tsushima further strained the social relations in Russia and pushed the peace discussions forward. The president of the United States, Theodore Roosevelt, had offered to act as a peace mediator for Japan and Russia before Tsushima. Japan was eager to end the war as they were stretched to their limits and wanted to end the conflict while they held the upper hand. Some in Russia wanted to continue the fight; however, unrest at home and defeat in the Far East had brought the Russians to the table. The Treaty of Portsmouth was signed on September 5, and ended the Russo–Japanese War. The Russians would retain the northern half of Sakhalin Island, situated between Japan and Russia. Russia acknowledged the interest of Japan in Korea. Japan would also obtain the Russian leases on the Laiotung Peninsula including Port Arthur. Furthermore, both nations agreed that Manchuria would be off-limits to both militarily. After 1905, Japan was positioned to act in Korea as they saw fit, which they did quickly.[30]

This painting depicts the Russian battleship *Oslyabya* being sunk in the opening moves of the Battle of Tsushima on May 27, 1905. *Author's Collection*

Top view of Cherry Blossom Badge document. The eagle, which resembles the eagle from the Order of the Golden Kite, is perched on two crossed Japanese flags. *Author's Collection*

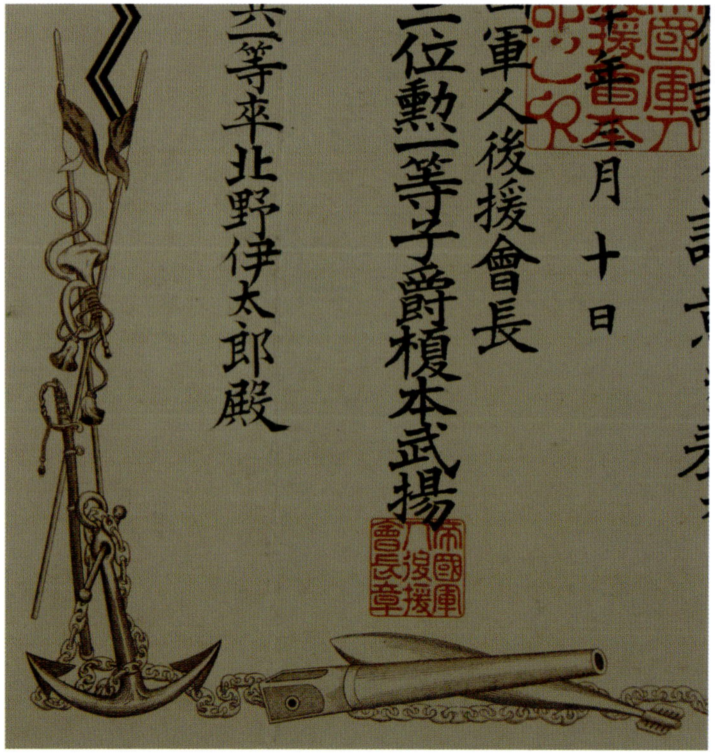

Left corner view of Cherry Blossom Badge document features an anchor, sword, bugle, and two lances with small flags attached. *Author's Collection*

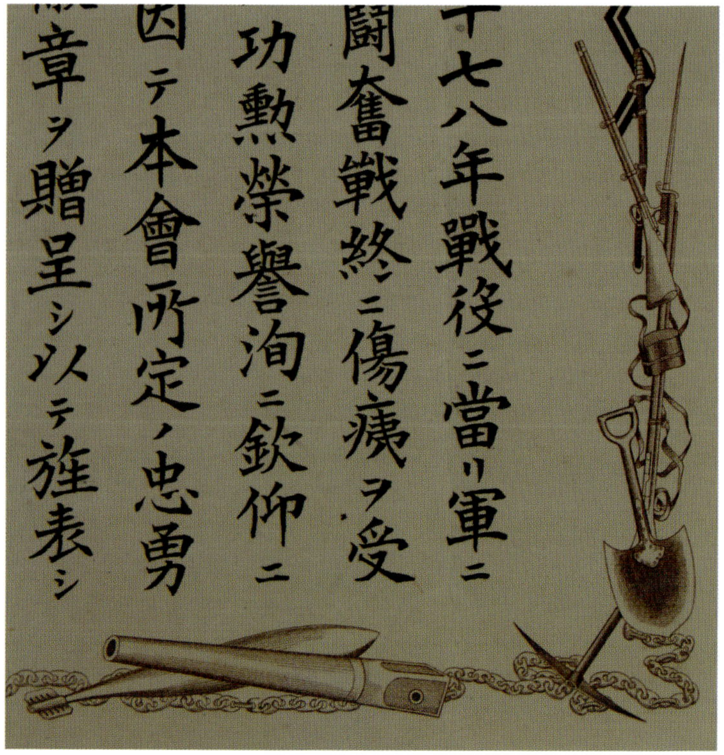

Right corner view of Cherry Blossom Badge document features a pickaxe, shovel, mess kit, two rifles, and a sword. *Author's Collection*

Annexation of Korea

Korea developed an order system much like Japan's, and they are all rare because of the short span of time that Japan was only "protecting" Korea. The two documents featured at the start of this section are associated with the Korean Order of the Eight Trigrams. The larger document is the Korean Order of the Eight Trigrams 6th Class, awarded in 1909, while the smaller document is the official permission to wear the document from the Japanese government given in 1910. The permission document was necessary for all foreign awards, including medals from Korea and later Manchukuo. A variation exists where the characters for "awarded to" are at the top center. This variation usually appeared on documents before 1907. Both of these documents are for the same person, army infantry Cpl. Morozumi Chiharu. Individually, these documents are hard to find and together they are extremely rare. The Order is actually signed by Emperor Sunjong. These documents also speak to the influence of Japan on Korea during the first decade of the twentieth century. You must remember that orders were awarded by social class. The accompanying permission to wear document indicates that Cpl. Morozumi had only been awarded the Order of the Rising Sun 8th Class (I have this document as well). Thus, he was considered to be socially equivalent to someone worthy of the 6th class order in Korean, but only the 8th Class in Japan. This comparison is an interesting example of how Japan worked to undermine the social structures of Korea before annexation.

The Japanese influence on Korea had started even before the First Sino-Japanese War and became more intense after Japan's victory over China. For instance, the orders and medals of the Korean Empire were fashioned after the Japanese model around 1900. The Japanese victory over Russia in 1905 solidified Japan's domination of Korea. Foreign agreements and treaties gave international legitimacy to Japan as a protectorate of Korea. Japan had a free hand to institute a variety of measures to reduce the autonomy of the Korean government. The initial demands that Japan placed on Korea were centered on internal and external security. This control was eventually extended to transportation, diplomacy, and then to most every institution in Korea. Emperor Gojong, who had ruled Korea since the 1860s, had lost all power.[31]

The Korean leaders tried desperately to regain their autonomy separate from Japan. Emperor Gojong even appealed to The Hague in the Netherlands in 1907 in the hope that the international community would put pressure on Japan to back off or lessen their efforts to dominate Korea. The international community was not moved by his plea and sided with Japan. This decision was significant for Japan since the international community essentially enshrined Japan's status as an empire and Korea as their colonial possession. Emperor Gojong was forced to abdicate in favor of his son.[32]

The small award document featured in this section was awarded to army infantry Capt. Kutsunoya Jirō for the Order of the Rising Sun 4th Class. The document

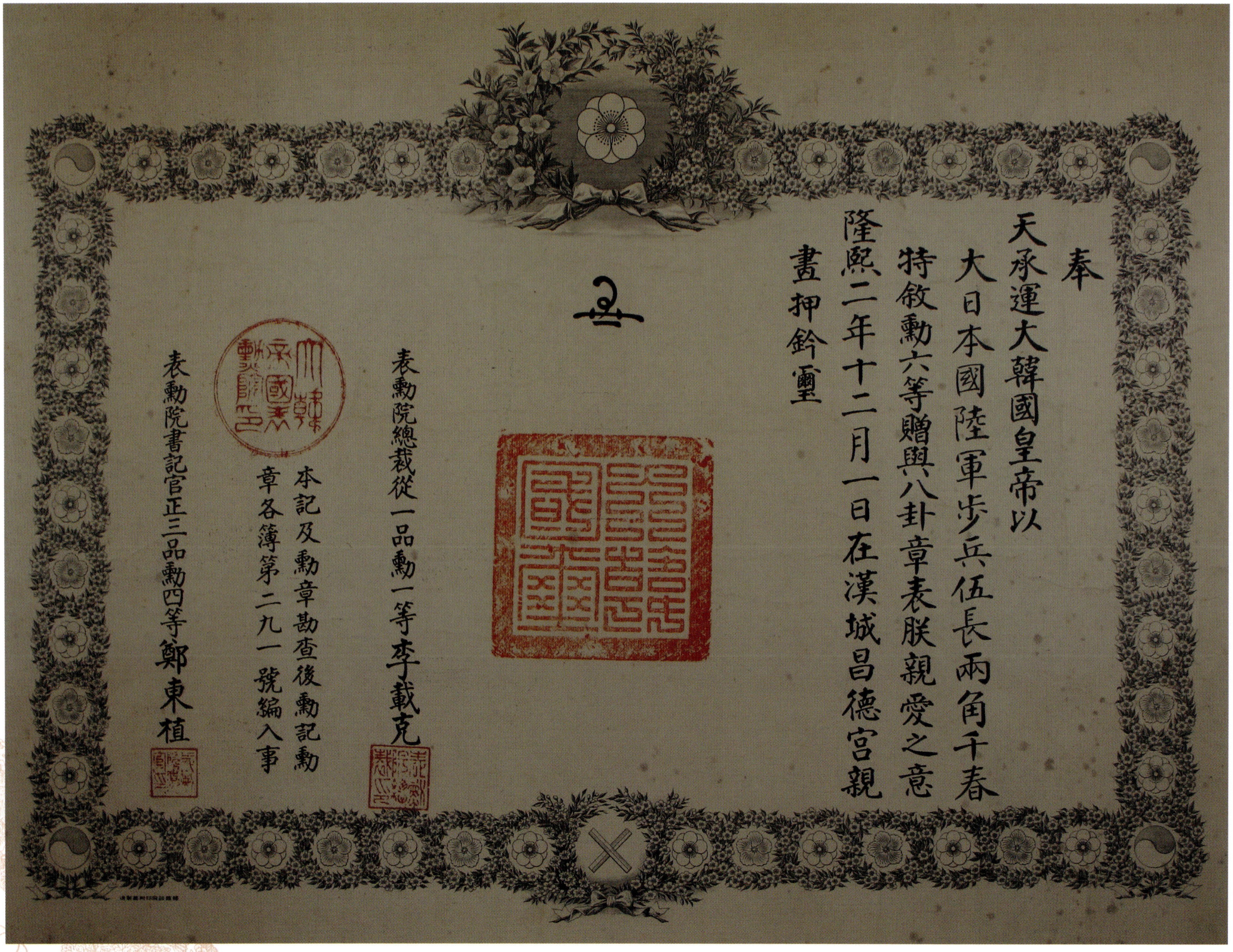

奉

天承運大韓國皇帝以

大日本國陸軍步兵伍長兩角千春

特敘勳六等贈與八卦章表朕親愛之意

隆熙二年十二月一日在漢城昌德宮親

畫押鈐璽

表勳院總裁從一品勳一等李載克

本記及勳章勘查後勳記勳

章各簿第二九一號編入事

表勳院書記官正三品勳四等鄭東植

Opposite: Translation of Korean Order of the Eight Trigrams 6th Class document, right side only: "December 1, 1909, by the grace of the Emperor of Korea, Great Japan Army Infantryman Corporal Morozumi Chiharu, a special award of the 6th Class Order of the Eight Trigrams is given." *Author's Collection*

Top view of the Korean Order document features a plum blossom surrounded by floral leaves. The documents for the Korean Order of the Taegeuk and Eight Trigrams were identical in form. Both of these orders were patterned after the Japanese Orders of the Rising Sun and Sacred Treasure. *Author's Collection*

View of Korean Emperor Sunjong's signature. This is his signature in Hangul (Korean). I have also seen his signature in the Hanja form of this birth name, presumably signed before he was completely enthroned as the emperor. The photograph also highlights the plum blossom watermark of this document. *Author's Collection*

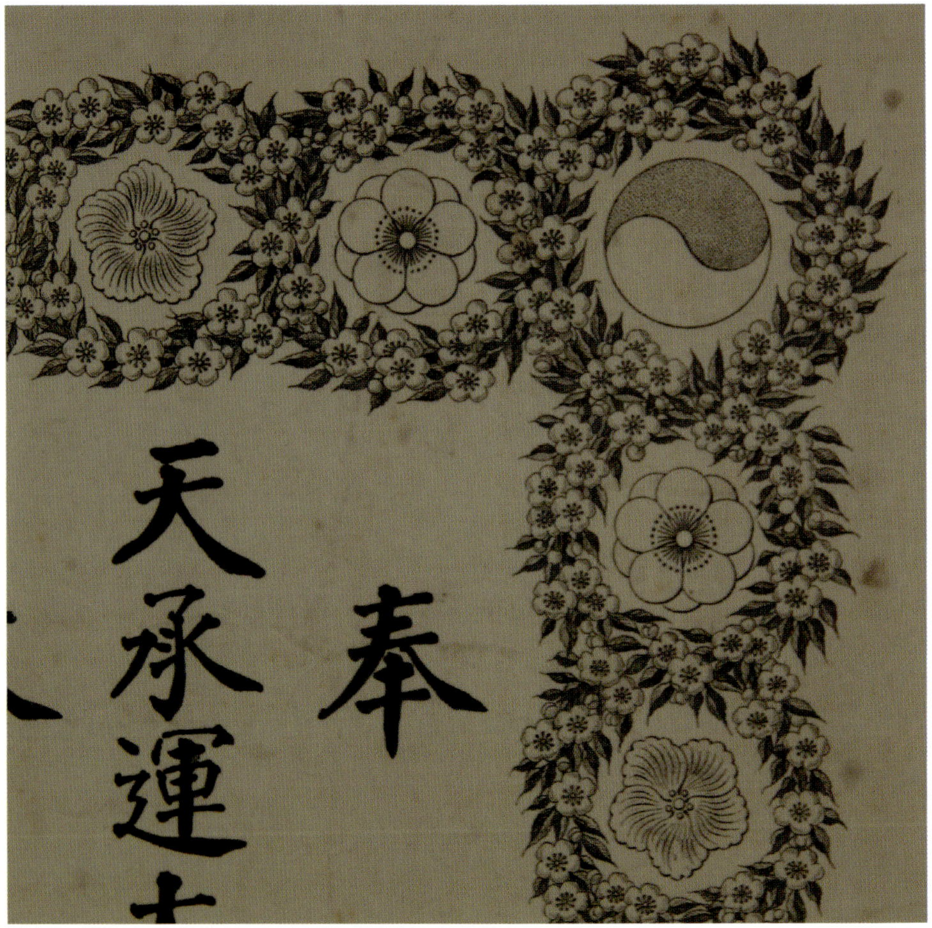

Corner view of the Korean Order document features alternative plum blossoms that form the whole border of the document. The corners of the border are anchored with the Yin and Yang symbol of Taoism. Much of the design of these documents resembles the Japanese order documents. *Author's Collection*

Bottom view of the Korean Order document features, what seems to be two crossed rulers surrounded by a floral wreath. *Author's Collection*

大日本帝國外國勲章佩用免許證

陸軍歩兵伍長勲八等兩角千春

韓國皇帝陛下ヨリ贈與シタル勲六等八卦
章ヲ受領シ及ヒ佩用スルヲ允許セラル

明治四十三年八月二十八日

賞勲局總裁従二位勲四等伯爵正親町實正

第七千六百十七號ヲ以テ外國
勲章佩用免許簿冊ニ記入ス

賞勲局書記官従四位勲三等横田香苗

賞勲局書記官従五位勲四等藤井善言

Opposite: Translation of Japanese permission to wear the Korean Order of the Eight Trigrams 6th Class document, right side only: "Great Japan Army Infantryman Corporal Morozumi Chiharu 8th Decorated Rank, permission to wear to the 6th Class Order of the Eight Trigrams is given. August 28, 1910." *Author's Collection*

shows the award was for his actions in suppressing insurgents in Korea in 1907–08. This is a rare document for both the high class of the order and the events surrounding the document. Capt. Kutsunoya was part of a very small but powerful contingent of soldiers who were in charge of internal security. These forces quashed any form of Korean resistance. Much of the resistance from insurgents was centralized in Seoul, the political heart of Korea.[33] Considering the illegal nature of the Japanese coercion of Korea, though the action was sanctioned by many other nations, the blunt wording of this document is quite surprising. This document leaves no doubt that Japan was serious about maintaining their control over Korea.

The abdication of Gojong and enthronement of Sunjong put Korea firmly in the hands of Japan. The last straw was the assassination of Prince Itō Hirobumi by a Korean national in 1909. Prince Hirobumi was a former prime minister of Japan and resident-general of Korea. The assassination provided the catalyst for the Japanese government to annex Korea into the Japanese empire. Japan wrote a treaty and coerced Korean leaders to sign it in August 1910.[34] The effect of the treaty was devastating to Koreans. The Japanese ruled Korea with an iron hand for thirty-five years, forcing the Koreans to endure many hardships.

The Korean Annexation Commemorative Medal was given to all of those who contributed to annexation event. This award document was given to governor general of Korea Railroad Secretary Oda Tokujiro. It is hard to find, and this document is numbered 29,999. The annexation of Korea was a celebrated event in Japan while Emperor Sunjong and much of the Korean court were given Japanese titles of nobility and stipends.[35] The Korean peninsula was officially opened up to Japanese military, merchants, and businessmen. Japan now had a real colony and could proudly stand on the world stage as an imperial power, not to be taken lightly.

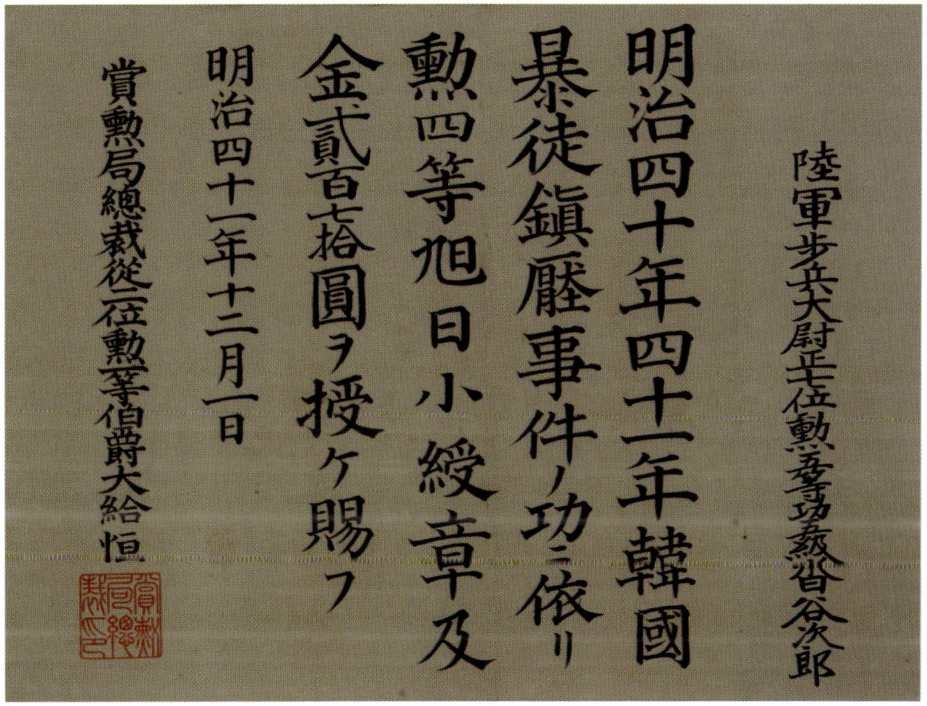
陸軍歩兵大尉正七位勲五等功五級沓谷次郎
明治四十年四十一年韓國
暴徒鎮壓事件ノ功ニ依リ
勲四等旭日小綬章及
金貳百七拾圓ヲ授ケ賜フ
明治四十一年十二月一日
賞勲局總裁従二位勲一等伯爵大給恒

Translation of small award document for Order of the Rising Sun 4th Class for actions in Korea, right side only: "Army Infantry Captain, 7th Senior Imperial Rank, 5th Decorated Rank, Order of the Golden Kite 5th Class, Kutsunoya Jirō. For your achievement in quelling Korean rioters in Meiji 40–41, the Order of the Rising Sun 4th Class and two hundred and seventy yen are conferred on you. Meiji 41 [1908], December 12." *Author's Collection*

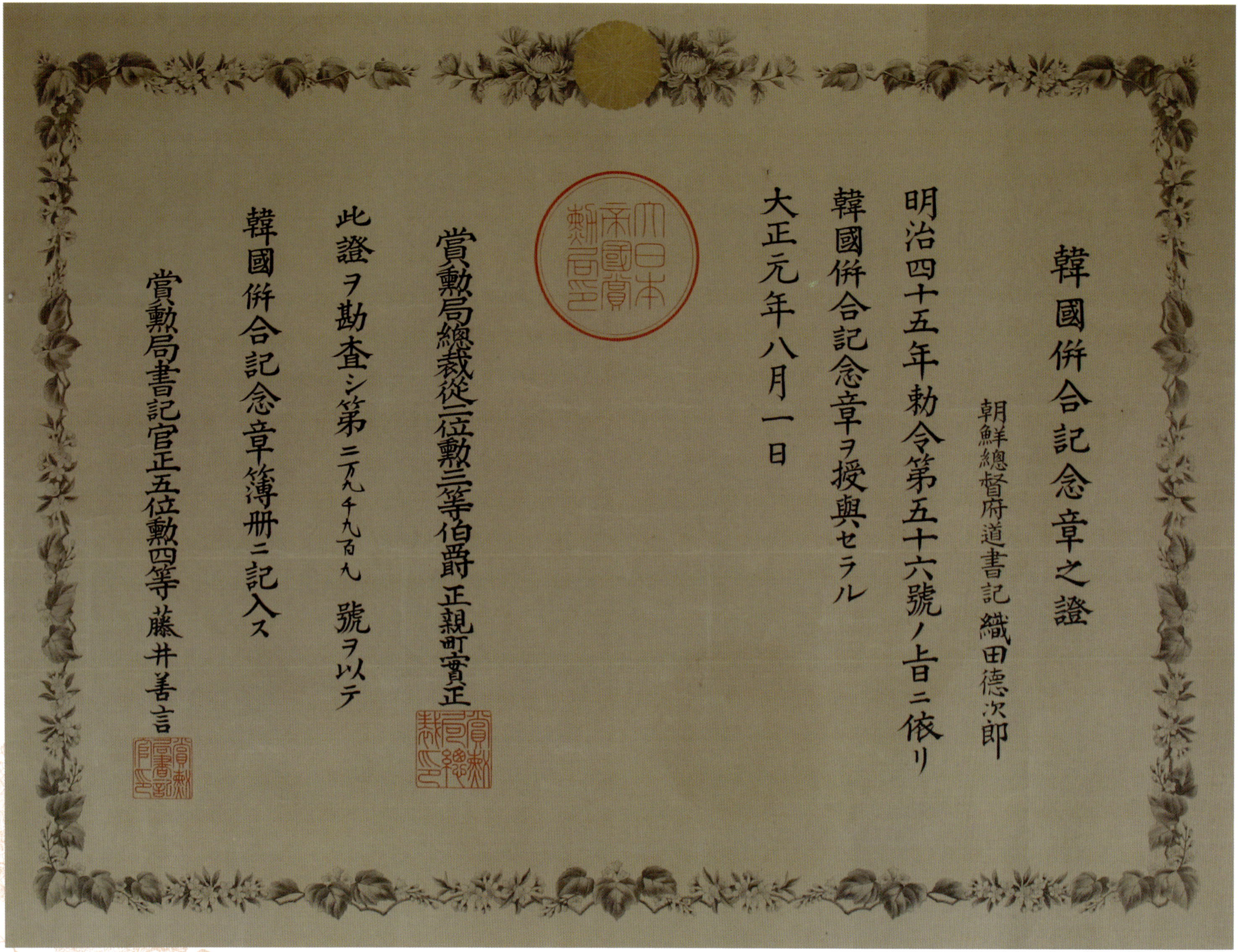
韓國併合記念章之證

朝鮮總督府道書記 織田德次郎

明治四十五年勅令第五十六號ノ旨ニ依リ
韓國併合記念章ヲ授與セラル

大正元年八月一日

賞勳局總裁從二位勳二等伯爵 正親町實正

此證ヲ勘査シ第二万九千九百九號ヲ以テ
韓國併合記念章簿冊ニ記入ス

賞勳局書記官正五位勳四等 藤井善言

Opposite: Translation of the Korean Annexation Commemorative Medal document, right side only: "According to the 1912 Imperial Ordinance number 56, the Korean Annexation Commemorative Medal is awarded to Governor-General of Korea Railroad Secretary Oda Tokujiro, August 1, 1912." *Author's Collection*

Top view of Korean Annexation Commemorative Medal document that features the gold imperial seal. The center red seal circle stamp, visible in the full photograph of the document reads, "Great Japan, Imperial Awards and Medals Department." *Author's Collection*

Side view of Korean Annexation Commemorative Medal document, which features an alternating flowers, presumably kiri leaves and cherry blossoms. *Author's Collection*

Chapter 2 Endnotes

1. S. C. M. Paine, *The Sino–Japanese War* (Cambridge, MA: Cambridge University Press, 2003), 116–121.
2. S. C. M. Paine, *The Sino–Japanese War* (Cambridge, MA: Cambridge University Press, 2003), 151.
3. R. B. Edgerton, *Warriors of the Rising Sun: A History of the Japanese Military*. (New York: W. W. Norton company, 1997), 45–46.
4. S. C. M. Paine, *The Sino–Japanese War* (Cambridge, MA: Cambridge University Press, 2003), 158–159.
5. S. C. M. Paine, *The Sino–Japanese War* (Cambridge, MA: Cambridge University Press, 2003), 165–168.
6. S. C. M. Paine, *The Sino–Japanese War* (Cambridge, MA: Cambridge University Press, 2003), 179–181, 202–203.
7. R. B. Edgerton, *Warriors of the Rising Sun: A History of the Japanese Military*. (New York: W. W. Norton company, 1997), 47–48.
8. S. C. M. Paine, *The Sino–Japanese War* (Cambridge, MA: Cambridge University Press, 2003), 235–236, 242–243.
9. S. C. M. Paine, *The Sino–Japanese War* (Cambridge, MA: Cambridge University Press, 2003), 177.
10. S. Makito, *The Sino-Japanese War and the Birth of Japanese Nationalism* (Tokyo: International house of Japan, 2009), 100–101.
11. S. C. M. Paine, *The Sino–Japanese War* (Cambridge, MA: Cambridge University Press, 2003), 271–277.
12. S. C. M. Paine, *The Sino–Japanese War* (Cambridge, MA: Cambridge University Press, 2003), 290–293.
13. R. B. Edgerton, *Warriors of the Rising Sun: A History of the Japanese Military* (New York: W. W. Norton company, 1997), 80.
14. C. Martin, *The Boxer Rebellion* (New York: Abelard-Schuman, 1968), 42–43.
15. C. Martin, *The Boxer Rebellion* (New York: Abelard-Schuman, 1968), 44–47, 58.
16. R. B. Edgerton, *Warriors of the Rising Sun: A History of the Japanese Military*. (New York: W. W. Norton company, 1997), 79–80.
17. R. B. Edgerton, *Warriors of the Rising Sun: A History of the Japanese Military* (New York: W. W. Norton company, 1997), 96–97.
18. A. Gordon, *A Modern History of Japan: From Tokugawa Times to the Present* (New York: Oxford Press, 2009), 144–145.
19. R. M. Connaughton, *The War of the Rising Sun and Tumbling Bear: A Military History of the Russo–Japanese War 1904–5* (New York: Routledge, 1988), 5–11.
20. Robert B. Edgerton, *Warriors of the Rising Sun: A History of the Japanese Military* (New York: W. W. Norton company, 1997), 101–103.
21. M. Connaughton, *The War of the Rising Sun and Tumbling Bear: A Military History of the Russo–Japanese War 1904–5* (New York: Routledge, 1988), 24–44.
22. R. M. Connaughton, *The War of the Rising Sun and Tumbling Bear: A Military History of the Russo–Japanese War 1904-5* (New York: Routledge, 1988), 47–65.
23. R. M. Connaughton, *The War of the Rising Sun and Tumbling Bear: A Military History of the Russo–Japanese War 1904–5* (New York: Routledge, 1988), 66–78, 80-–98.
24. R. M. Connaughton, *The War of the Rising Sun and Tumbling Bear: A Military History of the Russo–Japanese War 1904–5* (New York: Routledge, 1988), 100–101, 172–174.
25. R. M. Connaughton, *The War of the Rising Sun and Tumbling Bear: A Military History of the Russo–Japanese War 1904–5* (New York: Routledge, 1988), 125–167.
26. R. M. Connaughton, *The War of the Rising Sun and Tumbling Bear: A Military History of the Russo–Japanese War 1904–5* (New York: Routledge, 1988), 176–207.
27. R. B. Edgerton, *Warriors of the Rising Sun: A History of the Japanese Military* (New York: W. W. Norton company, 1997), 181–186.
28. R. B. Edgerton, *Warriors of the Rising Sun: A History of the Japanese Military* (New York: W. W. Norton company, 1997), 187–211.
29. Imperial Solider Relief Association, *History of the Imperial Soldier Relief Association* (Imperial Solider Relief Association: Japan, 1940).
30. R. M. Connaughton, *The War of the Rising Sun and Tumbling Bear: A Military History of the Russo-Japanese War 1904–5* (New York: Routledge, 1988), 273.
31. W. G. Beasley, *Japanese Imperialism, 1894–1945* (Oxford: Clarendon Press, 1987), 85–89.
32. W. G. Beasley. *The Modern History of Japan* (New York: Praeger, 1974), 175.
33. C. I. E. Kim and H. Kim, *Korea and the Politics of Imperialism, 1876–1910* (Berkley, CA: University of California Press, 1967), 196–197.
34. W. G. Beasley, *Japanese Imperialism, 1894–1945* (Oxford: Clarendon Press, 1987), 90.
35. C. I. E. Kim and H. Kim, *Korea and the Politics of Imperialism, 1876–1910* (Berkley, CA: University of California Press, 1967), 215–217.

3 JAPAN ON THE WORLD STAGE:

RISE OF THE EMPIRE (1910–1926)

The Taishō period, which stretched from 1912–1926, was a time of great change in Japan. The country made enormous strides toward modernizing as well as obtaining recognition on a par with the other great countries. It was a time of great industrial growth and accumulation of wealth. Yet, it was also a time of political intrigue and growing social instability. The military and social documents from the Taishō Period have great diversity.

This stylized drawing from 1916 features Allies from World War I. Japan had emerged as a world power at the same table as the most dominant powers in the world. However, the position of the Japanese in the back of the group also symbolizes the tension that Japan felt at the end of the war. This tension would lead to growing distrust between Japan and the West towards the end of the 1920s. The economic and social downturn in Japan during the Taishō's Democracy would further complicate the situation. *Author's Collection*

天佑ヲ保有シ萬世一系ノ帝祚ヲ踐タル
日本國皇帝ハ從四位勲四等鳥山虎也太ヲ明治
勲章ノ勲三等ニ敘シ瑞寶章ヲ授與ス
即チ此位ニ屬スル禮遇及ヒ特權ヲ有
セシム
神武天皇即位紀元二千五百七十四年
大正三年六月二十九日東京帝宮ニ於テ
親ラ名ヲ署シ璽ヲ鈐セシム

嘉仁

大正三年六月二十九日
賞勲局總裁從二位勲三等伯爵正親町實正
此證ヲ勘査シ第四十三万千四百四十八
號ヲ以テ勲等簿冊ニ記入ス
賞勲局書記官正五位勲四等藤井善言
賞勲局書記官　正七位　廣瀬温

Opposite: Translation of Order of the Sacred Treasure 3rd Class document, right side only: "Through the honor of the immortal Emperor, the Empire of Japan bestows this award. Junior 4th Imperial Rank, Order of Merit 4th Class, Toriyama Koyata. Order of the Sacred Treasure 3rd Class medal. Imperial Year 2574 [1914]. Taishō 3 [1914], June 29. Tokyo Imperial Shrine."
Author's Collection

Death of Emperor Meiji and Taishō's Enthronement

The Order of the Sacred Treasure 3rd Class is rare, though it is the most common of the 3rd class orders. This document is from 1914 and is signed by Emperor Taishō, more commonly known as Yoshihito. Emperor Taishō stopped signing this class of order for both the Scared Treasure and Rising Sun soon after. Presumably this action was taken to save time and preserve the prestige of the emperor's signature for people of the highest rank. This particular order was given to a man named Toriyama who had the 4th Junior Imperial Rank of class and had previously been awarded an order in the 4th class.

Emperor Meiji had reigned for forty-five years when his health started to fail in early 1912. He began to fatigue easily, and by July he became very ill. Emperor Meiji died on July 30 in the early morning hours. His son, Prince Yoshihito, began the accession process almost immediately. The Japanese government and public mourned his passing over the next five days as singing, dancing, and playing were forbidden and criminals were not executed or forced to do labor. The emperor was buried on September 13, and his final tomb was outside Kyoto. The most publicized mourning event was the suicide by seppuku (a samurai ritual self-disembowelment) of Gen. Nogi. Nogi felt he owed a debt to the emperor dating back to the Satsuma Rebellion when he lost his regimental banner in battles. His use of seppuku brought notoriety back to this old practice.[1]

The legacy of Emperor Meiji is undoubtedly his role in the Meiji Restoration. His influence goes beyond just having been emperor during a time of great change in Japan. We must recognize that the great accomplishments of the restoration happened because of many people; Emperor Meiji just happens to be the most visible as the ruling monarchy. Nonetheless, he worked to ensure that the changes could happen. He rejected many aspects of 500 years of tradition for Japanese emperors. Emperor Meiji did not revere the past and spend time in isolation; rather,

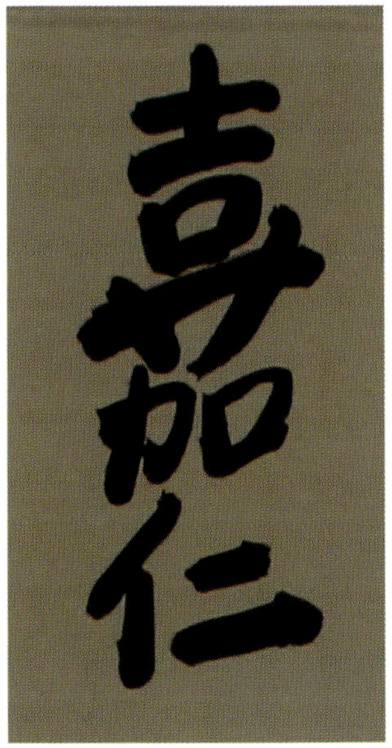

Emperor Taishō's Signature from the Order of the Sacred Treasure 3rd Class document. His signature is hard to find, although it may be easier to find than his son's signature, Emperor Hirohito.
Author's Collection

View of the Medal of Order of the Sacred Treasure 3rd Class document. This class of the Sacred Treasure Orders seemed to keep its same form on the award document from the 1890s through the imperial era. *Author's Collection*

he looked toward the future and foreign customs. This willingness to change set the example for the whole country and paved the way for one of the greatest transformations of a country in history. Japan emerged from a backward, feudal society to a modern, industrialized nation that commanded respect throughout the world.

The life of Prince Yoshihito and his early days as the newly enthroned Emperor Taishō are not as well documented as the reign of his father nor the subsequent history of his son, the eventual Emperor Hirohito. Prince Yoshihito was born in 1879, and became the heir to the throne by age nine. As a boy, he enjoyed Western customs, even to the point of annoying the emperor. Prince Yoshihito also suffered from numerous health problems that would plague him his entire life. These illnesses became worse as he got older. Consequently, he would make few public appearances as emperor. In 1900, Prince Yoshihito married Kujō Sadako, who was the daughter of a Japanese nobleman. Their first child, born in 1901, was Hirohito, the future Emperor Showa. Due to Emperor Taishō's chronic illness, Crown Prince Hirohito would take over more and more of the duties of his father.[2] The actual coronation process of Emperor Taishō did not occur until 1915.

The Taishō Enthronement medal and document was given rather freely to those who participated in the event. This document is numbered 52,039 and was awarded to Mayor of Taga Village, Shimizu Senjirou, in 1915. Crown Prince Yoshihito would become Emperor Taishō. The events around the coronation were quite ritualistic. The emperor assumed possession of the sacred treasures of the Japanese mythology. These include the sacred mirror, necklace, and sword. Though the actual coronation of Emperor Taishō did not take place until 1915, he began wielding his influence soon after his father's death. These events would be termed the Taishō Political Crisis and would be an auspicious start to the Taishō period.[3]

A photograph of Emperor Taishō at the start of his reign. *Author's Collection*

大禮記念章之證

滋賀縣犬上郡多賀村長清水仙治郎

大正四年勅令第百五十四號ノ旨ニ依リ
大禮記念章ヲ授與セラル

大正四年十一月十日

賞勲局總裁従二位勲二等伯爵正親町實正

此證ヲ勘査シ第六万二千百三十九號ヲ以テ
大禮記念章簿冊ニ記入ス

賞勲局書記官正五位勲四等藤井善言

Opposite: Translation of Taishō's Enthronement Commemorative Medal document, right side only: "Taishō Enthronement Commemorative Medal document Shiga Prefecture, Inukami District, Taga Village Mayor Shimizu Senjirou. In Taishō 4 [1916], the Taishō Enthronement Commemorative Medal is established by imperial edict 54. Taishō 4 [1916], November 10." *Author's Collection*

Top view of the Taishō Enthronement Medal document, which features a thin sprig of foliage surrounding the imperial seal. *Author's Collection*

A tied ribbon, the ends of which are wrapped around thin branches, forms the corner design of the Taishō Enthronement Medal document. *Author's Collection*

Bottom view of the Taishō Enthronement Medal document, which resembles what we might think of as a floral arrangement with small sprigs and flowers emerging from leaves. *Author's Collection*

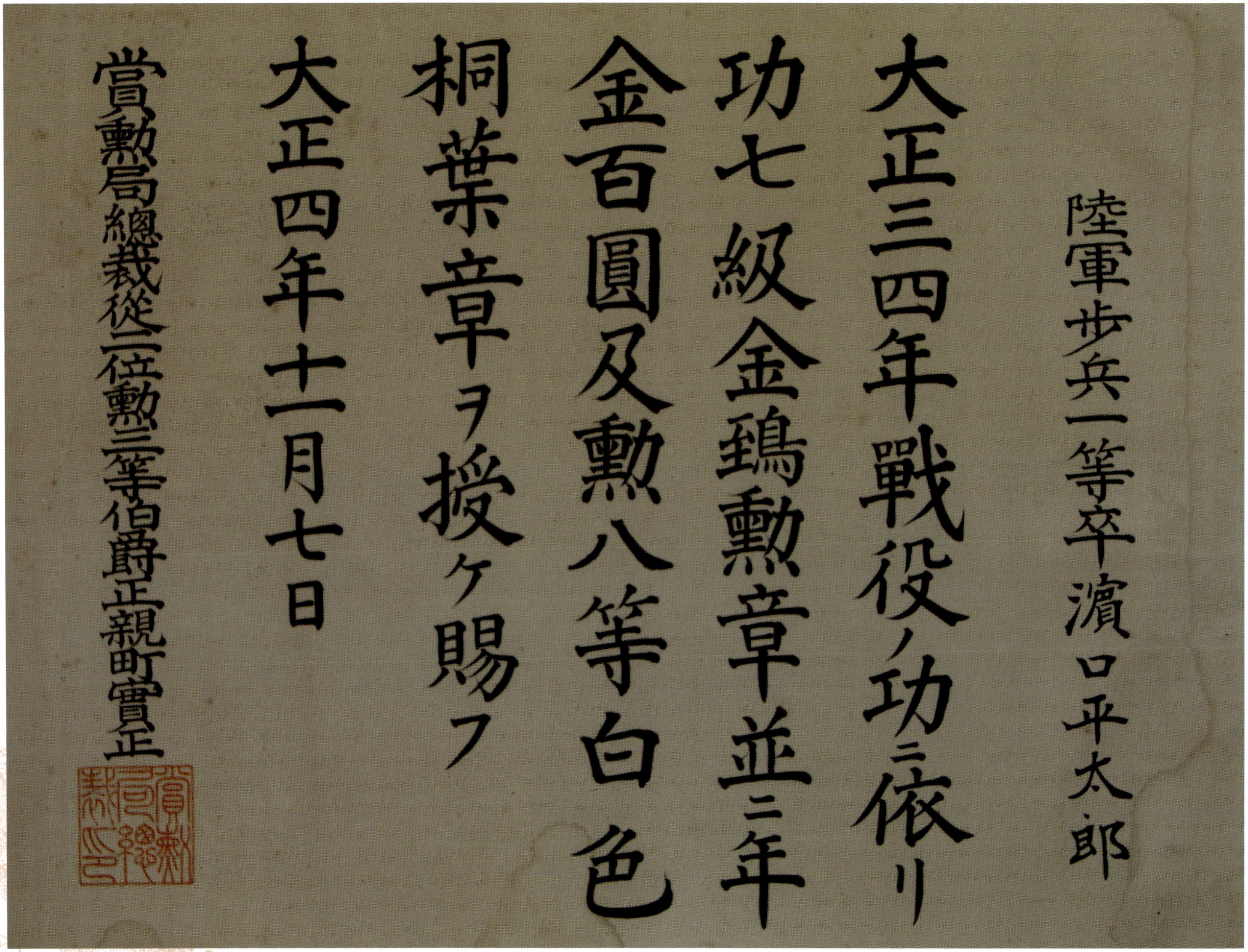

陸軍歩兵一等卒濱口平太郎

大正三四年戰役ノ功ニ依リ
功七級金鵄勲章並ニ年
金百圓及勲八等白色
桐葉章ヲ授ケ賜フ

大正四年十一月七日

賞勲局總裁從二位勲二等伯爵正親町實正

Opposite: Translation of small award document given to army infantry PFC Hamaguchi Heitaro. Translation: "For Bravery in the Taishō 3–4 [1914–15] War, the named person is awarded the Order of Golden Kite 7th Class medal, a cash award of 100 yen, and the 8th Class Rising Sun White Paulonia Leaves medal. Taishō 4 [1915], November 7." *Author's Collection*

World War I

The First World War provided an opportunity for Japan to claim territory from Germany with very little bloodshed. War documents from this conflict are harder to find because of the relatively low numbers of combatants. In fact, all combat-related documents can be traced to a single battle, the Siege of Tsingtao. This small document has an interesting story. It was awarded to army infantry PFC Hamaguchi Heitaro. He was awarded the Order of the Golden Kite 7th Class and Rising Sun 8th Class. Pvt. Heitaro undoubtedly helped dig the zigzag assault trenches that inched towards the German lines and culminated in a frontal assault in the usual Japanese style. Any Order of the Golden Kite document from this conflict is rare; however, smaller documents like these are quite affordable and offer more detail than their larger counterparts. The battle for which Private Heitaro won this distinction was the only land battle in which Japan had a major role in the First World War.

The start of World War I found the Japanese in a position of power in the Pacific. However, Japanese leaders were keenly aware of how fast the situation could erode. The European powers had turned their full attention to Europe, since a shift had left a vacuum of power in China. This situation provided a tempting opportunity for Japan to move against China in places like Manchuria. The Japanese realized that this move would eventually lead them to conflict with the European powers once World War I was over. Furthermore, attacking the Chinese would drive them closer to the Americans, who were quickly becoming Japan's rival in the Pacific. The Japanese decided to work with the Allied forces in Europe; they declared war on Germany. Japan had an alliance with Great Britain in 1902, although the British did not compel the Japanese to join the Allies. The British used the conditions of the alliance in early August 1914, when they asked for Japanese protection of the British naval interest around China and, more broadly, in the Pacific. The Germans had a small naval force situated in Tsingtao (now Qingdao) on the Shantung Peninsula on the northern Chinese coast. The Germans also possessed the northern part of New Guinea and a variety of small islands along the equator, including the Bismarck Archipelago and the North Solomon Islands. Japan used the start of World War I to take this territory from Germany. They demanded the Germans surrender their forces in Tsingtao and their naval forces in the Pacific on August 15, 1914. The Germans refused, and the Japanese declared war on Germany and Austria-Hungary on August 23, 1915.[4]

A group of Japanese soldiers pausing for lunch during the Siege of Tsingtao. *Author's Collection*

Japan moved quickly to besiege the German port of Tsingtao in China. The Japanese landed near the port on September 2, 1914. Japan moved quickly to complete the naval blockade of Tsingtao followed by the surrounding of the port on land by early October. The Japanese forces were supplemented by British troops. The siege featured an interesting historical first as Japan conducted the first air-to-sea attacks as their airplanes fired upon German ships in the harbor. The Allied naval force subdued the German forts through their artillery from October 31 through the first few days of November. Japanese and British troops had begun to attack the fort by November 3. The Germans held out until November 6 and surrendered the next day. The casualties on both sides were relatively light. The German garrison was bitter about the Japanese role in the siege, feeling racial superiority to the Japanese; however, the Germans were treated quite well in captivity and some even chose to remain in Japan after the end of World War I.[5]

Japan also moved quickly to take German islands in the Pacific. Germany had a number of colonies in the Pacific. The Allies, primarily Australia and Japan, moved to claim these territories. Japan occupied the Marshall and Caroline Islands by October 1914. These bloodless conquests were a political triumph that seemed to have little real value initially. Japan pushed its influence deep into the Pacific with these islands. The Japanese public was excited about the expansion of the empire though the islands provided little actual resources. However, as Japan began to plan on war in the Pacific, the islands would prove to be important staging areas for future actions. Later, the Marshall and Caroline Islands were sites of barbaric battles during the latter parts of World War II.[6]

The Allied victory in World War I was truly a worldwide effort. The victorious Allies decided to award a similar victory medal for all of the countries who sent combatants. The ribbon color pattern of the medal was the same for all countries while the medal designs varied by country. Many collectors actually try to obtain at least one World War One victory medal from each victorious nation, which makes this medal popular. The award document for the Japanese World War I Victory Commemorative Medal was also quite beautiful. This document was awarded to army engineer PFC Hirano Kou in 1919. The challenge with this particular document is the lack of an exact date and location specifying when and where PFC Kou served in World War I. We can only assume that he served in 1914 or 1918–19 and probably in far-east Asia.

Japan remained involved with the war in Europe for the next few years in a limited capacity. They did contribute materiel and limited military support from 1915 to 1917. Moreover, diplomatic efforts proved to be the biggest events during this time. Japan and Russia signed an alliance in 1916, which was meant to cool tensions in the historically contentious Manchurian region. The Japanese signed agreements with the rest of the Allies, which helped to secure Japanese claims on German islands taken in 1914. Within the next five years, two events would shape the immediate future of Japan: the Bolshevik Revolution in Russia in 1917 and the Treaty of Versailles in 1919.[7]

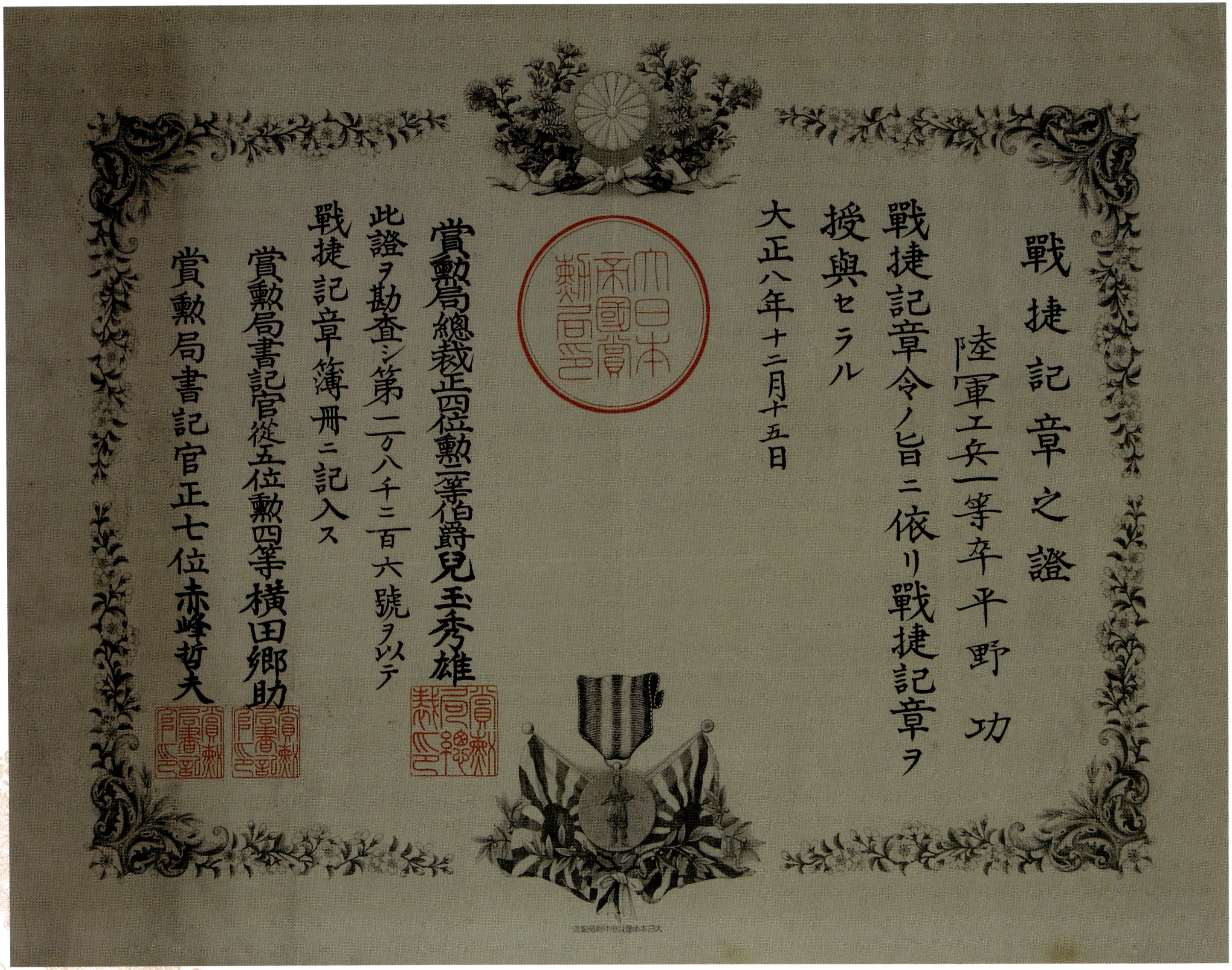

戰捷記章之證

陸軍工兵一等卒平野功

戰捷記章令ノ旨ニ依リ戰捷記章ヲ
授與セラル

大正八年十二月十五日

賞勳局總裁正四位勳一等伯爵兒玉秀雄

此證ヲ勘査シ第二万八千二百六號ヲ以テ
戰捷記章簿冊ニ記入ス

賞勳局書記官從五位勳四等横田郷助

賞勳局書記官正七位赤峰哲夫

Opposite: Translation of World War Victory Commemorative Medal document, right side only: "Record of Awarding the World War I War Victory Medal. Army Engineer Private 1st Class Hirano Kou. Given the World War I War Victory Medal. Taishō 8 [1919] December 15." *Author's Collection*

The top view of World War Victory Medal document features the imperial chrysanthemum surrounded by a floral arrangement. *Author's Collection*

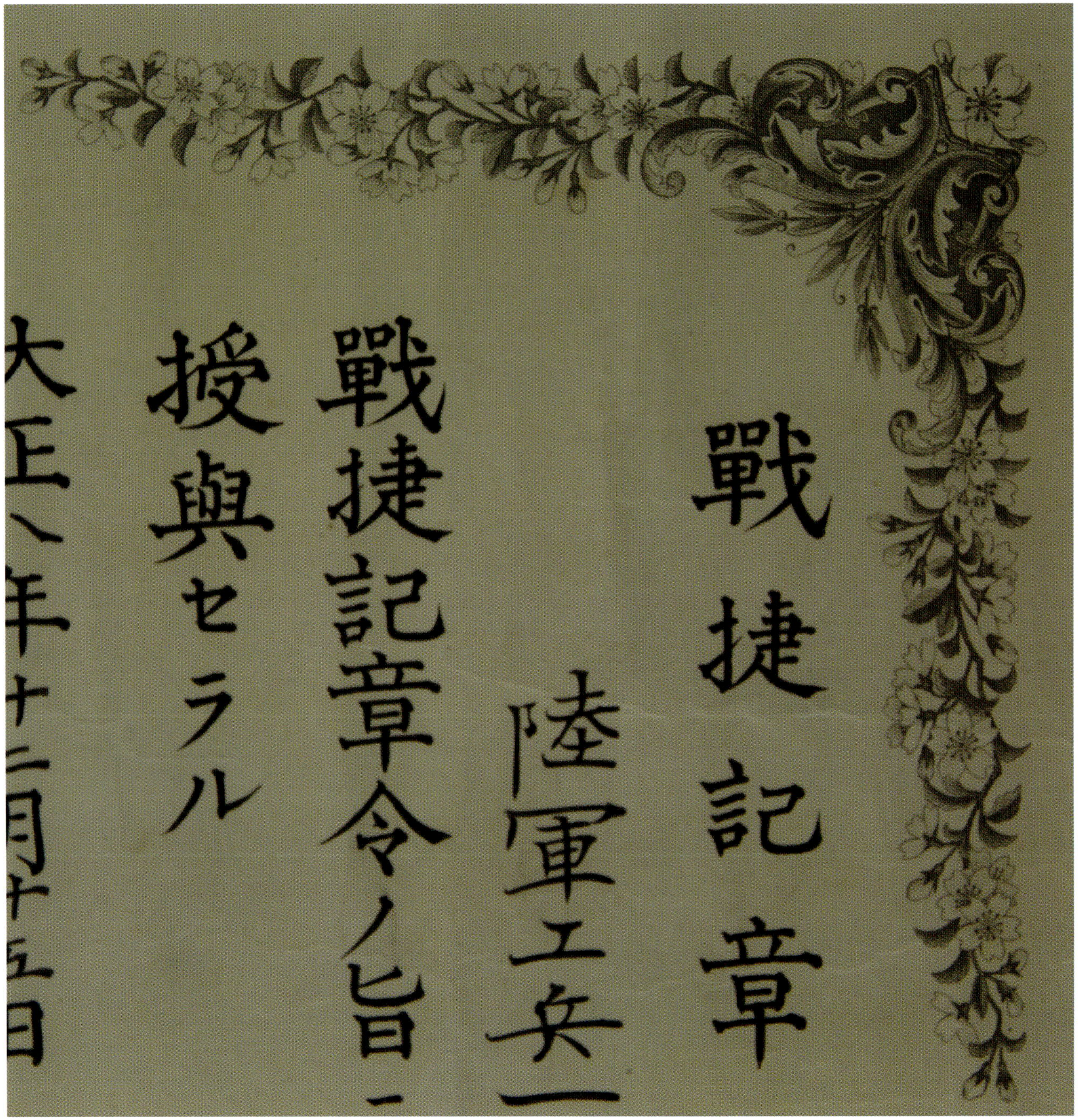
戰捷記章
陸軍工兵一
戰捷記章令ノ旨ニ
授與セラル
大正八年十二月十五日

The corner of the document has an interesting floral arrangement.
Author's Collection

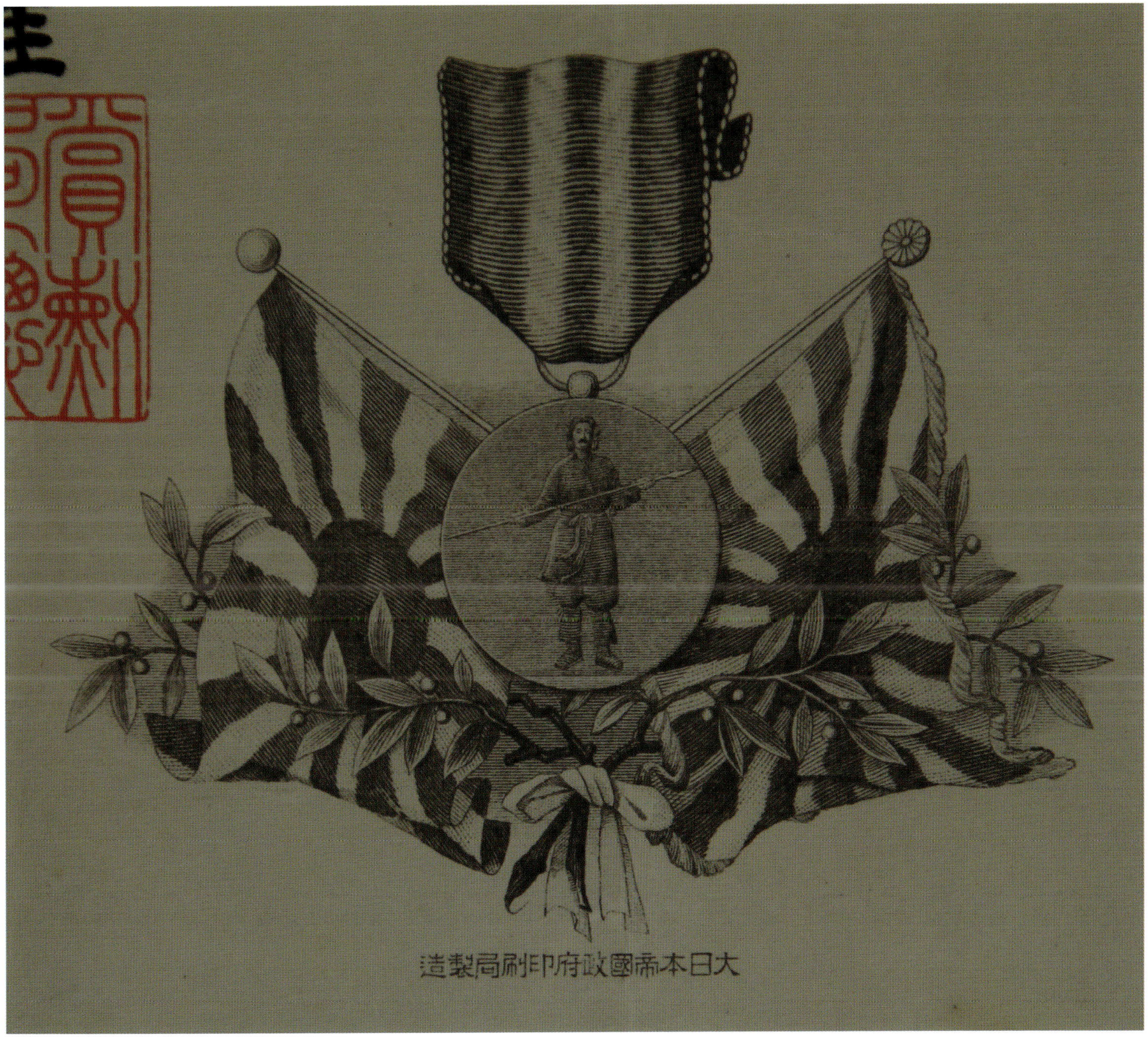

The drawing of the World War I Victory Medal on the document is quite stunning. The two Japanese flags bracket the medal with two olive branches beneath the medal. This design created one of the most detailed drawings of any documents. Interestingly, all of the victory medals for the Allies share the same ribbon colors and basic design on the obverse. This medal and document is quite popular with collectors. *Author's Collection*

The Japanese and Russian Alliance of 1916 was nullified with the Bolshevik Revolution in Russia. The Bolshevik Revolution was initially seen as an opportunity for Japan. In December 1917, just a month after the Russian Revolution, Japan decided to act against revolutionary ideals. Some in Japan wanted to go as far as to send military forces into Siberia to protect any Russian forces (also referred to as the Whites) fighting against the Bolsheviks. This idea was shelved until approval from the Allies, especially the United States, could be obtained. The Japanese were wary of spreading the conflict any further. It was not until the summer of 1918 that the Allies granted Japan permission to intervene in Siberia. Four to five Japanese divisions eventually landed in Siberia and operated along the trans-Siberian railway from Vladivostok to Amur in Far Eastern Russia. The Russian Civil War was going in favor of the Bolsheviks by 1920, and the Allies began to leave the parts of White Russia they still occupied. Japan was one of the last to leave in 1922. Japan occupied the northern half of the Sakhalin Island, situated between Siberia and Japan, but they returned control of this half of the island to the Soviets in 1925. Japan's intervention in Siberia was a costly affair and unpopular at home. The efforts of the Japanese were for naught as the Soviet's reclaimed Siberia and reestablished control. The actions of the Japanese in Siberia served to reignite tensions between the two countries, tensions that would ignite multiple times in the next twenty-five years.[8]

The Treaty of Versailles and subsequent League of Nations formation highlighted how world leaders both respected and resented Japan. Japan was given the honor of being one of the five nations to work in the peace terms in 1919. The former German Pacific Islands were granted to Japan. Japan's claim to the German colony in China on Shantung was not as easy to settle. The Chinese delegation rejected these claims and would not sign the treaty. Japan would remain in control of this area until the 1922 Washington Naval Conference settled the dispute and China regained control. The racial equality clause in the League of Nations, which Japan supported, was defeated. Japan had been sending people abroad for a number of years as its population increased. The United States and Australia were wary of such immigration and did not favor any language about racial equality in the League of Nations Charter. This clause, though it had support, was not accepted by the United States or Britain. Japan earned a permanent seat on the Council of the League of Nations and full representation on committees, but Japan also felt resentment based on the denial of racial equality.[9]

A group of Japanese deployed in Siberia ready for action. Interestingly, the caption claims that the Japanese soldiers are preparing to fight the Germans who were threatening Siberia. We know this assertion to be false today. These troops were stationed there to combat the spread of communism in Russia.
Author's Collection

天佑ヲ保有シ萬世一系ノ帝祚ヲ踐タル
日本國皇帝ハ從七位宮島良澄
ヲ明治勲章ノ勲六等ニ敍シ瑞寶章ヲ
授與ス即チ此位ニ屬スル禮遇及ヒ特權
ヲ有セシム
神武天皇即位紀元二千五百七十五年
大正四年十一月七日京都皇宮ニ於テ
璽ヲ鈐セシム

大日本國璽

大正四年十一月七日

賞勲局總裁從二位勲三等伯爵正親町實正

此證ヲ勘査シ第四十六万四千八十七
號ヲ以テ勲等簿冊ニ記入ス

賞勲局書記官正五位勲四等藤井善言

Opposite: Translation of Order of the Sacred Treasure 6th Class document, right side only: "Through the honor of the immortal Emperor, the Empire of Japan bestows this award. Junior 7th Imperial Rank, Miyajima Yoshisumi. Order of the Sacred Treasurer 6th Class medal. Imperial Year 2575 [1915].Taishō 4 [1915], November 7. Tokyo Imperial Shrine." *Author's Collection*

Liberal Movements

This Order of the Sacred Treasure 6th Class document was awarded to a man named Miyajima on November 7, 1915. The document gives no indication if he was a military man or civilian. Civilians were eligible for both the Order of the Sacred Treasure and Order of the Rising Sun. The vocations of civilians who could earn the Order of the Sacred Treasure 6th Class included post office department heads, fire department chiefs, police chiefs, bureaucrats, and various other government officials. Miyajima had received the junior 7th Imperial Rank, which was bestowed upon soldiers who had the rank of first lieutenant and sergeant major as well as the equivalent ranks in the navy. We cannot assume a military rank since civilians (bureaucrats, public employees, and nobility) obtained this rank also. We know that Miyajima was not a peasant and was probably someone who had some influence in his local area.

The Taishō period, which lasted from 1912 to 1928, spanned the reign of the Taishō emperor. It was a time of great social change in Japan. The first big event, termed the Taishō Political Crisis, started soon after Emperor Meiji's death in 1912–1913. The Japanese political system had calmed substantially since the 1890s. A dispute between the military and the Prime Minister Saionji Kinmochi, who belonged to the Seiyūkai party, occurred as Kinmochi made known his desire to cut army spending. The army leaders protested, and Kinmochi resigned soon after as the controversy continued. Taishō appointed a former prime minister and army Gen. Katsura Tarō as Prime Minister. The Seiyūkai party members, who held a majority of seats in the Diet (parliament), viewed the moves by the army as threatening to the constitutional government. The situation further exacerbated as Prime Minister Tarō asked Emperor Taishō to intervene on his behalf. This culminating action sent the nation into turmoil. Protestors marched throughout Japan to protect the constitutional form of government. Seeing the danger of the social unrest, Prime Minister Tarō resigned in later February of 1913 after only two months in office. The subsequent era of general political peace, entitled the Taishō Democracy, would last until Emperor Taishō's death.[10]

Medal view of Order of the Sacred Treasure 6th Class document. *Author's Collection*

第一四八八號
靜岡縣平民
木村松之助
嘉永三年四月三日生
明治三十一年一月二十五日登録
丙種運轉士免狀
明治二十九年法律第六十八號
船舶職員法ニ依リ之ヲ授與ス
大正二年二月二十六日
遞信大臣元田肇

Opposite: Translation of class driving license document for commercial naval vessels: "Number 1488th. Commoner from Shizuoka Prefecture. Kimura Matsunosuke. Born in Kaei 3 [1850], April 3rd. Registered Meiji 31 [1898], January 25th. 3rd Class driver's license. This license is awarded in accordance with the Meiji 29 [1896] shipping vessel crew law number 68. Taishō 2 [1913], February 26." *Author's Collection*

Civilian employees were given highly stylized documents, much like the military. The opposite document was awarded to Kimura Matsunosuke as a worker in the shipping industry. The work license is in the 3rd class. The document features a rare character set, the date characters for the Emperor Kaei. Kimura was born in the third year of Kaei, which is 1850. This document highlights the growth in Japanese economy during the Taishō period. The outbreak of World War I afforded Japan a unique opportunity. They acquired territory from the Germans, as outlined previously; however, Japan benefited economically as well. The colonial powers turned their attention to Europe, and Asian markets turned to Japan to fill the void. Industrial output in Japan increased from 1.4 billion yen in 1914 to 6.8 billion yen in 1918. Exports of goods like cotton rose as well. Unemployment dropped, and wages increased as workers became scarce. The economic boom benefited the banks and businessmen, but this era was not as prosperous for the common Japanese.[11]

The economic boom of World War I brought hardship for many Japanese consumers and workers. Even though wages were up and unemployment was down, inflation often outpaced these gains. This situation became more acute through the war and then worsened in 1920 when the Japanese stock market crashed. The economic boom then came to an end for even the wealthy in Japan. Industrial output shrank by almost 40% in some sectors, which led to massive layoffs. The economic disasters would continue throughout the decade, including the Great Kantō Earthquake in 1923 (discussed later), widespread bank failures in 1927, and then the worldwide stock market crash in

The corner view of driving license document features an anchor and ornate, symmetrical artwork. *Author's Collection*

This watermark found in the lower right corner features a cherry blossom outline with the kanji for "Stamp" in the center. This watermark can be found on many different documents. *Author's Collection*

The top view of the driving license for commercial naval vessels includes the Imperial Paulonia seal found on many documents. *Author's Collection*

1929. This time period was also filled with protests (e.g., the rice riots in 1918), strikes (e.g., the steel workers strike in 1920, which was put down by government troops), and political assassinations (e.g., Prime Minister Hara Takashi in 1921). The extended period of economic hardships and social unrest in Japan led many leaders, especially in the military, to distrust the liberal government and capitalism as a whole. This growing unease would morph into the militaristic society of Japan in the 1930s.[12]

The 1920s constituted an eventful decade for Japan. The first national census was carried out in 1920. Those who administered or helped to administer the census were eligible for the 1920 Census Commemorative Medal. This document for a medal was awarded to Okada Keisuke and was numbered 42,403. Those who received this medal, including Mr. Okada, would have either been an official census taker, and, therefore, a prominent member of his community or he would have been one of the many behind-the-scenes workers who directed the event. The total number of medals must have exceeded the stated numbers of volunteers (260,000) since even behind-the-scenes workers and others would have received the award.

The 1920 census was another milestone on the way to Japan becoming a modern nation. A census of this scale is truly a national effort. A practice census was conducted in 1879 in just one prefecture. This trial run revealed issues that took some time to eliminate. A national census was scheduled for 1895 and then postponed to 1905 because of the First Sino–Japanese War. The census was then postponed again in 1905 and then again in 1915 because of the Russo-Japanese War and then World War I. It was not until 1920, 130 years after America's first census, that Japan conducted its own census. This momentous event did not go unheralded. Commemorative goods were also made of every sort: paperweights, iron kettles, postcards, porcelains, photograph books, handbooks, and sake cups. And on the much-anticipated time, midnight on October 1, sirens blared, cannons fired, bells at temples and shrines rang, and *taiko* drums thundered to signal the beginning of this momentous occasion. Once the census began, volunteers spread to the households. These appointed officials were prominent citizens from the cities and villages. It was considered prestigious to be selected for such an unprecedented achievement.

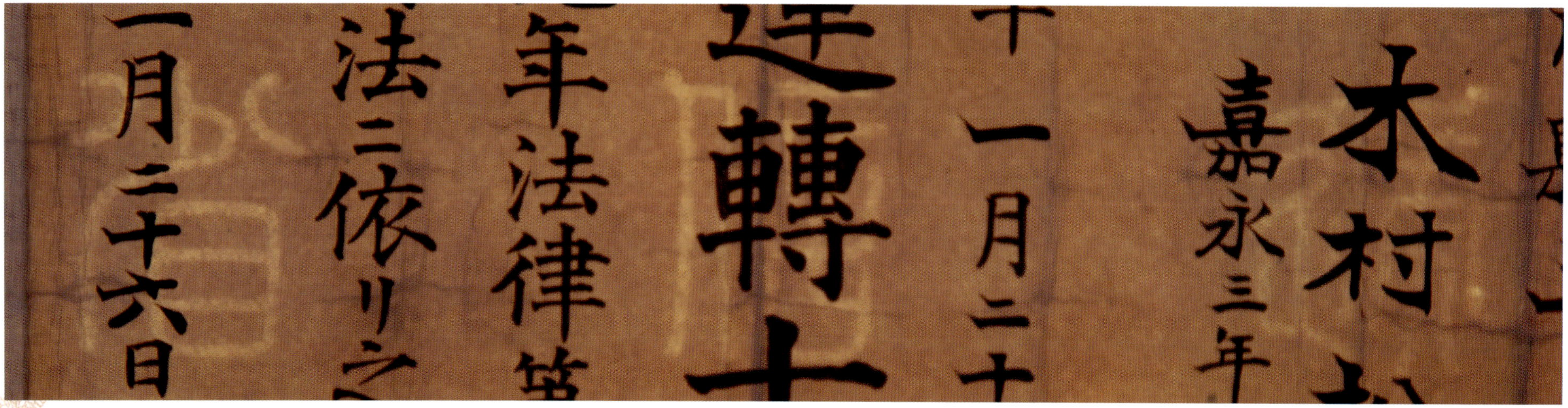

The document features a unique three-character watermark, reading "Ministry of Communications." *Author's Collection*

Opposite: Translation of 1920 Census Commemorative Medal document, right side only: "Record of Awarding the First National Census Commemorative Medal. Okada Keisuke. According to the 1920 imperial ordinance 272, the First National Census Commemorative Medal is awarded. Taishō 10 [1921] July 1." *Author's Collection*

第一回國勢調査記念章之證

岡田惠助

大正十年勅令第二百七十二號ノ旨ニ依リ
第一回國勢調査記念章ヲ授與セラル

大正十年七月一日

賞勳局總裁正四位勳一等伯爵兒玉秀雄

此證ヲ勘査シ第四万二千四百三號ヲ以テ
第一回國勢調査記念章簿冊ニ記入ス

賞勳局書記官正五位勳四等横田郷助

賞勳局書記官正六位郡山智

The chrysanthemum of the imperial seal was featured on the top of the 1920 Census document. *Author's Collection*

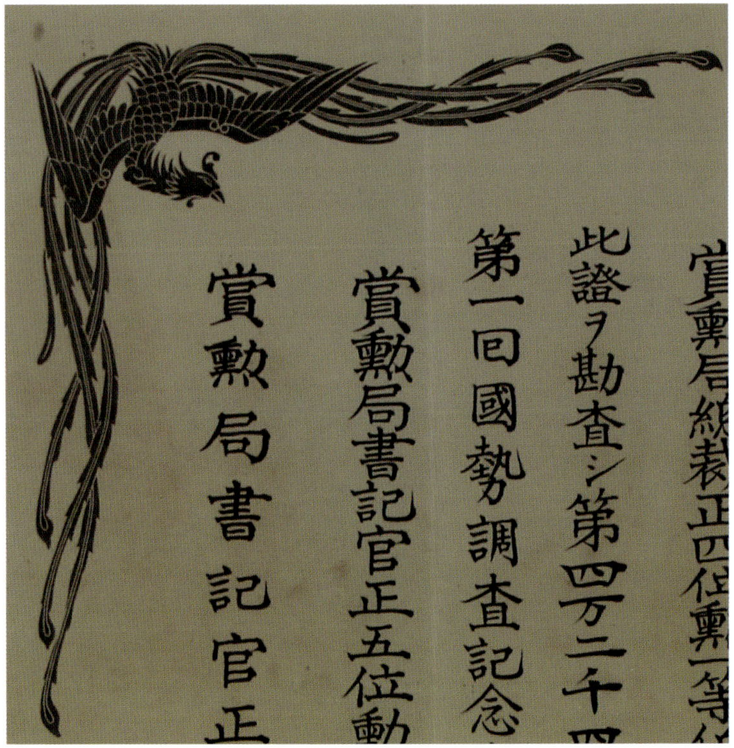

The corner of 1920 Census document features a peacock with its back feathers stretching around the corners. The peacock has a variety of meanings around the world, including Japan, because of its beauty and nature. *Author's Collection*

A close-up of the 1920 Census Medal on the document. *Author's Collection*

川邊尋常高等小學校校舍增築ニ
關シ功勞尠カラス茲ニ記念
品ヲ贈リ感謝ノ意ヲ表ス

大正十一年[illegible]月二十一日

加茂郡川邊町長従七位勲六等西村才三郎

町會議員
平岡直吉殿

Translation of a citation for helping a school, right side only: "For the number of meritorious deeds pertaining to the enlargement of the Kawabe Ordinary and Advanced Elementary School house, we hereby give this souvenir and present this certificate as an expression of our gratitude. Taishō 11[1921], January 21." *Author's Collection*

Certificates of appreciation were popular documents during this era. This particular document was awarded to Hiraoka Naokichi for helping enlarge an elementary school in 1922. I have a document also awarded to the same Hiraoka in 1943 for donating bicycles to the war-wounded. Hiraoka seems to have been a generous man. The document makes mention of a gift along with the document, but we have no way of knowing what the gift was. This document highlights the economic and educational tension in Japan. A letter to a newspaper editor from an elementary school teacher in 1918 testifies to the struggles that seemingly middle-class employees had. The letter describes the economic hardships that the elementary teacher had to endure due to the teacher's low salary. He had difficulty feeding his family. The family could not buy new clothes and had not taken a bath in over a month. This situation paired with the document provides us a glimpse into the unstable nature of Japanese society during the Taishō period.[13]

This Imperial Capital Rehabilitation Commemorative Medal document was awarded to Kato Sadakichi in 1931. The documents are usually dated May 1, 1931. The award is rather rare, and this particular document is numbered 17,108. It was only awarded to those who specifically helped with the rebuilding of the capital after the earthquake. Of all the official Japanese medals, both war and commemorative varieties, this is the only one not included in the official order of precedence issued by the Decorations Bureau. In other words, the recipients were not expected to wear the piece. In addition, the document itself differs greatly from the other medal documents. One difference is the color of the printing—this was done in light green, a rather unassuming color. The border decoration is basic and standard fare, just the traditional cherry blossoms and leaves that are the main symbols of Japan. This award highlights two significant events in Japanese history, the Great Kantō Earthquake in1923 and subsequent rebuilding of Tokyo.

The earth shook mightily under Tokyo and Yokohama on September 1, 1923. The Great Kantō Earthquake was a magnitude 7.9 quake. Between the earthquake and ensuing fires, immense areas in both cities were razed to the ground. The human death toll was extremely high: an estimated 140,000 deaths plus further casualties caused by the riots against Korean nationals. It was a terrible time, to be sure. Furthermore, 570,000 personal homes were destroyed. Recovering from such an extreme event took an enormous toll on both private citizens and the government. A Rehabilitation Ministry was established in early 1924, a department that continued to exist in some form until 1932. Streets were remade, districts were rebuilt, public schools were built; undeveloped areas were cleaned and restored. Green areas and parks were made in special layouts to prevent any rapid spread of fires. In fact, most districts were completely redrawn in order to prevent such fires. For instance, people today can visit Yamashita Park in Yokohama, which was built using the rubble from a commercial district. This famous park was opened on March 15, 1930. Countless more improvements appeared in almost all areas devoted to public life. In March 1930, the Imperial Capital Rehabilitation festivities were beginning, and these were to be attended by the emperor as well as many other imperial family members and assorted dignitaries.

帝都復興記念章之證

勲四等加藤定吉

昭和五年勅令第百四十八號ノ旨ニ依リ
帝都復興記念章ヲ授與セラル

昭和六年五月一日

賞勲局總裁正四位勲二等下條康麿

此證ヲ勘査シ第一万七千百八號ヲ以テ
帝都復興記念章簿冊ニ記入ス

賞勲局書記官従五位伊手衛

Opposite: Translation of Capital Rehabilitation Commemorative Medal document, right side only: "Record of Awarding the Capital Rehabilitation Commemorative Medal. Kato Sadakichi, 4th Decorated Rank. According to the 1930 imperial ordinance 148, the Capital Rehabilitation Commemorative Medal is awarded. Showa 6 [1931] May 1." *Author's Collection*

The top of the Capital Rehabilitation Commemorative Medal document features the imperial chrysanthemum seal. *Author's Collection*

The bottom design of the Capital Rehabilitation Commemorative Medal document features a similar floral arrangement as the corners. *Author's Collection*

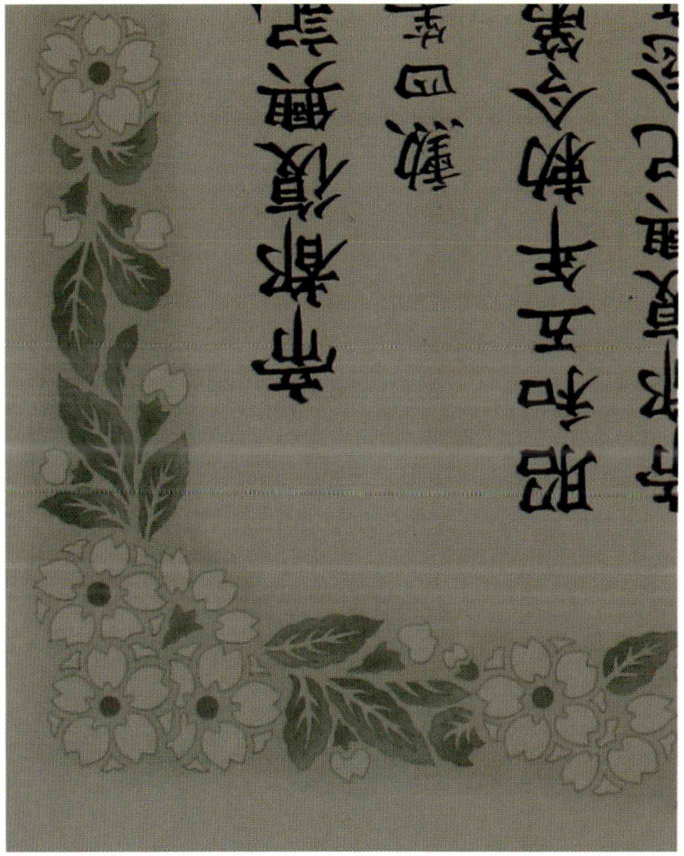

A three flower arrangement in light green forms the corners of the Capital Rehabilitation Commemorative Medal document. *Author's Collection*

This photograph shows the Metropolitan Police Office burning near Hibiya Park after the earthquake. *Author's Collection*

Illness and Death of Taishō

This document is an extremely rare document. It is an award document for the Grand Cordon of the Supreme Order of the Chrysanthemum. It was given to Prime Minister Katō Takaaki (also known as Katō Kōmei) on the date of his death. The average collector should not expect to find this document for their collection as it is the highest award in Japan and only around fifty Japanese civilians (not including the imperial family) have received the award. The rareness is partially due to the fact that the recipient was awarded it after his death. Prime Minister Katō was a member of the conservative Kenseikai party and served from June 1924, until his death in January 1928. One of his lasting actions as prime minister was extending suffrage in Japan. The signature on the document also tells a story. It is a double signature of Emperor Taishō and Crown Prince Hirohito. The Crown Prince, acting as the Regent, actually signed the document as his father had become incapacitated by this time.[14]

The illness of Emperor Taishō became progressively worse through the 1910s. His actions in public, which he rarely made, were often odd and disturbing. For example, Emperor Taishō climbed down from his viewing stand during the annual military maneuvers and unpacked a soldier's kit out of curiosity. He soon suffered cerebral hemorrhages or blood clots that essentially incapacitated him. Crown Princc Hirohito became regent in 1921 and ruled in place of his father. Emperor Taishō would live until 1926 when he died of a heart attack in late December.[15]

天佑ヲ保有シ萬世一系ノ帝祚ヲ踐タル
日本國皇帝ハ正二位勲一等伯爵加藤高明
ヲ明治勲章ノ大勲位ニ敍シ菊花大綬章ヲ
授與ス即チ此位ニ屬スル禮遇及ヒ特權
ヲ有セシム
神武天皇即位紀元二千五百八十六年
大正十五年一月二十八日東京帝宮ニ於テ
親ラ名ヲ署シ璽ヲ鈐セシム

嘉仁
裕仁

大日本國璽

大正十五年一月二十八日

賞勲局總裁從三位勲二等宇佐美勝夫

此證ヲ勘査シ第五十一號ヲ以テ
大勲位簿冊ニ記入ス

賞勲局書記官正五位勲四等　郡山智

賞勲局書記官正六位　伊手衡

Opposite: Translation of the Grand Cordon of the Supreme Order of the Chrysanthemum, right side only: "Through the honor of the immortal Emperor, the Empire of Japan bestows this award. Senior 2nd Imperial Rank, Order of Merit 1st Class, Katō Takaaki. Grand Cordon of the Supreme Order of the Chrysanthemum. Imperial Year 2586 [1926]. Taishō 15 [1926], January 28. Tokyo Imperial Shrine." *Courtesy of an Anonymous Collector*

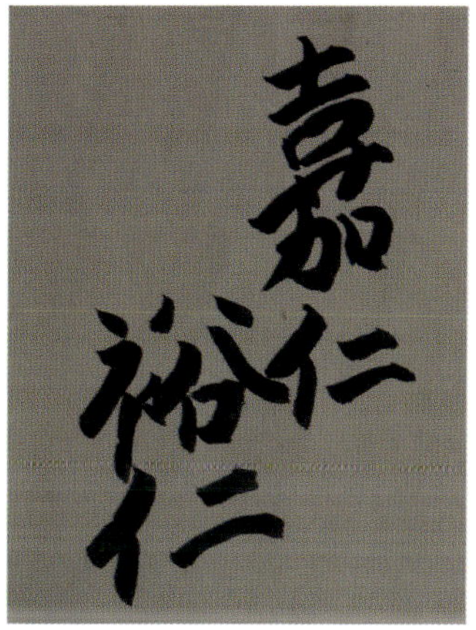

The double signature of documents from this era was actually Crown Prince Hirohito signing his signature (the lower) and his father, Emperor Taishō's, signature (the upper). Documents with the double signature are one of the clearest pieces of evidence that collectors have of Emperor Taishō's illness. *Courtesy of an Anonymous Collector*

The drawing of the Grand Cordon of the Supreme Order of the Chrysanthemum is arguably the most beautiful of all order documents and one of the rarest. *Courtesy of an Anonymous Collector*

Chapter 3 Endnotes

1. D. Keene, *Emperor of Japan: Meiji and His World, 1852–1912* (New York: Columbia University Press, 2002), 699–710.

2. D. Keene, *Emperor of Japan: Meiji and His World, 1852–1912* (New York: Columbia University Press, 2002), 552–554.

3. D. Bergamini, *Japan's Imperial Conspiracy* (New York: William Morrow and Company, 1971), 290–291.

4. W. G. Beasley, *The Modern History of Japan*. (New York: Praeger, 1974), 196–202.

5. *The Times History of the War, Vol. II* (London: The Times, 1915), 412–420.

6. *The Times History of the War, Vol. II* (London: The Times, 1915), 423–424.

7. W. G. Beasley, *The Modern History of Japan* (New York: Praeger, 1974), 204–206.

8. W. G. Beasley, *The Modern History of Japan* (New York: Praeger, 1974), 208–210.

9. W. G. Beasley, *The Modern History of Japan* (New York: Praeger, 1974), 206–208.

10. A. Gordon, *A Modern History of Japan: From Tokugawa Times to the Present* (New York: Oxford Press, 2009), 128–129.

11. A. Gordon, *A Modern History of Japan: From Tokugawa Times to the Present* (New York: Oxford Press, 2009), 139.

12. A. Gordon, *A Modern History of Japan: From Tokugawa Times to the Present* (New York: Oxford Press, 2009), 139–143, 162–163.

13. A. Gordon, *A Modern History of Japan: From Tokugawa Times to the Present* (New York: Oxford Press, 2009), 158.

14. J. Benson and T. Matsumura, *Japan, 1868–1945: From Isolation to Occupation* (Essex, UK: Pearson Education, 2001), 35.

15. D. Bergamini, *Japan's Imperial Conspiracy* (New York: William Morrow and Company, 1971), 306.

4 JAPAN'S IMPERIAL PLAN:

SOLIDIFYING THE EMPIRE (1927–1936)

The first few years of the Showa Era witnessed a continued and dramatic militarization of Japanese culture through the mid-1930s. The conquest of Manchuria and foundation of Manchukuo presented the Japanese with economic opportunities abroad. The increased military spending also helped to pull the Japanese economy up from the Depression. However, the military actions in Manchuria cost Japan prestige on the world stage and brought them into a conflict that would last for fifteen years.

A group of women wave Japanese and Manchukuo flags. The Japanese government continually emphasized the friendship between the two groups; however, Manchukuo was almost always treated as a puppet state. *Author's Collection*

大禮記念章之證

陸軍砲兵上等工長勲八等濱田重吉

昭和三年勅令第百八十八號ノ旨ニ依リ
大禮記念章ヲ授與セラル

昭和三年十一月十六日

賞勲局總裁正四位勲三等天岡直嘉

此證ヲ勘査シ第三万六千四百三十一號ヲ以テ
大禮記念章簿冊ニ記入ス

賞勲局書記官從五位伊手衛

Opposite: Translation of Showa Enthronement Commemorative Medal document, right side only: "Record of Receiving the Showa Enthronement Commemorative Medal. According to Imperial Rescript #188 of Showa 3 [1928]. The Showa Enthronement Commemorative Medal is awarded to Order of Merit 8th Class Hamada Shigekichi. Showa 3 [1928]. November 16." *Author's Collection*

Emperor Hirohito's Enthronement

The Showa Enthronement Commemorative Medal document was given quite freely to any who participated in the number of different celebration events. This particular document was given to a Warrant Officer Superior Hamada Shigekichi. He served in the artillery. He had previously been awarded an order in the 8th class. The enthronement celebrations happened throughout Japan in a variety of events.

Emperor Hirohito found himself in a difficult situation when he ascended upon the Chrysanthemum throne in 1928. The cult of the emperor, which had been growing since Emperor Meiji, had increased to the point where Emperor Hirohito was believed to be the descendent of the sun-goddess Armaterasu. Yet, his powers were actually limited according to tradition and constitution. He would often not voice his opinion to his ministers, including military decisions. Emperor Hirohito was a "living god" who would be best described as a figurehead in Japan. The complicated political situation would cause much debate in the decades following the end of World War II as people contemplated Emperor Hirohito's role in the war.[1]

A butterfly is positioned at the corner of this document. *Author's Collection*

The bottom of the Showa Enthronement Commemorative Medal document features two birds with outstretched wings that are touching in the center. *Author's Collection*

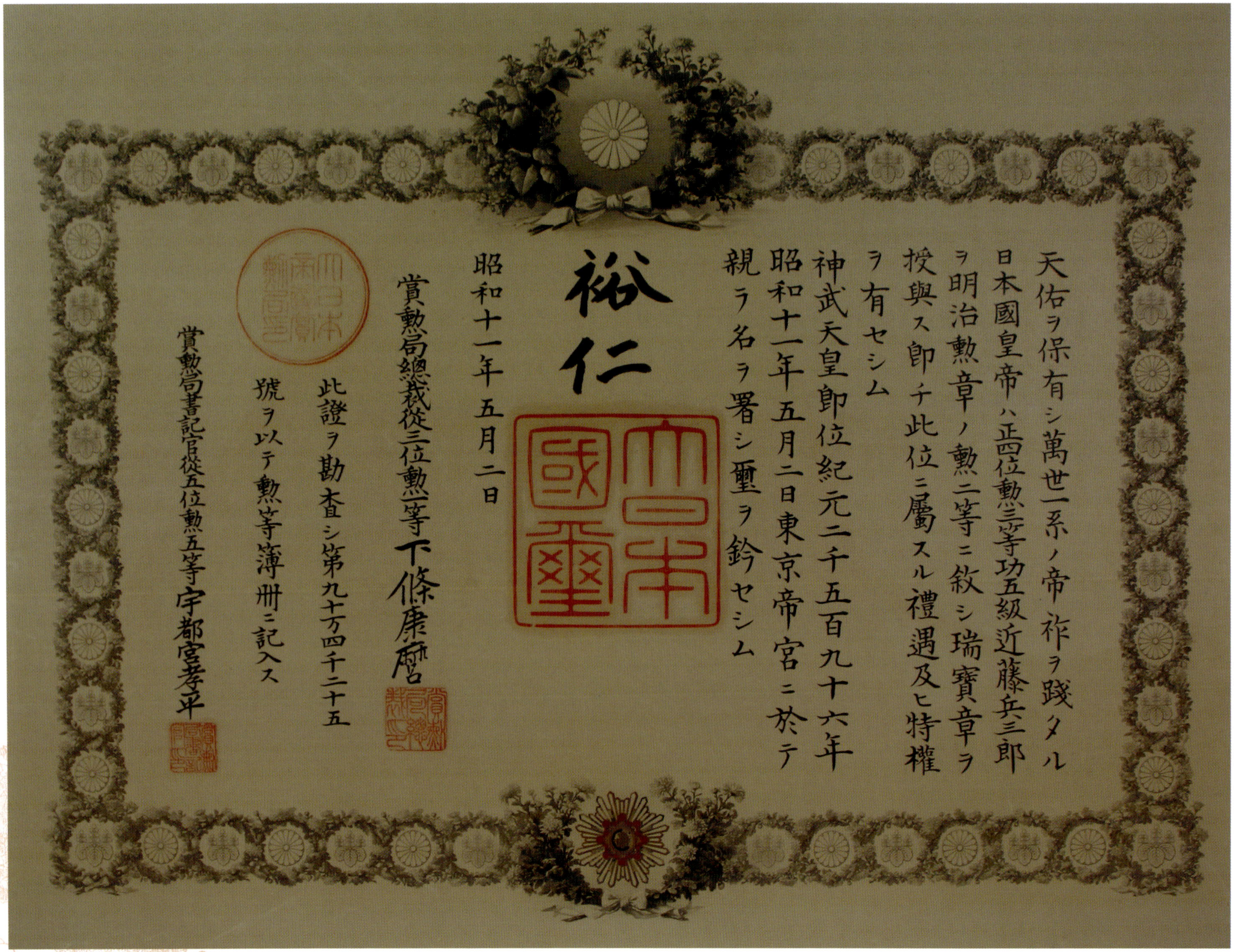

天佑ヲ保有シ萬世一系ノ帝祚ヲ踐メル
日本國皇帝ハ正四位勲三等功五級近藤兵三郎
ヲ明治勲章ノ勲二等ニ敍シ瑞寶章ヲ
授與ス即チ此位ニ屬スル禮遇及ヒ特權
ヲ有セシム
神武天皇即位紀元二千五百九十六年
昭和十一年五月二日東京帝宮ニ於テ
親ラ名ヲ署シ璽ヲ鈐セシム

裕仁

昭和十一年五月二日

賞勲局總裁従三位勲一等下條康麿

此證ヲ勘査シ第九十万四千二十五
號ヲ以テ勲等簿冊ニ記入ス

賞勲局書記官従五位勲五等宇都宮孝平

Opposite: Translation of Order of the Sacred Treasure 2nd Class document, right side only: "Through the honor of the immortal Emperor, the Empire of Japan bestows this award. Senior 4th Imperial Rank, Order of Merit 3rd Class, Order of the Golden Kite 5th Class, Kondo Hyouzaburou. Order of the Sacred Treasure 2nd Class. Imperial Year 2596 [1936]. Showa 11 [1936], May 2. Tokyo Imperial Shrine." *Courtesy of Author's Collection*

All orders in the 2nd class were breast badges and are extremely rare. This document is for the Order of the Sacred Treasure 2nd Class. It was given to Kondo Hyouzaburou in 1936. He was a person of rank and veteran status had been awarded as an order in the 3rd class and Order of the Golden Kite 5th Class as well as being Senior 4th Rank. The document also features Emperor Hirohito's large signature. Hirohito's signature is very hard to find from the imperial age because he signed only the highest classes of orders. I have even seen documents of this same order and class not signed by the emperor.

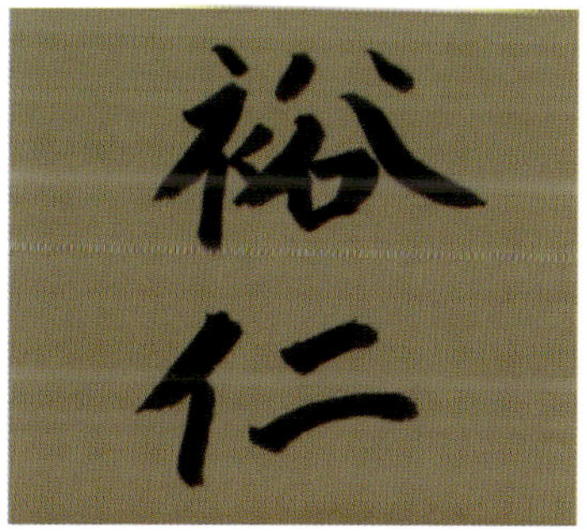

The striking signature of Emperor Hirohito. *Author's Collection*

The drawing of the Order of the Sacred Treasure 2nd Class that is featured on this document. Note the damage in the center of the medal. *Author's Collection*

This photograph from the early 1930s shows Emperor Hirohito walking past a line of saluting soldiers. He always seemed ill fitted to military uniforms. In fact, his involvement and role in the military affairs of Japan during World War II has been a point of contention for historians. He was not tried for war crimes like other leading political figures in Japan after the war. Hirohito was better suited for the society of Japan after 1945 as he helped rebuild the Japanese economy and society though the 1980s. *Author's Collection*

Rise of Militarism

The economic and social turmoil of the late 1910s and 1920s set the stage for Japan's turn to militarism in the 1930s. There were some winners in this era, including Togō Tori from the document above. The early 1930s also saw an increase in Japanese production and overall economic improvement. The cause of this economic improvement included Japan's return to the gold standard. This move dropped the value of the yen and opened more markets aboard to Japanese products. In 1931, a yen could buy two dollars' worth of goods; by 1932, a yen could buy five dollars' worth of goods. The second major cause was Japan's reliance on deficit spending to fund the military and expansion into Manchuria. The military budget went from one-third of the government's spending in 1930 to three-fourths in 1937. The economic result was considered an economic miracle. Industrial output rose 82% from 1931–34 and the economy as a whole grew 50% from 1930–36. Thus, Japan was able to escape from the Great Depression faster than most.[2]

感謝狀

貴下ハアサヒ地下足袋専賣店トシテ
専念弊社製品ノ普及擴充ニ盡
瘁セラレ洵ニ感激ニ不堪候
尚共存共榮ノ趣旨ニ則リ販賣
能率ノ向上ニ努メ一層ノ御援助
相願度茲ニ謹而感謝ノ微意
ヲ表シ候

昭和四年三月

日本足袋株式會社
社長 石橋徳次郎

専賣店
都甲トリ殿

Translation of the appreciation document, right side only: "Togō Tori as the exclusive distributor of Hamasahi Work Tabi, have given your undivided attention in the assistance of distribution of our company's product and have indeed aspired to the same aim of co-existence and co-prosperity. For the elevation of efficiency in sales, and for endearing to support us, we hereby present this small token of our sincere gratitude. Showa 4 [1929] March." *Author's Collection*

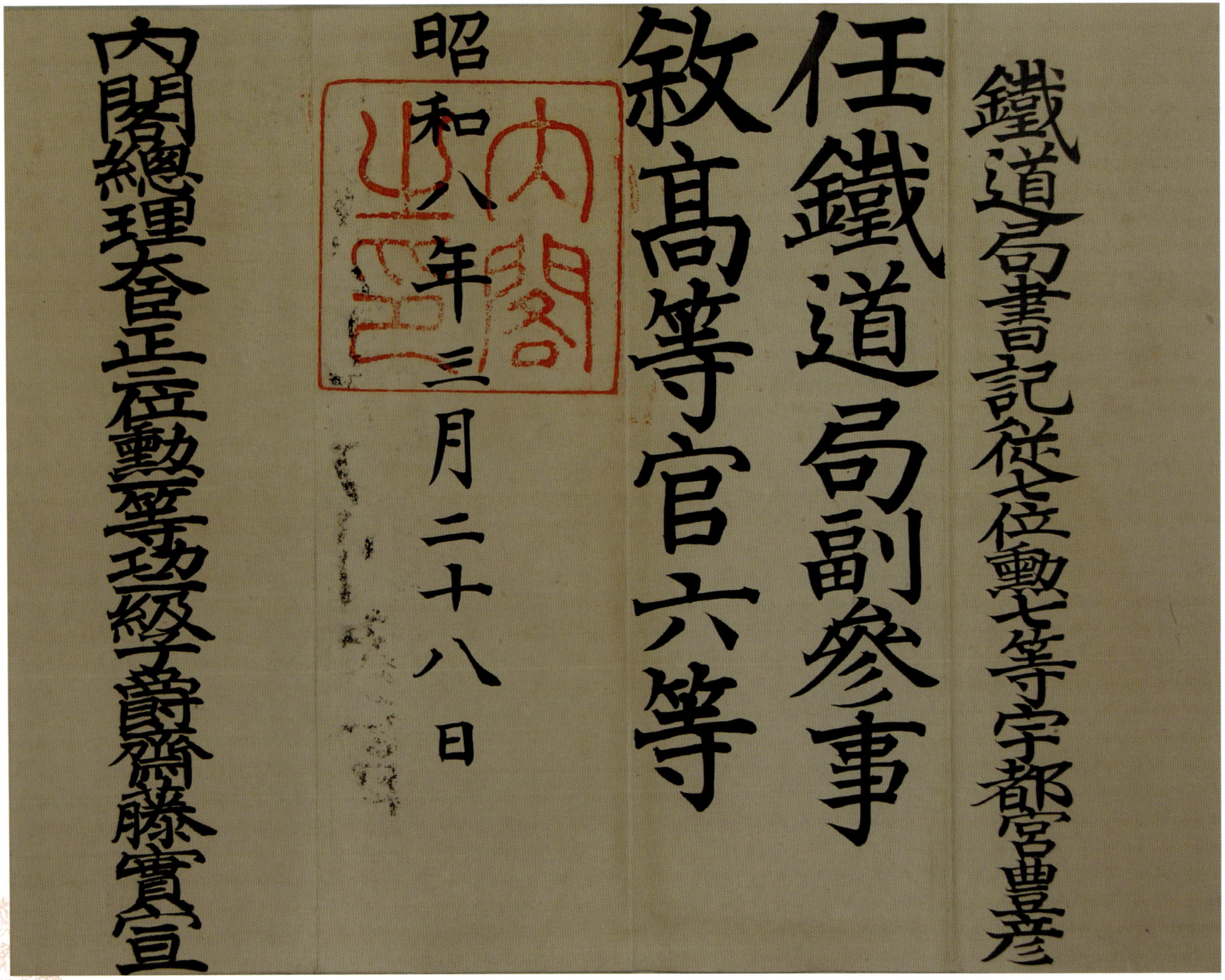

鐵道局書記從七位勳七等宇都宮豊彦
任鐵道局副參事
敍高等官六等
昭和八年三月二十八日
内閣總理大臣正二位勳一等子爵齋藤實宣

Translation of Railroad Ministry promotion document: "Railroad Bureau Clark, Junior 6th Rank, Order of Merit 7th Class, Ubemiya Toyohiko. Appointed Vice Councilor of the Railroad Bureau and conferred Senior 6th Rank. Showa 8 [1933], March 28." *Author's Collection*

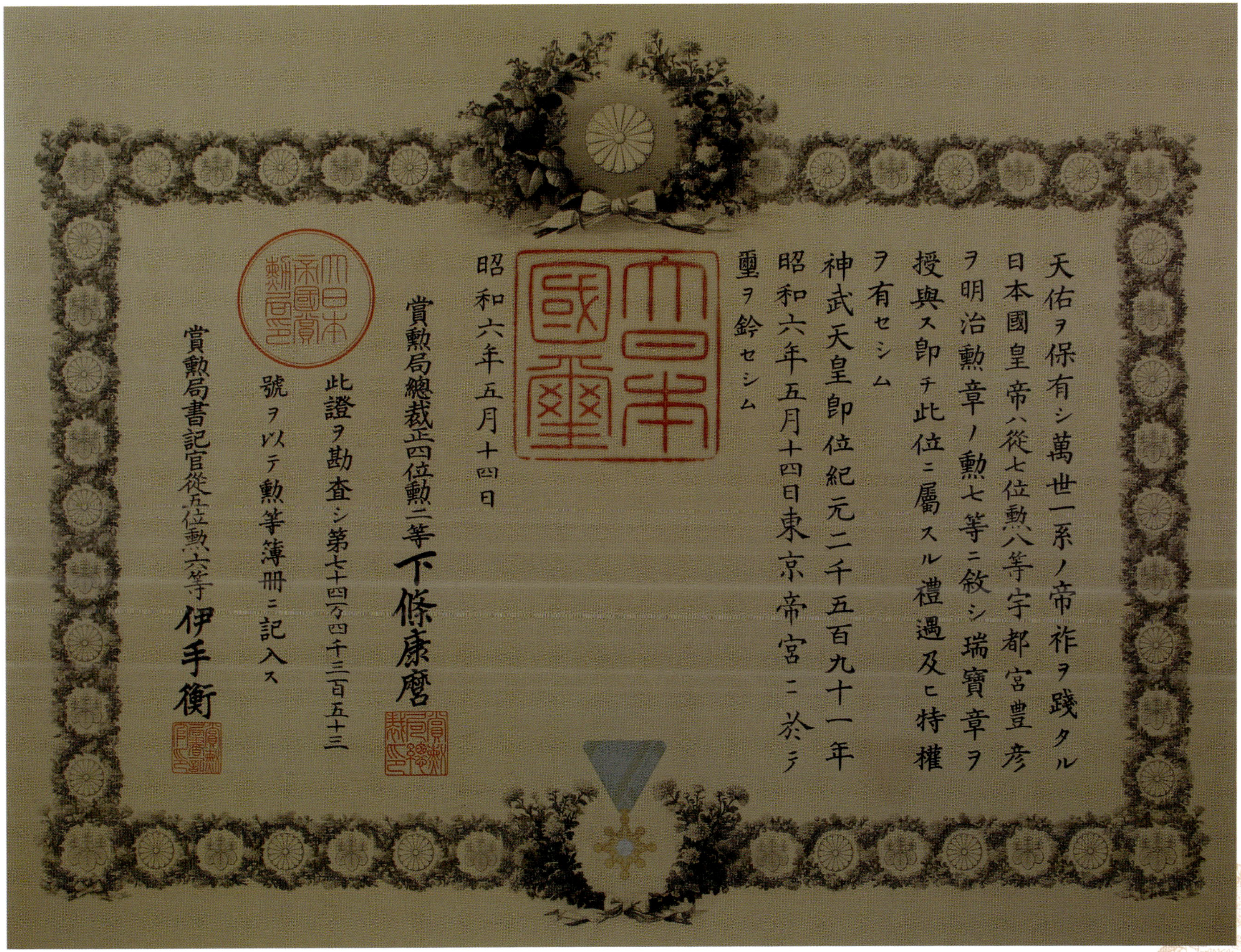

天佑ヲ保有シ萬世一系ノ帝祚ヲ踐タル
日本國皇帝ハ從七位勲八等宇都宮豊彦
ヲ明治勲章ノ勲七等ニ敘シ瑞寶章ヲ
授與ス即チ此位ニ屬スル禮遇及ヒ特權
ヲ有セシム
神武天皇即位紀元二千五百九十一年
昭和六年五月十四日東京帝宮ニ於テ
璽ヲ鈐セシム

昭和六年五月十四日

賞勲局總裁正四位勲二等下條康麿

此證ヲ勘査シ第七十四万四千三百五十三
號ヲ以テ勲等簿冊ニ記入ス

賞勲局書記官從五位勲六等伊手衡

Translation of Order of the Sacred Treasure 7th Class document, right side only: "Through the honor of the immortal Emperor, the Empire of Japan bestows this award. Junior 7th Imperial Rank, Order of Merit 8th Class, Ubemiya Toyohiko. Order of the Sacred Treasure 7th Class. Imperial Year 2591 [1931]. Showa 6 [1931], May 14. Tokyo Imperial Shrine." *Author's Collection*

The previous two documents were both awarded to the same person, Ubemiya Toyohiko. The first is his promotion document for a position as a vice councilor in the Railroad Ministry from 1933. The second is his Order of the Sacred Treasure 7th Class from 1931. I have a document for Toyohiko that dates back to World War I for his service during the war in the Ministry of Railroads. The document from 1920 does not mention him earning any orders. By 1931, Toyohiko had earned the Order of the Sacred Treasure 8th Class and then 7th class. The time span of these documents highlights the length of service required to earn the Order of the Sacred Treasure as a civilian. The class to be awarded depended on the social status of the person as well. The various roles he had in the Railroad Ministry also highlighted the high level of bureaucracy in the Japanese economy.

The color version of the medal is centered on the bottom of this document. Some versions of this document feature medals that are black and white. *Author's Collection*

The economic gains of the early 1930s signified the shift in political ideology within Japan. Japan lost faith in capitalism and had always feared communism. Japan sought to find a middle ground. This included sponsoring and influencing large corporations to act in accordance with the government's wishes. These corporations would work closely with the military in Japan and Manchuria. This top-down approach to economics and policy led to a crackdown on political dissidence. By 1937–38, labor unions were on the decline, often by force, as the government sponsored labor councils, which viewed the factory as a community. These councils were fashioned after Nazi Germany's political response to unions and essentially removed much of the power from workers in favor of factory owners and managers. This move created some public dissidence; however, the general move towards a fascist society was taking hold in Japan, and these reforms took hold.[3]

The politics of Japan also became more fascist through the 1930s. This movement was sparked by deadly coup attempts that did not change the government completely, but did keep pushing the politics towards militarism. First, parliamentary rule was greatly reduced with the assassination of Prime Minister Tsuyohi by right-wing military men in 1932. The new cabinet that formed was dominated by the military. The most famous of the failed coups was the 2–26 Incident. On February 26, 1936, 1,500 troops took control of the government sector of Tokyo. A string of assassinations struck fear in the government over the next couple of days. Even though the coup was quickly crushed and the leaders of the 2–26 Incident were executed, the action strengthened the position of the military. The military promised to purge its ranks of radicals and this move was welcomed by civilians and government officials. The shift towards the political right was also seen in the day-to-day political attitude of Japan. Police began to crack down on political speech that criticized the new political order. This control and terror spread even to the most popular of political parties. The Seiyūkai party, which had won the 1932 general election, was dissolved in 1940 in favor of Japan's movement toward a single-party state.[4]

Opposite: Translation of iron works license document: "Blacksmith License. Kumamoto Prefecture, Mr. Honda. Established on Meiji 23 [1890], Law Number 23, Blacksmith Regulations Article 2, Clause 2. [License given] Showa 11 [1937], January 8." *Author's Collection*

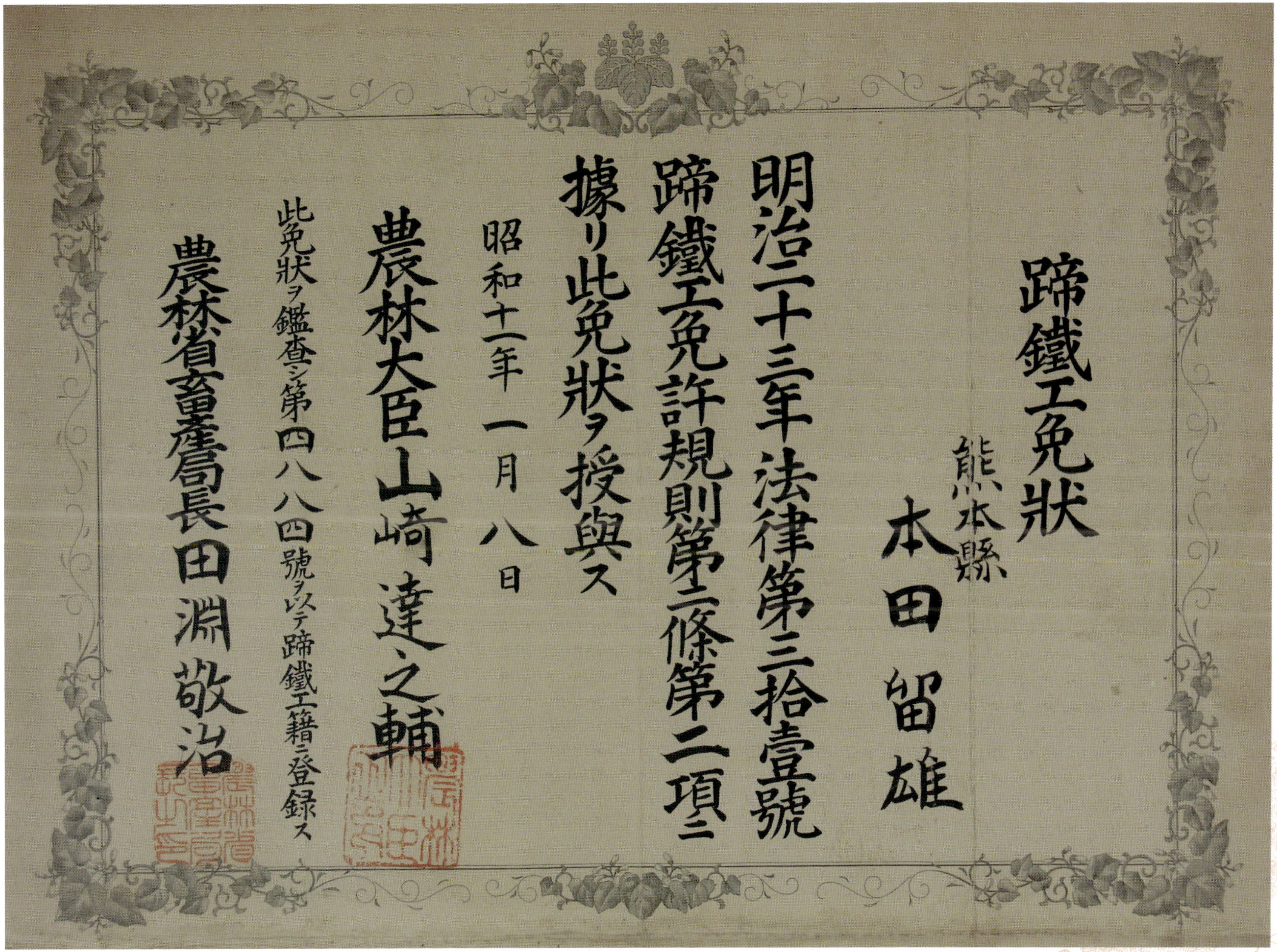

蹄鐵工免狀

熊本縣
本田留雄

明治二十三年法律第三拾壹號
蹄鐵工免許規則第二條第二項ニ
據リ此免狀ヲ授與ス

昭和十一年一月八日

農林大臣山崎達之輔

此免狀ヲ鑑查シ第四八八四號ヲ以テ蹄鐵工籍ニ登録ス

農林省畜産局長田淵敬治

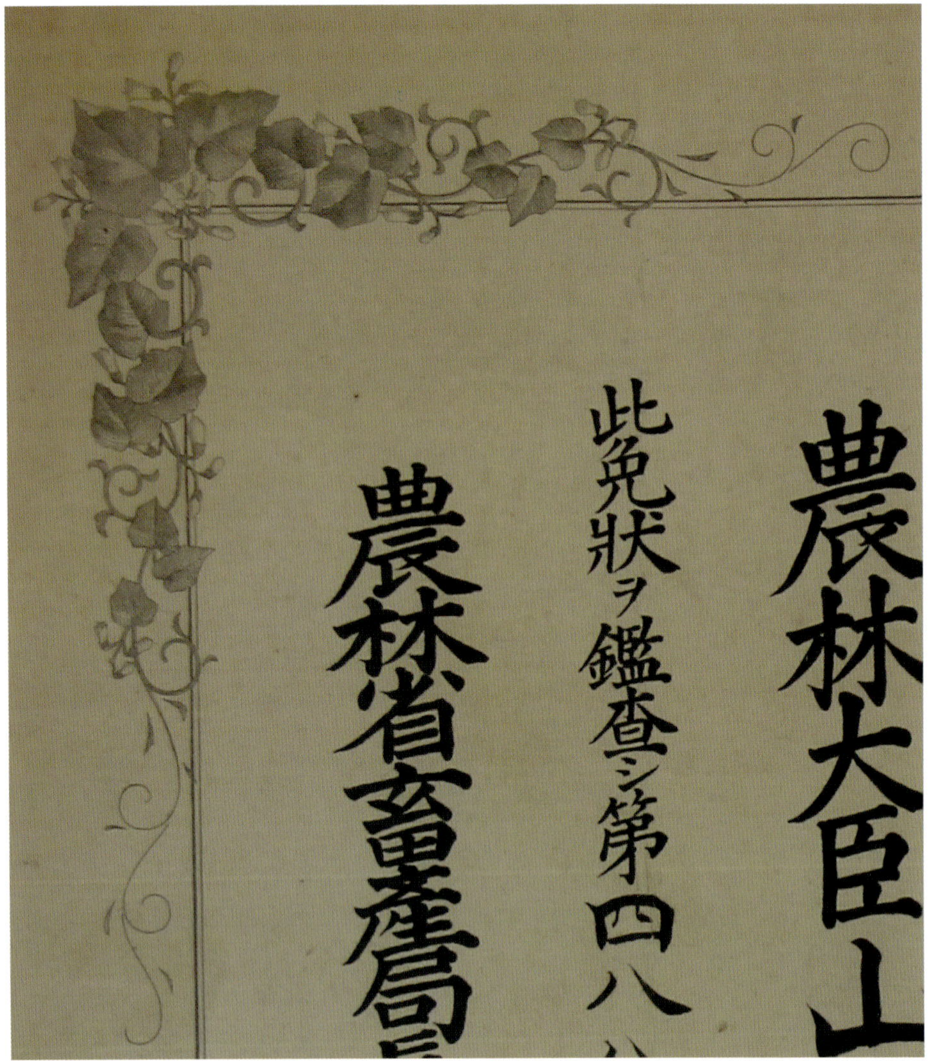

The corner of this document is decorated with less stylized paulownia leaves, which comes from the kiri tree and vines. *Author's Collection*

The imperial seal of stylized paulownia leaves is the top design of this iron works license document. *Author's Collection*

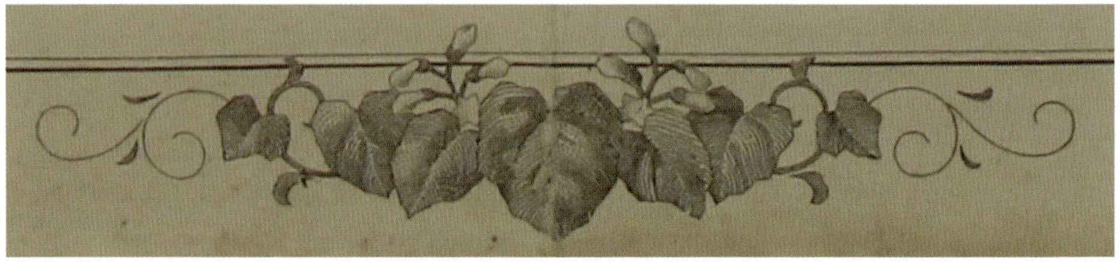

The bottom center of this particular license document features more paulownia leaves. *Author's Collection*

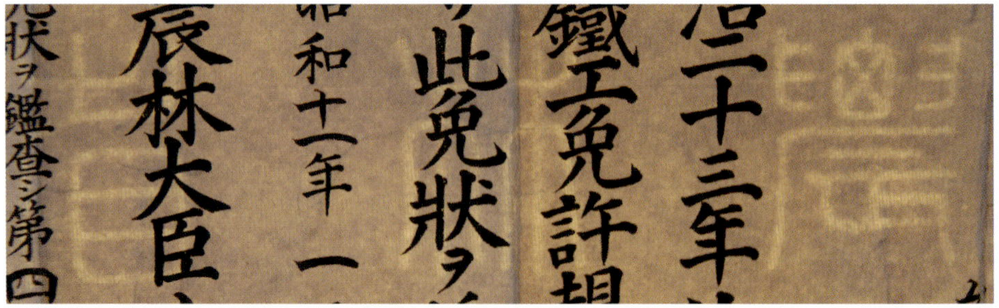

The iron works license document includes a watermark of three characters that is unknown to me. *Author's Collection*

Civilians obtaining licenses from the government could also receive very detailed and beautiful documents. The document featured above is a blacksmith license given in 1937 to Mr. Honda. Industry in Japan was a complicated situation. The industrial infrastructure in Japan had very large firms like Toyota and Nissan. However, a majority of the industrial and manufacturing firms had fewer than five employees. The aforementioned document highlights this reality. This situation drove Japan to seek territory and colonies for natural resources and increased industrial capacity.[5]

The economic and political situation at the time did not mean that life in Japan was extremely brutal. In fact, Japanese society in the 1930s found interesting ways to counter the conservative militaristic movement. Western fashions and activities became popular. For example, baseball in Japan became extremely popular and drew huge crowds. American jazz was also popular as well as Western styles of dress and hairstyles. Millions of Japanese had radios and over a million had telephone service. While the government had become firmly militaristic, the Japanese people had yet to be completely militarized by the end of the 1930s. This would change with the onset of Japan's Great East Asian War in 1941.[6]

This period photograph illustrates the tensions in Japan at the time. The Western and traditional fashions of Japanese women are both on display. The Western styles had been popular in Japan since the later part of the nineteenth century. Western clothing was actually encouraged by Japanese leaders. However, the rise of militarism in Japan brought prominence back to traditional Japanese styles, which included kimonos. Japanese leaders had to find ways to balance between Western culture that had taken hold in Japan and their eventual war against what they called the Western cultural and military imperialism in the Asian west. *Author's Collection*

昭和六年乃至九年事變從軍記章之證

海軍二等水兵 古川公一

昭和六年乃至九年事變從軍記章令ノ
旨ニ依リ從軍記章ヲ授與セラル

昭和九年四月二十九日

賞勲局總裁従二位勲一等 下條康麿

此證ヲ勘査シ第十四万八千六百四十號ヲ以テ昭和六年
乃至九年事變從軍記章簿冊ニ記入ス

賞勲局書記官正五位勲四等 伊手衡

Opposite: Translation of Manchurian Incident War Medal document, right side only: "Showa 6-9 [1931-34] War Incident Dispatch Medal. Navy Ensign 2nd Class Furukawa Kōichi. Record of Awarding the Showa 6–9 [1931–34] War Incident Dispatch Medal. Showa 9 [1934], April 29." *Author's Collection*

Manchurian Conquest

Navy Ensign 2nd Class Furukawa Kōichi earned the Manchurian Incident Medal in 1934 for his service during the Manchurian invasion from 1931–1934. This conflict, which started with treachery and little strategic aims, would drag Japan into a long conflict in northern China. The name of this conflict in Japan, the Manchurian Incident, highlights the tension of this conflict as Japan did not declare war on the Republic of China. Yet, Ensign Furukawa probably did not understand the complex nature of the conflict nor foresaw devastation it would bring. He spent his time patrolling the Yellow Sea between Korea, Manchuria, and northern China. Ensign Furukawa might have even helped train the new Manchurian Navy. The victory in Manchuria in 1932 was a celebrated event in Japan; however, when the celebrations ended and the conflict continued into 1934 and then beyond, the long war had begun.

The Manchurian invasion in 1931 was a result of numerous factors. The political nature of Japan would become more militarized in the latter half of the 1920s as the military leaders had forged more independence from the politicians. The world economic situation also changed the thinking in Japan. The American Wall Street crash of 1929 sent world markets plummeting. Japanese leaders started to turn their back on capitalism and looked to create their own markets for trade. These factors coupled with Japan's continual need for more land and resources for its growing population and industry meant conflict in Manchuria was highly likely.

Furthermore, Japanese intrigue into Manchuria had grown since 1904 as Japan saw Manchuria as a prime colonial conquest. Tension in the area was not new. Manchuria had been ruled by a warlord and Japan had strong influence in this region in the 1920s. However, by the end of the 1920s, China, under the Nationalist leadership of Chiang Kai-shek, had regained influence over the area. The Japanese military did not sit idly by at this time. There were numerous intrigues and even a high-level assassination. The pressure from political and economic factors in Japan, which were mentioned above, made many in Japan open to the idea of taking Manchuria. The area was still void of military strength. Yet, few politicians in Japan had the audacity to force a military takeover of Manchuria. The military leaders of the prestigious Kwantung Army, who controlled the South Manchurian Railway, would light the fuse of the conflict by their own initiative. They planted a bomb on the railway just south of Mukden on September 18, 1931, and blamed the act on the Chinese. This false pretext prepared the way for the Kwantung Army to invade southern Manchuria, despite protests of some politicians in Japan.[7]

The top of this document features the standard chrysanthemum flower seal in the reddish color of the whole document. *Author's Collection*

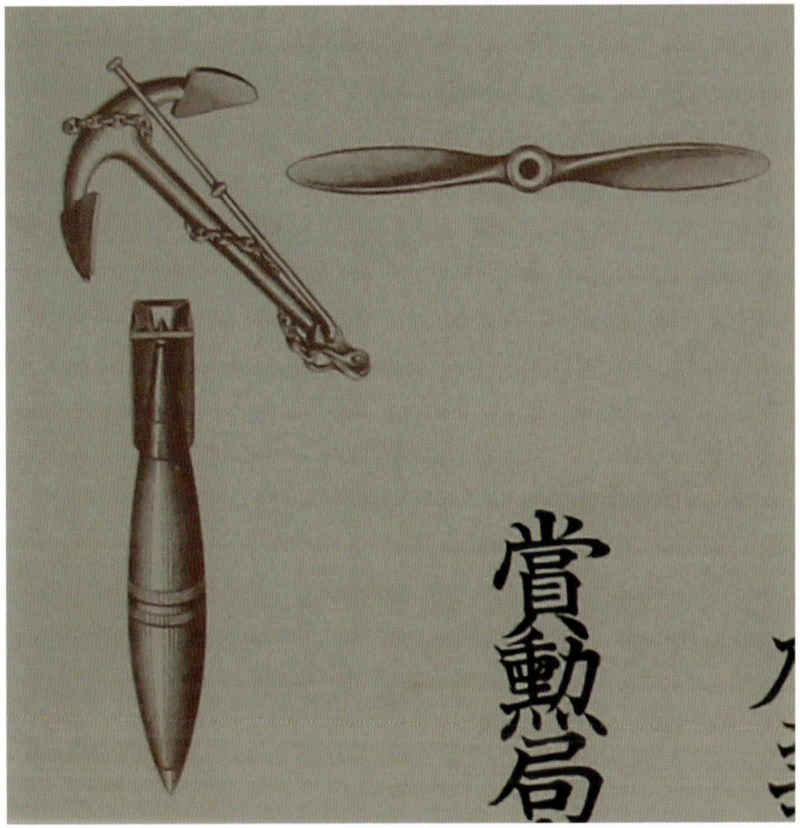

The corner of this document features airplane propellers and bombs bracketing an anchor. Notice how this newer style of war document still closely resembles the older versions. *Author's Collection*

The bottom center of the Manchurian Incident War Medal document features the medal with an intense and interesting array of the tools of war, including a tank, two planes, guns, etc. *Author's Collection*

The invasion of Manchuria was rapid. The Japanese had secured the major cities in southern Manchuria along a front that spread hundreds of miles. The whole region was under Japanese control within a week of the invasion. The Kwantung Army immediately began to support secessionist groups that argued for a Manchuria free from Chinese influence. These movements would culminate in the establishment of Manchukuo in 1932. The Japanese advance through northern Manchuria was also rather quick. The city of Tsitsihar, now Qigihar, fell on November 19, after a prolonged Japanese assault. The Japanese also took Harbin from Chinese forces in early February, which led to the ending of hostilities in northern Manchuria by the end of the same month. Meanwhile, the Japanese continued their advance into southern Manchuria on to the Great Wall of China itself.

天佑ヲ保有シ萬世一系ノ帝祚ヲ践タル
日本國皇帝ハ正五位勲三等辻　邦助
ヲ明治勲章ノ功三級ニ敍シ金鵄勲章ヲ
授與ス即チ此位ニ屬スル禮遇及ヒ特權
ヲ有セシム
神武天皇即位紀元二千五百九十四年
昭和九年四月二十九日東京帝宮ニ於テ
親ラ名ヲ署シ璽ヲ鈐セシム
裕仁
昭和九年四月二十九日
賞勲局總裁從二位勲一等下條康麿
此證ヲ勘査シ第十二万六千八百二十三
號ヲ以テ功級簿冊ニ記入ス
賞勲局書記官正五位勲五等森山鋭一

Opposite: Translation of Order of the Golden Kite 3rd Class, right side only: "Through the honor of the immortal Emperor, the Empire of Japan bestows this award. Senior 5th Imperial Rank, Order of Merit 3rd Class, Tsuji Kunisuke. Order of the Golden Kite 3rd Class. Imperial Year 2594 [1934]. Showa 9 [1934], April 29. Tokyo Imperial Shrine." *Courtesy of an Anonymous Collector*

The preceding document was awarded to Tsuji Kunisuke for his deeds during the Manchurian Invasion. The document features the signature of Emperor Hirohito, which makes this document quite rare because Emperor Hirohito only signed fifty Order of the Golden Kite 3rd Class documents. This award highlights the speed at which Japan conquered and subjugated Manchuria and later northern China. The Chinese government was unable to respond to these developments effectively. The Republic of China had its own issues at the time, including a civil war against the Communist Chinese. The initial conquest by the Japanese was completed very quickly, especially during the winter months in Manchuria. Japan now had the territory it had coveted for forty years. Manchuria would become a very profitable venture for many Japanese military and businessmen. However, the success of these initial operations came at a price. The conflict with China would continue for the next fifteen years. Furthermore, the reputation of Japan was tarnished in the world's eyes.

The medal designs of the Order of the Golden Kites can be quite appealing. This 3rd class version is the wrapped as normal of the Showa era. The earlier version of the Order of the Golden Kite 3rd Class was a flared style with the neck ribbon flowing away from the medal. The Order of the Golden Kite was abolished after World War II. *Courtesy of an Anonymous Collector*

建國功勞章證書

茲依大同二年教令第十一號建國
功勞章條例贈與大日本帝國陸軍三等主計正
萩原與三郎建國功勞章以彰勞勣
此證

康德元年三月一日

國務總理大臣鄭孝胥

查此證書以第貳壹貳壹九六號
記入建國功勞章簿冊

國務院總務廳恩賞處長皆川豐治

Opposite: Translation of Manchukuo Foundation Commemorative Medal document, right side only: "Record of Receiving the National Foundation Merit Medal. According to Imperial Rescript #11 of Daidou 2 [1933] the National Foundation Merit Medal is awarded to Greater Japanese Empire citizen Army Paymaster 3rd Class, Hagiwara Kōsaburō. Kōtoku 1 [1934], March 1." *Author's Collection*

The Foundation of Manchukuo

The foundation of Manchukuo was a celebrated event in Japan. A commemorative medal was instituted for the event and given relatively freely in Manchukuo and to those Japanese who had a role in the event. This Manchukuo Foundation Commemorative Medal document was given to Hagiwara Kōsaburō on March 1, 1934. The Manchukuo foundation document, along with the Nohomen Border Incident War Medal document, seem to be the two most common Manchukuo documents.

Manchukuo was officially founded in 1932 under scrutiny from around the world. The question of whether to annex the Manchurian territory or to create a new state was difficult. The Kwantung Army had more freedom of action in Manchuria than did the Japanese government. Many in the army preferred outright annexation of the territory to Japan; however, political considerations with China and the member nations of the League of Nations prevailed. The creation of Manchukuo was to be perceived by the world as a compromise and legitimation of the unlawful invasion. Manchuria would be ruled by Manchurians. The world ultimately saw through the Japanese plans though. Manchukuo was not a truly independent nation; rather, it became a puppet state of Japan. The internal affairs of Manchukuo were controlled by the Japanese acting alongside Manchukuo government officials. The Japanese even installed the last emperor of China, Pu Yi, as the Emperor of Manchukuo. Very few countries actually recognized Manchukuo as a sovereign nation during its short history.[9]

The creation of Manchukuo became the cornerstone of the Japanese ideology of the East Asian League, which later became the Greater East Asian Co-prosperity Sphere. The core claim of the ideology was an Asia free from Western colonization. Yet, the ideology also espoused the dominance of the Japanese over their Asian brethren. This ideology would become a cornerstone of Japanese actions in the Great East Asian War (1941–1945). The early years of Manchukuo highlighted economic policies of the ideology. Manchukuo was viewed in Japan much like western expansion in America in the previous century. Japanese viewed Manchukuo as a place where investors and businessmen could make money in industry, agriculture, and natural resource extraction. The Japanese invested billions of yen into Manchukuo from 1932 to 1941. Furthermore, the Japanese government sponsored migration plans for ethnic Japanese to colonize Manchukuo. The goal of these initiatives, beyond just colonial exploitation, was to create a self-sustaining and Japanese-friendly government on the Asian continent.[10]

The top of the Manchukuo Foundation Commemorative Medal document featured a plum blossom in a gold stamp form. *Author's Collection*

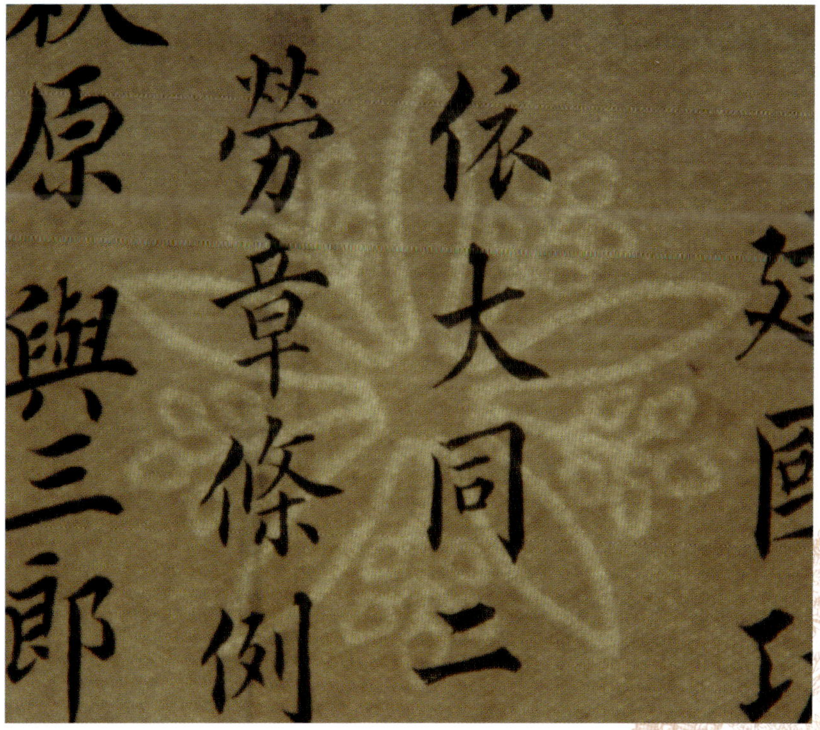

Many Manchukuo documents featured a plum blossom watermark. *Author's Collection*

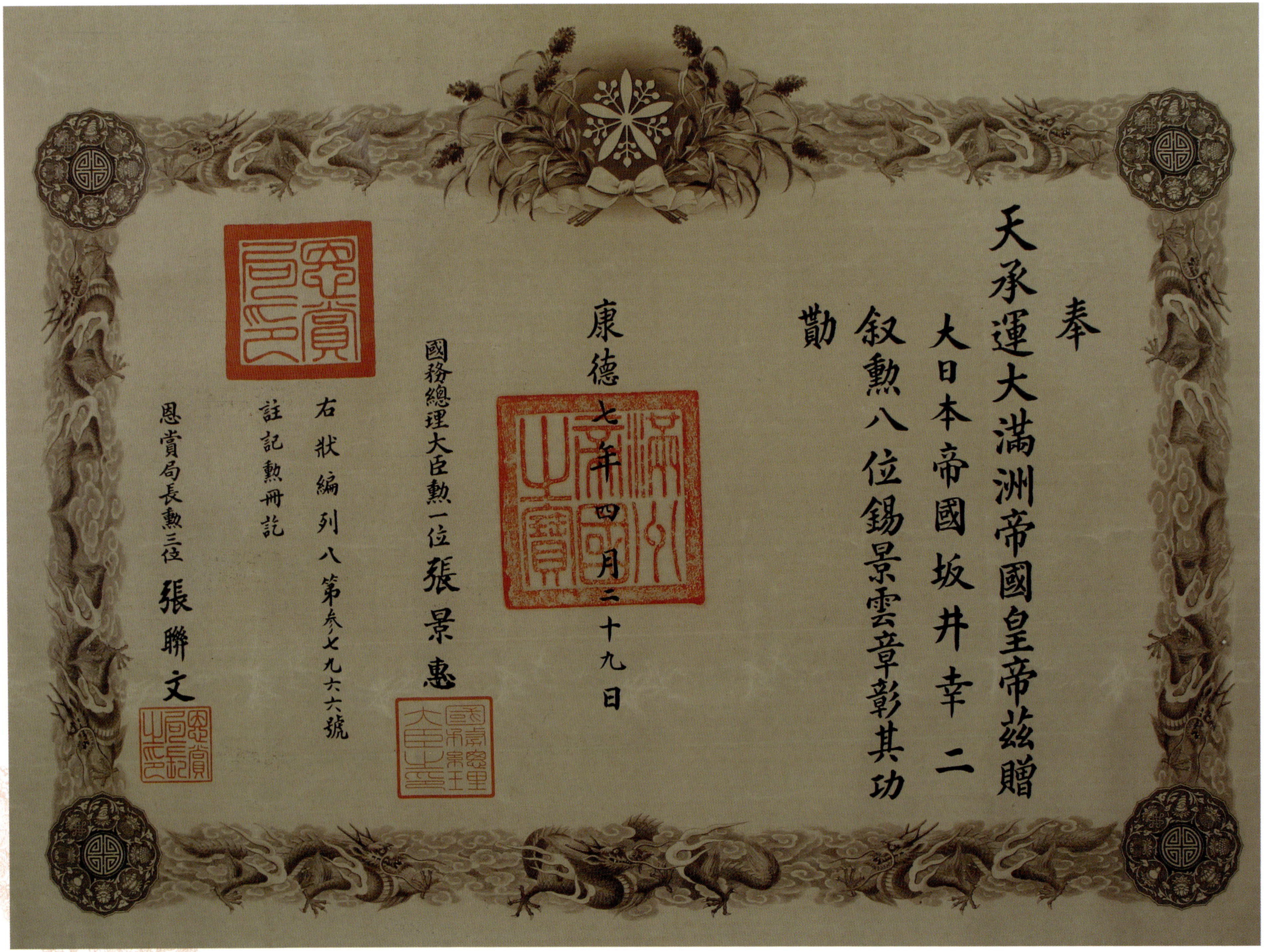

奉
天承運大滿洲帝國皇帝茲贈
大日本帝國坂井幸二
叙勳八位錫景雲章彰其功
勳

康德七年四月二十九日

國務總理大臣勳一位張景惠

右狀編列八第叁七九六六號
註記勳冊訖

恩賞局長勳三位張聯文

Opposite: Translation of Order of the Auspicious Clouds 8th Class document, right side only: "Emperor the Manchuria Empire, who governs with the Mandate of Heaven, declares that he herein presents Eighth-class decoration, Order of the Auspicious Clouds to Sakai Kōji of the Empire of Japan in order to commend his contribution. Kōtoku 7 [1940], April 29." *Author's Collection*

Manchukuo initiated a system of orders under the influence of Japan. The preceding document is a Manchukuo document for the Order of the Auspicious Clouds. This order was instituted in 1934 and mimicked the Order of the Rising Sun in Japan. The order came in eight classes. This document is for the 8th class. Much like Korea, Manchukuo copied much of the Japanese system of orders, which was probably done at the suggestion of the Japanese. Manchukuo also instituted the Order of the Pillars of State that followed the Japanese Order of the Sacred Treasure. The documents for both the Order of Auspicious Clouds and Pillars of State were identical. The indication of the order is in the wording of the document. These documents are hard to find and this document has a low award number, 7966. The document was given to private superior Sakai Kōji in 1941 for his actions during the Nohomen Incident. We know more details about Pvt. Sakai because I have more documents from this same person. The Nohomen Incident is discussed in the next chapter and two more of Sakai's documents are also featured. The creation of Manchukuo Orders was an attempt to socially legitimize the empire of Manchukuo, as it would be called by 1934. The installation of Emperor Pu Yi was meant to provide legitimization of the empire to the world.

All Manchukuo Order documents, both Auspicious Clouds and Pillars of State, feature the same design elements. You have to be able to read the characters to tell the two orders apart. The top center of the order document features the plum blossom flower of the Manchukuo state. The blossom is surrounded by what appears to be cattails though it probably is not cattails. *Author's Collection*

The corner of these order documents have dragons facing a design which appears to be of east Asian influence. *Author's Collection*

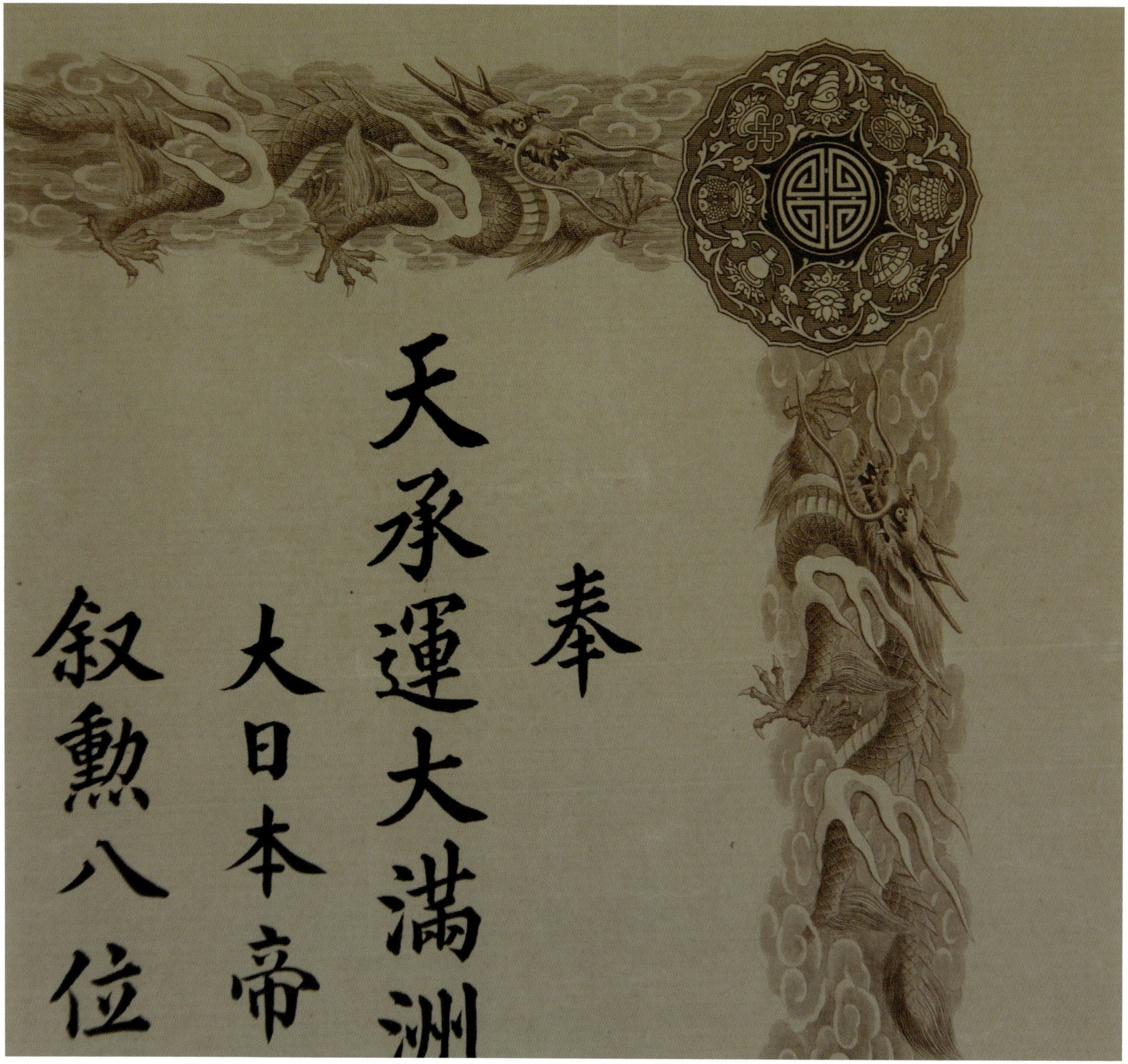

奉
天承運大滿洲
大日本帝
叙勳八位

The bottom of Manchukuo documents features a drawn dragon that is found around the border. The overall design of this document is very attractive. *Author's Collection*

The large watermark in these orders features four characters that read "Empire of Manchuria." *Author's Collection*

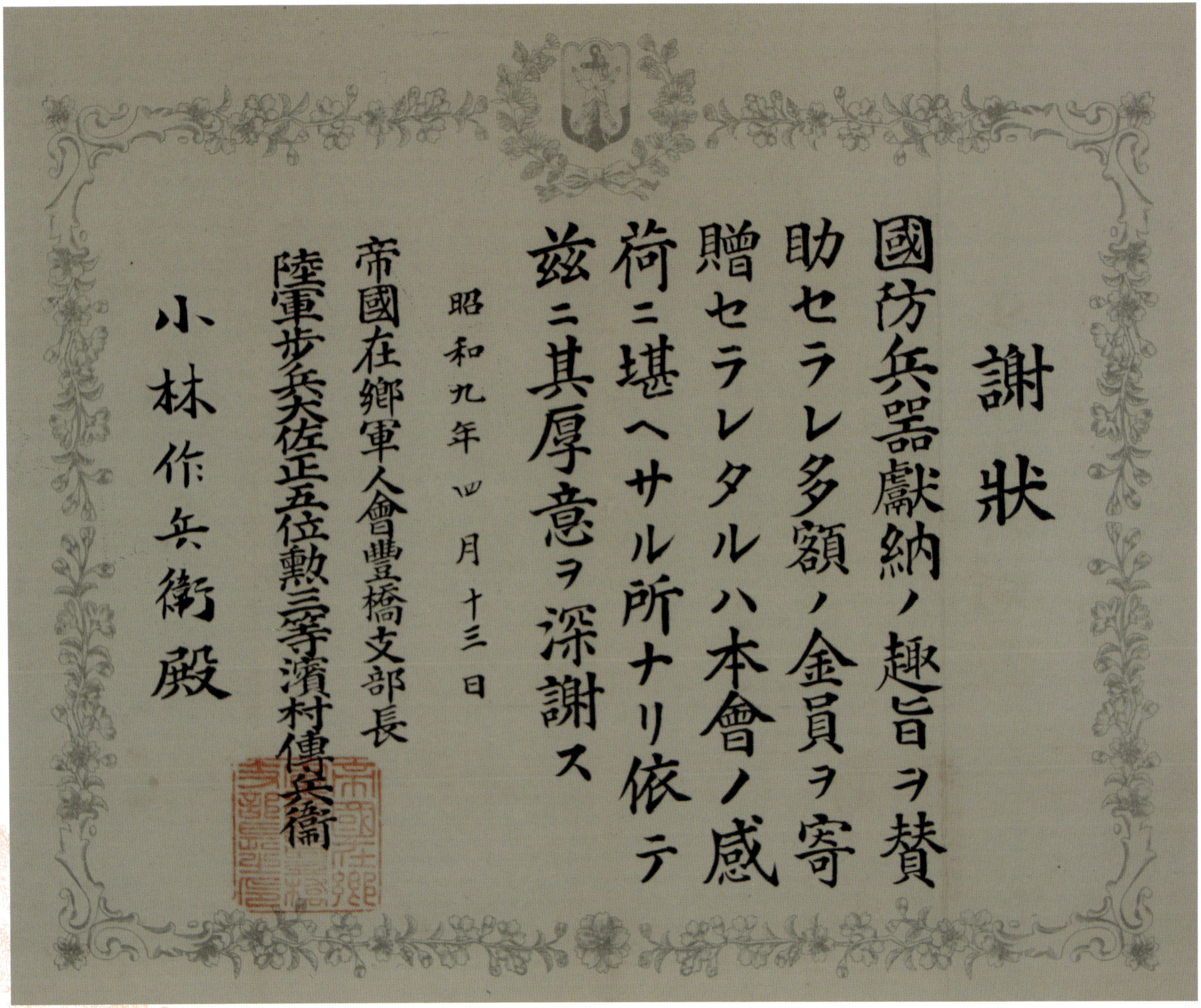

謝状

國防兵器獻納ノ趣旨ヲ賛助セラレ多額ノ金員ヲ寄贈セラレタルハ本會ノ感荷ニ堪ヘサル所ナリ依テ茲ニ其厚意ヲ深謝ス

昭和九年四月十三日

帝國在鄉軍人會豊橋支部長

陸軍歩兵大佐正五位勲三等濱村傳兵衛

小林作兵衛殿

Opposite: Translation of appreciation document for donating money in a war drive, right side only: "Kobayashi Sakubei, the association owes you a debt of gratitude for a large sum of financial contribution that you made in support of the cause of offering weapons (to the Emperor) to protect the nation. Therefore, we hereby express our sincere gratitude for your kindness. Showa 9 [1934], April 13." *Author's Collection*

Widening the War in China

The Manchurian Incident should not be considered a total war. The Japanese public was not expected to contribute everything to the war effort like the Great East Asian War. Nonetheless, those who did contribute were often recognized with documents. The example document in this section was given to Kobayashi Sakubei in 1934 for donating money to a war drive. Interestingly, this document was awarded by the Imperial Military Reserve Association. The Imperial Military Reserve Association was formed in 1910 with the goal to raise military preparedness of conscripts. The membership reached 2,000,000 at its peak. The group also helped install nationalism in Japan through further militarism.[11]

The foundation of Manchukuo did not mean the end of hostilities. Japan controlled the strategic important cities and transportation systems. However, hundreds of thousands of armed Chinese remained in the vast countryside of Manchuria. This problem would be repeated in 1937. The problem for now was more isolated and could be more easily dealt with by the Japanese and the new Manchukuo State. These forces, now labeled bandit, needed to be dealt with for a variety of reasons. Frist, the new state of Manchukuo needed to demonstrate its authority within its own borders. Second, the Japanese feared these rebels would become communist guerillas. These forces numbered over 350,000 and required thousands of Japanese soldiers a number of years to pacify. The pacification campaign also included the use of Manchukuo troops, though these troops were generally unreliable as they were usually from the same stock as the very bandits they were hunting. Nonetheless, this campaign had great success through the early 1930s as the number of bandits decreased to around 25,000 by 1935 and then to 7,300 by 1938.[12]

The war against China continued past 1932 as well. This war took multiple forms. There was the military action in the Inner Mongolian province of Jehlol. The Japanese launched their attack against the Chinese forces in the area in late February of 1933 with hostilities ending a month later. The sparse province became part of Manchukuo. The Japanese also fought a clandestine war to gain political influence in regions of north China, which were either in flux or controlled by warlords. They set up puppet governments, which were merely warlords with little

This appreciation document was awarded by the Military Reservist's Association and features their emblem at the top center. This emblem is the same as the pin given to members of the association. *Author's Collection*

Opposite: This interesting photograph shows Japanese soldiers marching somewhere in northern China. The multicolored striped flag signifies that the area is probably in the East Hebei Autonomous Council. This particular puppet regime lasted from 1935–1937 and was one of the many puppet regimes set up by the Japanese during World War II. *Author's Collection*

influence beyond their immediate regions. These puppet governments did instigate numerous skirmishes between the Chinese Nationalists under Chiang Kai-shek. These operations, which continued through 1937, spread the influence of Japan in northern China, but did little else.[13]

Finding a date to declare victory in the Manchurian conflict was an issue for the Japanese. The award documents from this conflict would list the Manchurian incident as stretching from 1931–1934. The actions in this area stretched beyond 1934 though. Historians would argue that the clandestine and proxy wars continued in China up to the Marco Polo Bridge Incident in July 1937.

The Manchurian Incident (also referred to as the Mukden Incident) in 1931 formed the beginning of fifteen years of war for Japan, culminating in their 1945 surrender to the Allies and signifying the end of World War II. Many Japanese historians refer to this time as the Fifteen–Year War, though Westerners are less aware of the events from 1931 to 1937. For the Japanese nation as a whole, the extended presence of Japan in China and subsequent battles resulting from their instigation of World War II, were not welcomed as the Japanese military and economy were not prepared to fight a protracted full-scale war in China or throughout the rest of the world.

The Japanese military began to change in the 1930s. The obvious change was the growth in size. The continued and escalated wars in China required more and more divisions. Another subtle change came in the rise of militarism in Japan. Bushido or the "way of the warrior" became more important and the combat art of kendo, which could include the bayonet or sword. Army infantry PFC Matsushita Sou was extremely talented at kendo. I have quite a few competition certificates from Sou even a document for him winning the Kendo Badge 2nd Class. This document was from 1935 as he obtained a high score in kendo competition within the 14th Regiment. The variations to these types of military documents are numerous and visually appealing.[14]

賞状

陸軍歩兵一等兵 松下操

昭和十年度聯隊
劍術競技會ニ於テ
其成績優秀ナリ
因テ茲ニ之ヲ證ス

昭和十年七月十二日

歩兵第十四聯隊長陸軍歩兵大佐從五位勲三等 今村勝次

Opposite: Translation of army kendo award document: "Award certificate. Army Private 1st Class Matsushita Sou. This certifies that you demonstrated excellent performance in the regimental swordsmanship competition held in Showa 10 [1935]. Showa 10 [1935], July 12." *Author's Collection*

The top center of this document features two crossed Japanese flags with the army star in the center. *Author's Collection*

The corners of this army kendo document feature a hybridized army badge. The badge appears to be a cross between the kendo badge and marksmanship badge. *Author's Collection*

This photograph from the 1930s shows Japanese soldiers practicing their bayonet fighting skills. Bayonet fighting fell under the discipline of kendo and soldiers could win the army kendo badge for their bayonet skills. *Author's Collection*

The world's reaction to Japan over the Manchurian Incident was an important stepping stone to the outbreak of World War II, and some historians even mark the incident as the start. Japan clearly broke the international mandates of the League of Nations, which they had signed. The Lytton Report, which was an investigation conducted by a League of Nations committee, found the Manchukuo was not legitimate and that Japan was really in control. Yet, the world had no real response to Japan's unprovoked and illegal takeover of Manchuria other than sanctions. Japan withdrew from the League of Nations in 1933. Japan's view of the situation was different. They saw themselves acting much like the Western counties did during their imperial years. Furthermore, their actions in Manchuria represented the strong militaristic and nationalistic ideologies fermenting in Japan. However, Japan's venture in Manchukuo was a generation too late by those standards. While people in Japan celebrated their recent conquests the world took notice of the new threat in Asia.

Chapter 4 Endnotes

1. Reader's Digest, *The World at Arms: The Reader's Digest Illustrated History of World War II* (New York City, NY: Reader's Digest, 1989), 132.
2. A. Gordon, *A Modern History of Japan: From Tokugawa Times to the Present* (New York: Oxford Press, 2009), 191–192.
3. A. Gordon, *A Modern History of Japan: From Tokugawa Times to the Present* (New York: Oxford Press, 2009), 193–194.
4. A. Gordon, *A Modern History of Japan: From Tokugawa Times to the Present* (New York: Oxford Press, 2009), 195–197.
5. J. Benson and T. Matsumura, *Japan, 1868–1945: From Isolation to Occupation* (Essex, UK: Pearson Education, 2001), 101.
6. A. Gordon, *A Modern History of Japan: From Tokugawa Times to the Present* (New York: Oxford Press, 2009), 198–200.
7. P. Duara, *Sovereignty and Authenticity: Manchurian and the East Asian Modern* (Lanham, MD: Rowman & Littlefield, 2003), 51.
8. P. Duara, *Sovereignty and Authenticity: Manchurian and the East Asian Modern* (Lanham, MD: Rowman & Littlefield, 2003), 42–86
9. L. Young, *Japan's Total Empire: Manchuria and the Culture of Wartime Imperialism* (Berkely, CA: University of California Press, 1998), 21–52.
10. A. Gordon, *A Modern History of Japan: From Tokugawa Times to the Present* (New York: Oxford Press, 2009), 135.
11. P. S. Jowett, *Rays of the Rising Sun: Armed Forces of Japan's Asian Allies, 1931* (Solihull, England: Helion & Company, 2004), 19.
12. P. S. Jowett, *Rays of the Rising Sun: Armed Forces of Japan's Asian Allies, 1931* (Solihull, England: Helion & Company, 2004), 25.
13. Reader's Digest, *The World at Arms: The Reader's Digest Illustrated History of World War II* (New York City, NY: Reader's Digest, 1989), 133.

5 JAPAN'S SUPERNOVA:
COLLAPSE OF THE EMPIRE (1937–1945)

The war against China that started in 1937 would take Japan to the breaking point even before their attack on the Allies in late-1941. The enormous invasions by Japan in late-1941 and early 1942 were acts of desperation stemming from resource shortfalls and a stalemate in China. The gains by Japan by mid-1942 were staggering. They briefly became the imperial masters of much of the Pacific. However, these gains were short lived and the territorial acquisition was just a supernova of the imploding Japanese empire. Japan would suffer a complete defeat by 1945 as their empire was broken.

Soldiers appear to be celebrating by shouting the traditional banzai chant. Banzai is a term that has roots in China and in Japan was used to express respect for the emperor. The term was also sometimes used by Japanese before they began an assault. This particular picture comes from the early phases of the Great East Asian War. Soldiers celebrated victories with banzai chants all over the Pacific. These victories were tactical successes that were almost unheralded in modern amphibious warfare; however, the victories were also strategic blunders as Japan was unable to defend the large area they had just conquered. The stress of defending such a vast area surrounded by numerous large bodies of waters proved too much for Japan even in the latter part of 1942 as they quickly lost the naval initiative to the West.
Author's Collection

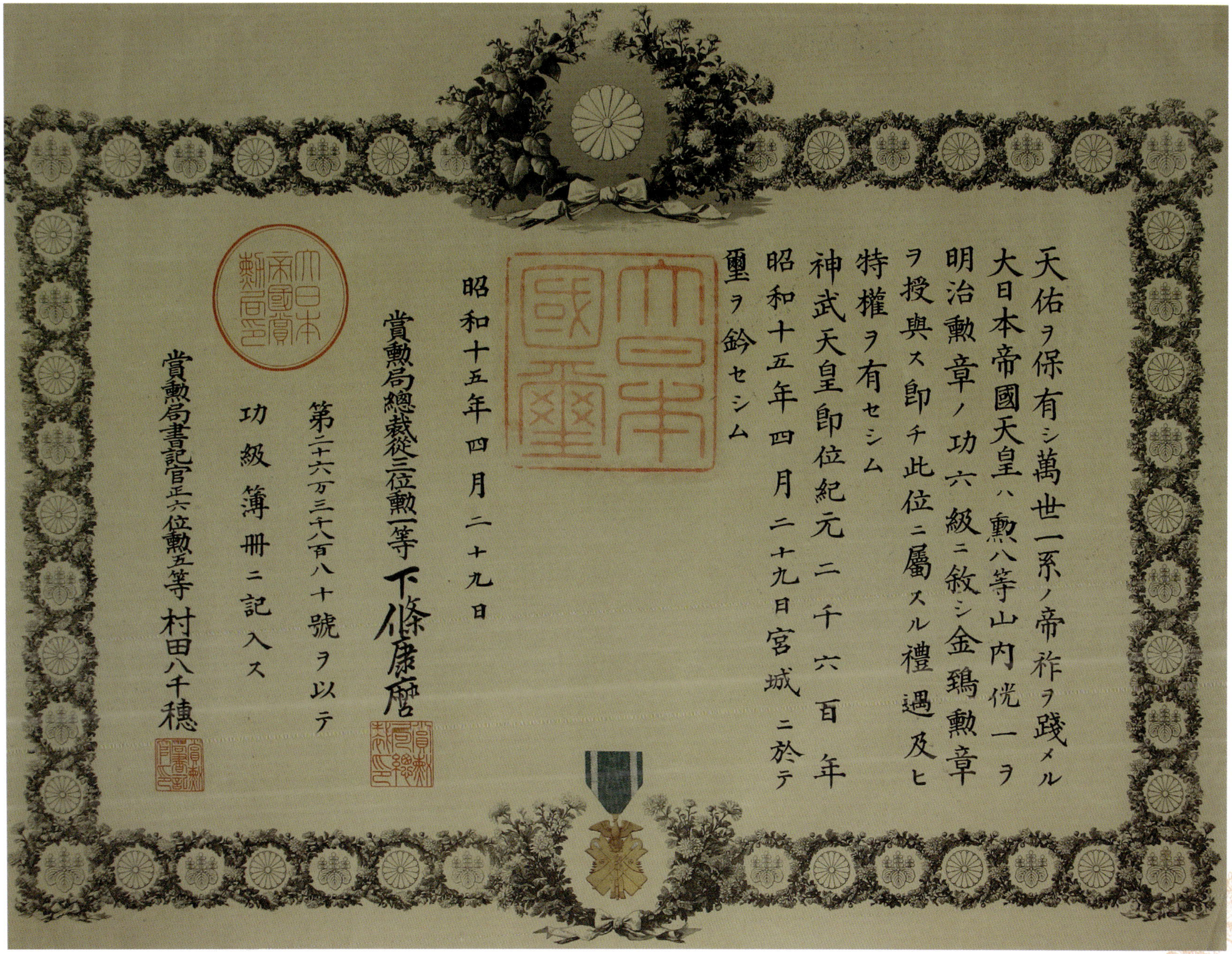
天佑ヲ保有シ萬世一系ノ帝祚ヲ踐メル
大日本帝國天皇ハ勲八等山内侊一ヲ
明治勲章ノ功六級ニ敍シ金鵄勲章
ヲ授與ス卽チ此位ニ屬スル禮遇及ヒ
特權ヲ有セシム
神武天皇卽位紀元二千六百年
昭和十五年四月二十九日宮城ニ於テ
璽ヲ鈐セシム

昭和十五年四月二十九日
賞勲局總裁從三位勲一等 下條康麿
第二十六万三千八百八十號ヲ以テ
功級簿冊ニ記入ス
賞勲局書記官正六位勲五等 村田八千穂

Translation of Order of the Golden Kite 6th Class document, right side only: "Through the honor of the immortal Emperor, the Empire of Japan bestows this award. Order of Merit 8th Class, Yamauchi Kouichi. Order of the Golden Kite 6th Class. Imperial Year 2600 [1940]. Showa 15 [1940], April 29. Tokyo Imperial Shrine." *Author's Collection*

Second Sino-Japanese War

The Order of the Golden Kite in the 6th class was given to enlisted men and non-commissioned officers for outstanding acts during war. The Golden Kite pictured is from the Second Sino-Japanese War. It was awarded to Yamauchi Kouichi who had previously earned a different order in the 8th class. There are two interesting points about this document. First, we do not know the rank of this military man as military ranks were no longer listed on order award documents after around 1920. This can be frustrating for the collector. Second, this document was given on April, 29 1940. The Japanese government gave many orders and medals related to this conflict on this date. I have seen relatively few China Incident War Medal documents with a date before April 1940. The reasons for this are various; yet, all reflect the difficult course of the conflict. The war could not be ended quickly. All other war medal awards were instituted after a victory or at least after an event which could be claimed as a victory. The Japanese government probably held back on awarding orders and medals, waiting for the war to end, and then decided that 2½ years was long enough and the backlog of awardees was too long to wait anymore.

Japan's war against China, which had hardly ended, restarted on July 7, 1937, at the Marco Polo Bridge just north of Peking (now Beijing). The incident did not immediately lead to all-out war as both sides discussed terms for a cease-fire. The discussions faltered as smaller incidents erupted in the Peking and Shanghai region. The Japanese continued to send reinforcements to the Peking region as tensions escalated. The Japanese began a full assault of Peking and the surrounding region by late July. Small scale skirmishes began around July 25, and fresh Japanese reinforcements began to probe Chinese defenses. Peace still seemed to be a small possibility as the delegations discussed terms to end the disputes. Yet, by July

The medal view of the Order of the Golden Kite 6th Class document. The difference between the 7th class and 6th class medals was in the color of the medal, silver for 7th class versus gold for 6th class. The Order of the Golden Kite only had seven classes versus eight classes for the Orders of the Rising Sun and Sacred Treasure. *Author's Collection*

27–28, these efforts were ended as Japan began a full assault against Chinese forces around Peking. The strategically important port of city of Tianjin fell after two days of fighting on July 30. Chinese forces in Peking were essentially cut off after Tianjin fell. Within a few days the Chinese fell back to the east and Peking fell by August 8. The fall of Peking would leave the northern China Plain, south of Peking, open to the Japanese as there were few natural defensive positions. The Japanese would soon launch an assault on Shanghai.

Japan wanted to knock China out of the war with a few quick victories in 1937. Capturing Peking, Shanghai, and Nanking were key to this plan. While Peking fell quickly, the last two cities would turn the tide from the advance of the Japanese offensive to a bloody stalemate. The Battle of Shanghai would last for three bloody months as up to one million soldiers fought for the city. The battle included tenacious house-to-house fighting, which can be compared to the Battle of Stalingrad. The Chinese were hoping to draw the wider world against Japan through the stubborn defense of Shanghai. The Japanese brought the might of their air, land, and navy weaponry against a force of Chinese, which were primarily equipped with infantry weapons. The intense combat at Shanghai drained both sides. The Chinese forces had sporadic successes until Japanese anti-tank guns, tanks, and flamethrowers helped clear Chinese positions. The Chinese actually had faced a tougher situation with supplies and reinforcements. They could not resist the pressure from Japanese forces and continually, though slowly, gave ground. The Japanese quickly realized that the Chinese were not going to give up without a bloody fight. The Japanese would capture the city by November 26, 1937, at a high cost of over 90,000 casualties. The Chinese also succeeded in drawing world attention to their struggle as countries began to condemn Japan for their acts of aggression.[1]

Japanese soldiers on the march through a Chinese city. The immense size of China quickly wore the Japanese military down, and the Japanese offensive in China halted within a year. These soldiers appear to be exhausted and by many accounts, the war in China became a test of endurance for many Japanese soldiers. *Author's Collection*

The Japanese pushed deep into northern China after the capture of Peking. They secured much of northern China by November 1937 with the capture of Shanxi province. The conquest of this region forced the Chinese Nationalists under Chiang Kai-shek and Communist Chinese under Mao Zedong to put aside their internal conflict for China to fight the Japanese. The Japanese would now face guerrillas in their occupied areas. The Japanese forces that had captured Shanghai were now free to march toward the capital for the Nationalists' Chinese capital of Nanking (now called Nanjing). The march from Shanghai towards Nanking, around 160 miles, and the subsequent battle was extremely quick, occurring between December 1 and 13, 1937. The Chinese troops were unprepared for a long siege and could not break out of the Japanese siege when ordered to on December 12. The end of the battle did not end the violence in the city. The Japanese occupiers committed mass murder and rape of tens and hundreds of thousands of Chinese prisoners of war and Chinese civilians. The number of victims will never be known and is still a matter of debate. The facts are clear and straightforward regarding the brutality of the Nanking Massacre. Accounts from foreigners, members of the German Nazi party, attest to the murder and rape of thousands during the month long horror. The Nanking Massacre hurt the prestige of Japan around the world and still resonates today as some in Japan refute the scope of the atrocities.[2]

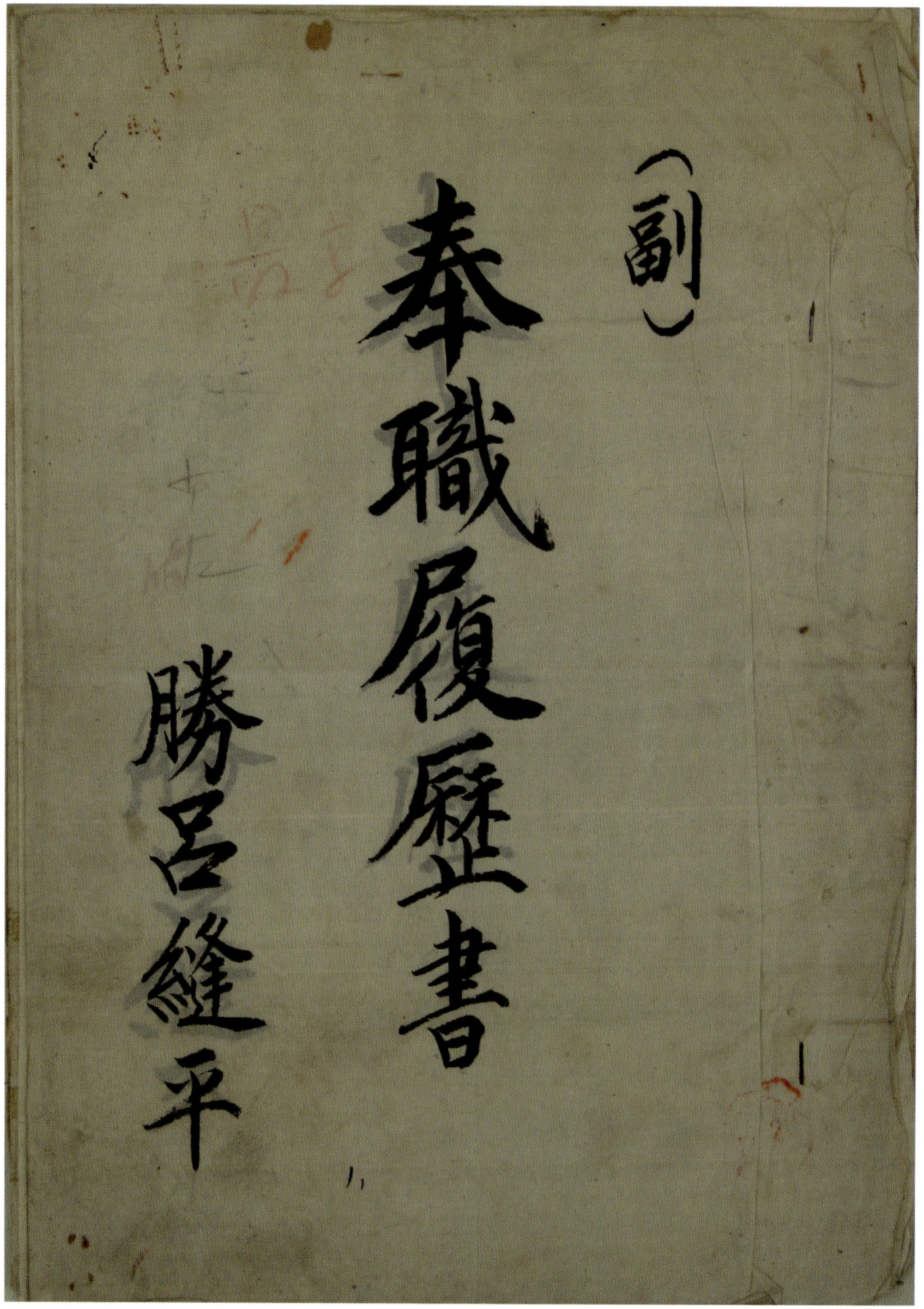

The cover of the Japanese Navy *rireki-hyou* of Katsuro Nuihei. A rireki-hyou is a notebook that is similar to the Japanese Army Techo. This particular rireki-hyou is quite long as his career spanned from 1904–1945. The rireki-hyou is made of soft rice paper that has survived quite well being over 100 years old. *Author's Collection*

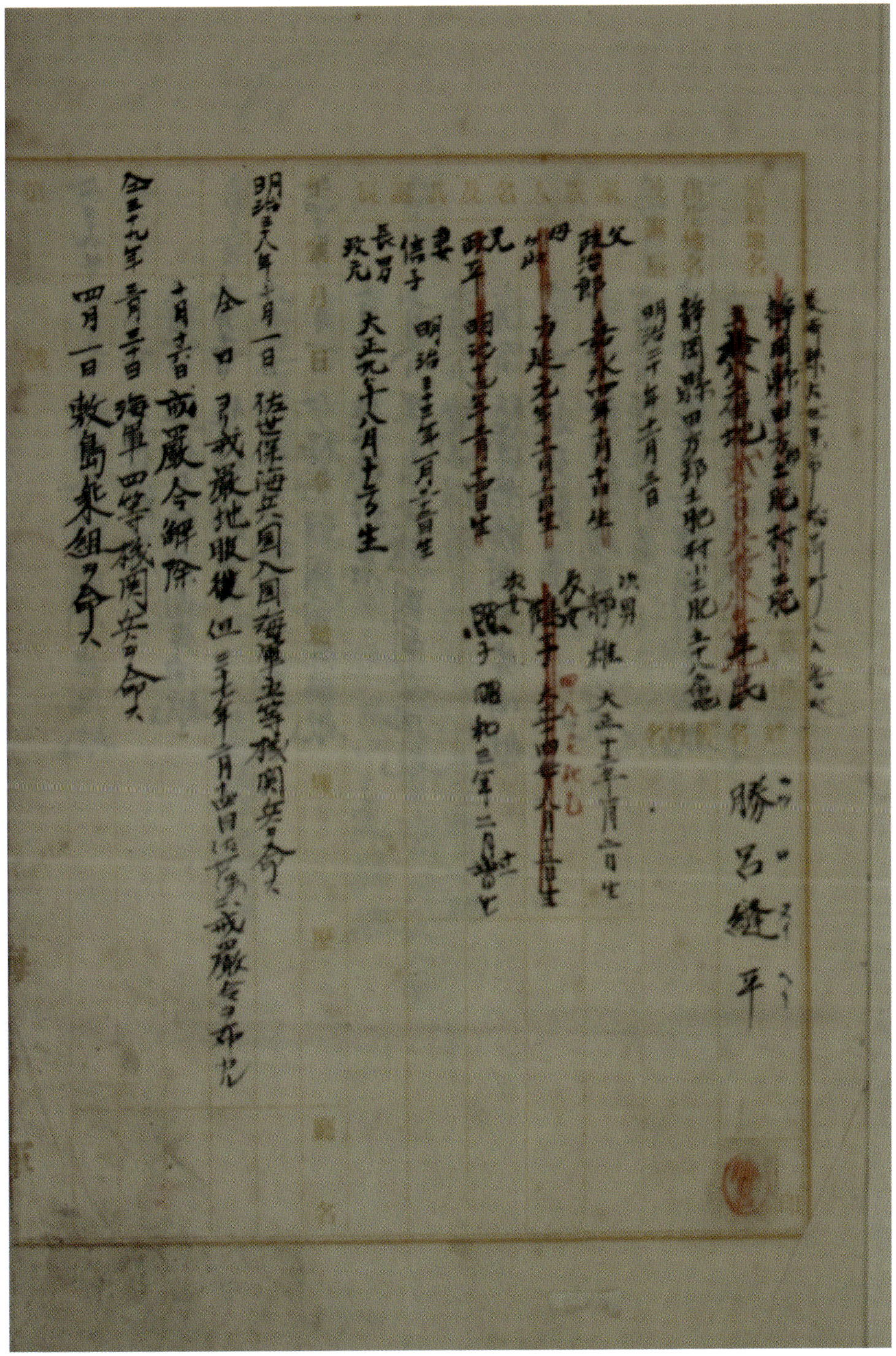

The opening page of Katsuro's CV (rireki-hyou) contains much of his personal information. A complete translation of this whole page as well as the whole document, which is sixteen pages long, is beyond the scope of this text. Katsuro was born in 1887 and served as engineer in the navy. He started his career in the Japanese military in 1906 as a navy seaman 4th class, which is the lowest rank of an enlisted man. Katsuro would rise through the ranks, become a mustang (navy slang for an enlisted man that becomes an officer), and ended up as a captain in 1942. Katsuro was also awarded many medals and orders and medals, including the Sacred Treasure (8th, 6th, 5th & 4th), Rising Sun (7th, 5th & 4th), War Medals (1914–15, 1914–1920, 1931–1934, China Incident), Commemorative Medals (Showa Enthronement & Manchukuo Foundation), and Imperial Ranks (Junior 7th through Senior 6th). *Author's Collection*

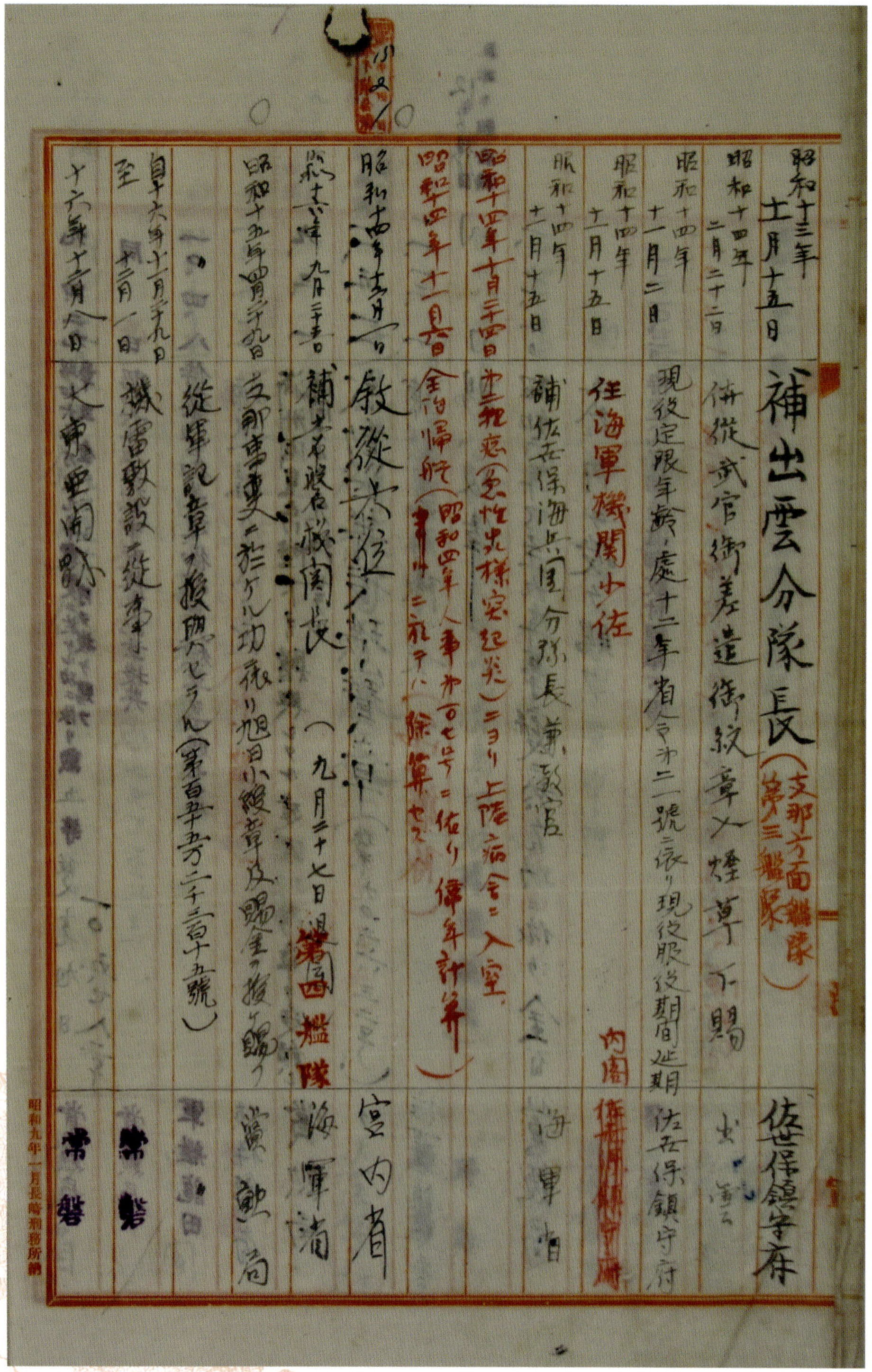

This page is testimony to how difficult translating these handwritten documents can be. The 4th column from the right is dated Showa 14 [1939], November 15, and says he was promoted to lieutenant commander. The 8th column from the right is dated Showa 14 [1939], December 1 and says he earned the Imperial Rank of Junior 6th. These two examples are relatively easily to translate. The 10th and 11th column from the right proves to be more of a challenge. The date and context is the first clue. The date is Showa 15 [1940], April 29. Katsuro had also served in China in 1938. This helps us identify what he wrote as he earned the China Incident Medal. Further examination of these columns reveals that he also earned the Order of the Rising Sun 4th Class at the same time. These documents can be a rewarding challenge for a collector, especially if you find a career military man like Katsuro. *Author's Collection*

The casualty rate experienced by the Japanese during the opening moves of their war against China caught Japan by surprise. Previous wars had been relatively quick, though sometimes bloody. The war in China seemed to have no end in sight and documents like the one above became increasingly issued to next-of-kin of fallen soldiers. The capture of Nanking did not bring the Nationalist Chinese to the peace table. Japan's foes actually became more determined to resist. The Japanese attempted to push farther west into the heart of China in 1938. The Japanese won a victory at Xuzhou in May but were unable to annihilate the Chinese forces completely. The escaping Chinese troops were able to regroup for future battles. Farther to the north, the Japanese lost the Battle of Taierzhuang in early April 1938. This battle shook Japan's morale and provided a much needed boost to Chinese moral. The first turning point of the Second Sino–Japanese War came during the Battle of Wuhan which lasted from June to late October 1938. Wuhan was a strategically important city along the Yangtze in central China. The Nationalist Chinese brought well over a million soldiers into the battle while Japan brought 350,000 of their troops. Casualties on both sides were remarkably high. The ferocity of the battle was extreme as well. The Japanese used poison gas, which drew international condemnation. The Japanese succeeded in capturing and securing Wuhan and the surrounding area. However, the victory was purely tactile and the strategic victory belonged to China. The Japanese had lost the offensive initiative in China because of the great number of causalities in the first year of combat. There would be further battles from 1939 through 1943 of which the Chinese won quite a few. The Japanese did not undertake another large scale offensive in China until 1944.[3]

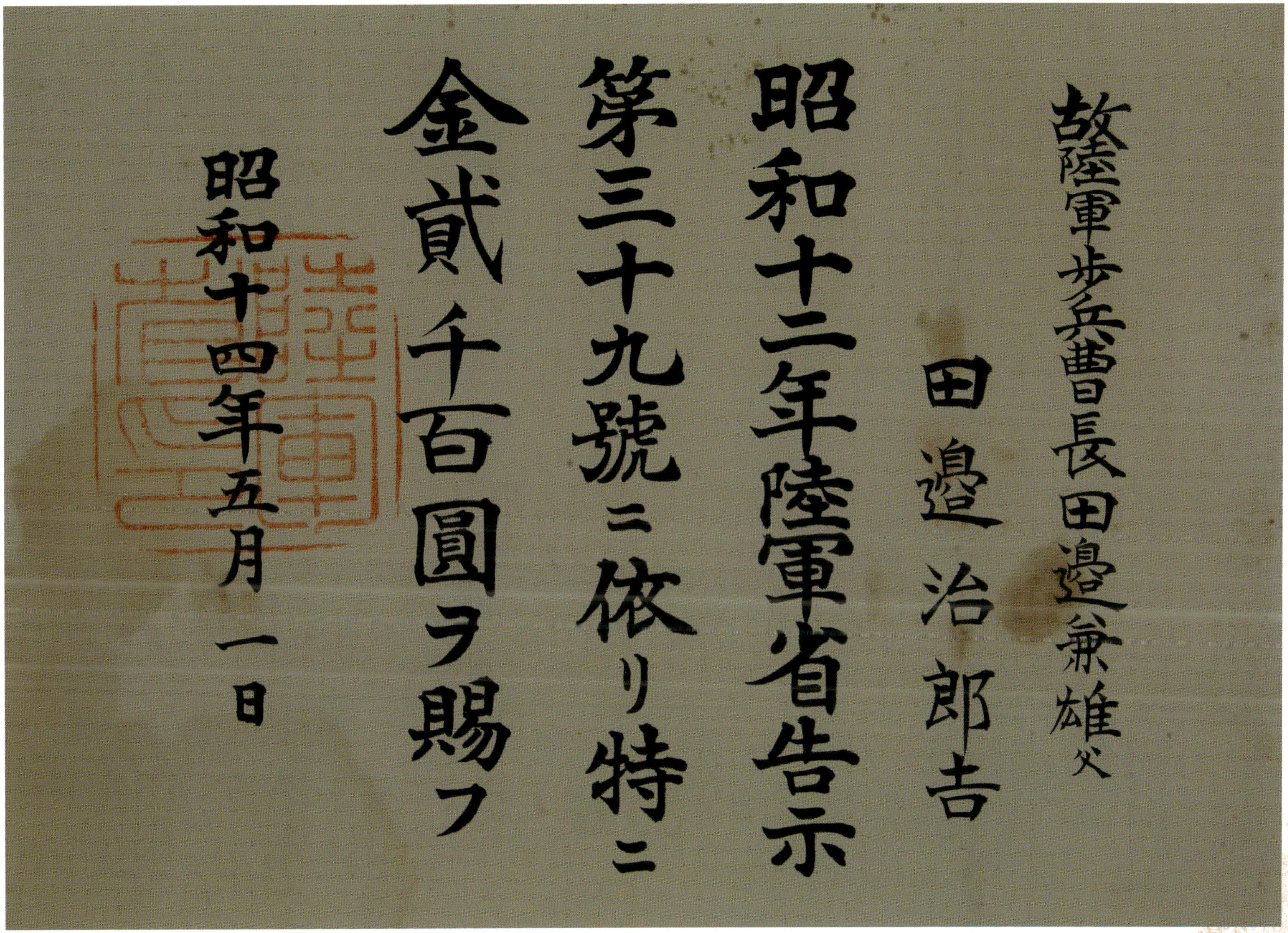

故陸軍歩兵曹長田邉兼雄父
田邉治郎吉
昭和十二年陸軍省告示
第三十九號ニ依リ特ニ
金貳千百圓ヲ賜フ
昭和十四年五月一日

Translation of killed-in-action pension document: "[To] The father of the late army infantry sergeant Tanabe Kaneo, Tanabe Jirōkichi. In accordance with the number 39 announcement issued by the Ministry of the Army in Showa 12, 2100 yen is granted (to you). Showa 14 [1939], May 1." *Author's Collection*

Translation of the Golden Kite Pension document, top side: "Certificate of the Order of the Golden Kite Pension. Issuance number 231173. This certificate cannot be transferred or offered as security/collateral." Next is the translation of the right side of the bottom half of the document. "Annual amount, 150 yen. Army infantry private first Class (name erased). Order of the Golden Kite 7th Class and permanent pension are conferred [on you]. This certificate is granted for that [reason]. Showa 14 [1939], August 26." *Author's Collection*

金鵄勲章年金之證

第貳參壹壹七參號

此證書ハ讓渡シ又ハ擔保ニ供スルヲ得ス

年額金百五拾圓

陸軍歩兵上等兵

功七級ニ敍シ金鵄勲章ヲ賜ヒ終身

年金ヲ給スルヲ以テ此證ヲ付與ス

昭和十四年八月二十六日

賞勲局總裁 下條康麿

賞勲局書記官 宇都宮孝平

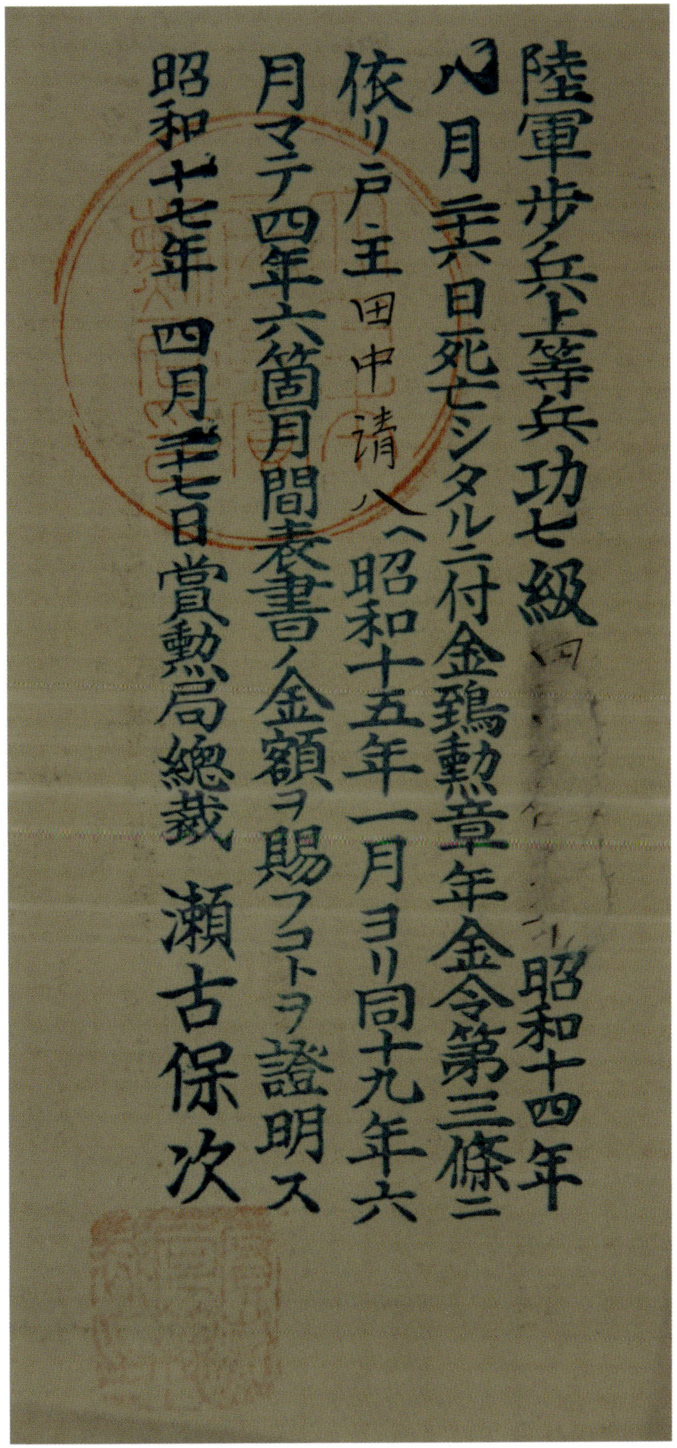
陸軍歩兵上等兵功七級　昭和十四年
八月廿六日死亡シタルニ付金鵄勲章年金令第三條ニ
依リ戸主田中清八ヘ昭和十五年一月ヨリ同十九年六
月マテ四年六箇月間表書ノ金額ヲ賜フコトヲ證明ス
昭和十七年四月廿七日
賞勲局總裁　瀬古保次

The Imperial Japanese government was faced with some of the same problems as that of modern states, including taking care of veterans. The awarding of the Order of the Golden Kite also included a pension for that solider. This pension rate would rise periodically. This happened in 1939. The army infantry private superior, whose name was scratched out, had earned the Order of the Golden Kite 7th Class. His Golden Kite pension increased August 26, 1939. This was not the first time such pensions were increased; pensions were increased in 1927. The interesting extra part of this document is that the original pension holder, the infantry private, had passed away and the reverse of the document awards the pension to his next-of-kin.

Translation of reverse of the Golden Kite Pension document: "Army infantry private first Class, Order of the Golden Kite 7th Class, (name erased) died on Showa 14 [1939], August 26. Therefore, in accordance with Article 3, the Order of the Golden Kite Pension Ordinance, the amount stated on the front side will be granted to Tanaka Seihachi, the householder, for four and one-half years, from Showa 15 [1940] to Showa [1944] January. This certificate confirms that. Showa 17 [1942], April 27." *Author's Collection*

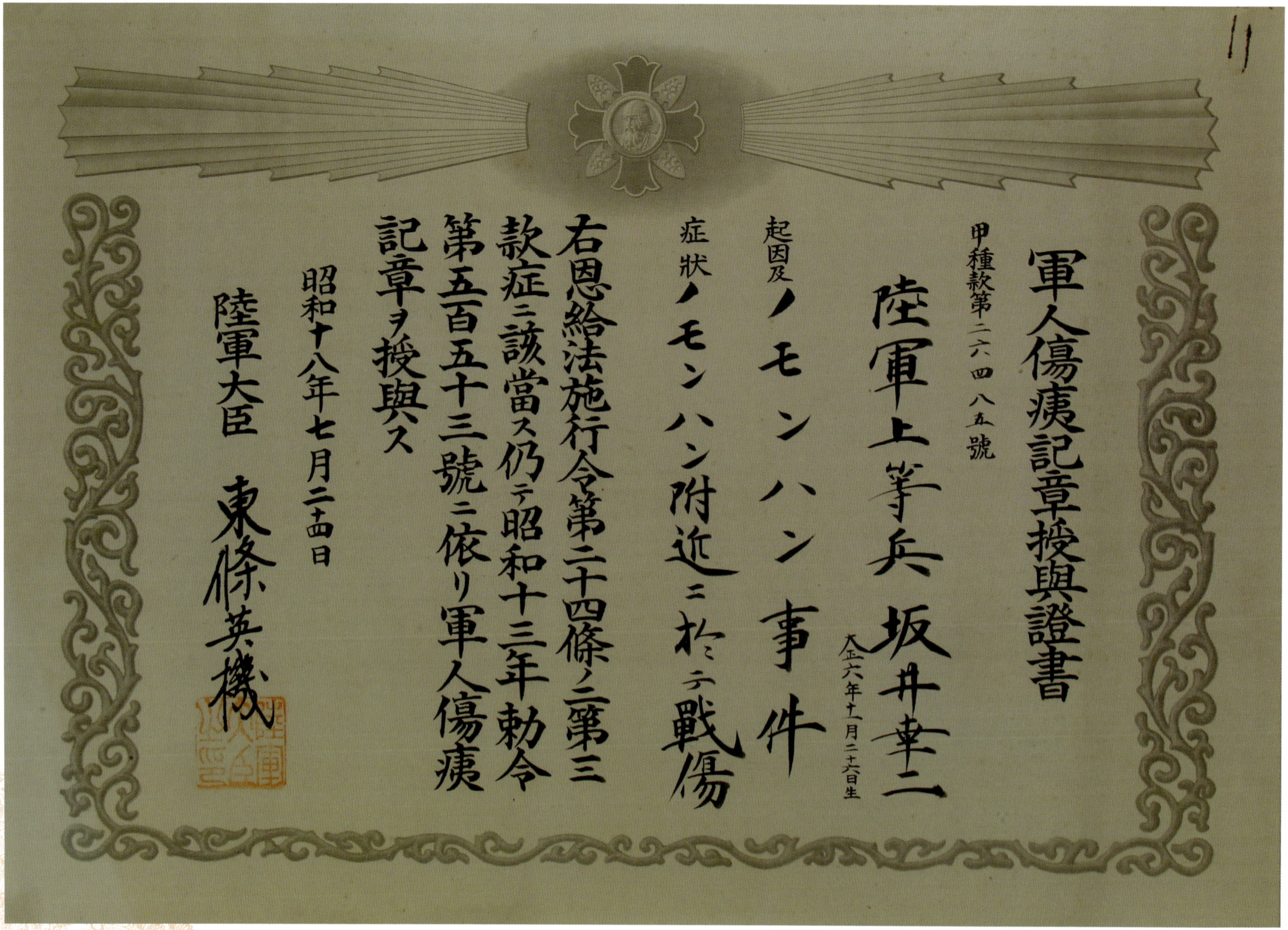

軍人傷痍記章授與證書

甲種款第二六四八五號

陸軍上等兵 坂井華一

大正六年十一月二十六日生

起因及 ノモンハン事件

症状 ノモンハン附近ニ於テ戰傷

右恩給法施行令第二十四條ノ二第三款症ニ該當ス仍テ昭和十三年勅令第五百五十三號ニ依リ軍人傷痍記章ヲ授與ス

昭和十八年七月二十四日

陸軍大臣 東條英機

Opposite: Translation of War Wound document from Nomonhan, right side only: "Certificate of granting a Disabled Veteran's Badge. First Class (*Kō*) category 26485. Army private 1st Class Sakai Kouji born in Taishō 6 [1917] November 26. Cause – Nomonhan Incident. Condition – Wounded near Nomonhan. [The condition of] the person stated to the right falls under the one set forth in Provision 3, Article 24, Order of Enforcement of the Pension Act. Therefore, a disabled veteran's badge is granted in accordance with #553, the Imperial Ordinance issues in Showa 13 [1938]. Showa 18 [1943], July 24." *Author's Collection*

Border Incident with Soviet Union

Being wounded in battle is the dread for many soldiers and sailors. Many would prefer a quick death rather than receiving a debilitating wound. Private Superior Sakai Kouji was wounded during the Nomonhan Incident in 1939 between Japan and the Soviet Union. This battle was the worst defeat the Japanese military had experienced to that point. The battle was also bloody, with 73% of the Japanese soldiers suffering casualties with about half being fatalities. Private Sakai was one of the wounded casualties of the battle. He experienced the wide array of shortcomings that the Japanese military had at that time. This included a lack of anti-tank weapons, vehicles and infrastructure for supplies, and a gross underestimation of their opponent's ability. The secretive nature of this conflict, which is little known in the West, is evident by the dates of the documents. Pvt. Superior Sakai did not receive the Nomonhan Incident (also called Border Incident and it was actually a Manchukuo War Medal) War Medal from Manchukuo (it was not a Japanese medal) until 1941 (see document below) and then his permission to wear the Nomonhan Incident Medal from the Japanese government (also in my collection) and this War Wound Badge until 1943. The document also includes the signature of prime minister, though using his title of army minister, Hideki Tōjō. The defeat and limited nature of the conflict forced the Japanese government to move slowly in recognizing the efforts of soldiers who fought in 1939.

The tension between the Soviet Union and Japan stretched back to before the Russo-Japanese War of 1904–05. The Soviets were keen to remember their embarrassing defeat from thirty years prior and were fearful of Japanese ambitions in Siberia. The Japanese were fearful of communist intrigue from the Soviet Union, Mongolia, and Communist China. Small conflicts had occurred periodically along the Manchukuo and Soviet/Mongolian border since Manchukuo's founding. A full-scale war broke out in 1938 at the border of Japanese-controlled Korea and the Soviet Union called the Changkufeng Incident, though many in the West refer to it as the Battle of Lake Khasan. The Japanese were defeated in this limited

The War Wound document from this time period featured the War Wound badge on the top center. This was the second style of the war wound badge. *Author's Collection*

engagement and the whole incident was kept relatively quiet. The cease-fire between the two belligerents would end in less than a year. Mongolian cavalrymen looking for pasture for their horses encroached into Manchukuo in May 1939, which set in motion events that would start a full scale battle.[4]

The Japanese cavalry of the Kwantung Army sent a small contingent to scare the Mongolians. However, these cavalry troops came under fire from the far side of the Khalkhin–Gol River from Soviet forces. The Japanese were forced to retreat and the Soviet forces remained. By early July the Japanese launched a major assault via a northern flanking maneuverer and straight assault. The fighting was intense, but the Japanese suffered from a lack of anti-tank weapons. The Japanese assault was thwarted and followed-up by a limited Soviet counteroffensive. Both sides paused for reinforcements until the Japanese renewed the assault in mid-July. The Japanese tried to soften the Soviet positions with a massive artillery barrage. This barrage failed, and Japanese assaults were repulsed again. The two opposing forces settled down battle resembling the First World War. The Soviets would break the stalemate with an offensive under Gen. Georgy Zhukov, who would become the most decorated officer of the Soviet Union. The Japanese were surprised and a division was surrounded. They had fought with typical fanaticism, but suffered heavily with over 17,000 casualties, about 73%. A cease-fire was called on September 16, 1939.[5]

The Border Incident document pictured was given by the Manchukuo government rather than the Japanese. This was done to keep the incident as low key as possible. The recipient was Private Superior Sakai. His rank is not listed on this document. We know

Japanese infantry approach behind and in front of two tanks. The tanks appear to be two Type 89 I-Go tanks. These medium tanks were one of the most prevalent types used by the Japanese in the Battle of Nomonhan. *Author's Collection*

Opposite: Translation of Manchukuo Border Incident document, right side only: "Record of Receiving the Border Incident War Dispatch Medal. According to Imperial Rescript #310 of Kōtoku 7 [1940]. The Border Incident War Dispatch Commemorative Medal is awarded to Sakai Kouji the Border Incident War Dispatch Commemorative Medal. Kōtoku 7 [1940] November 25." *Author's Collection*

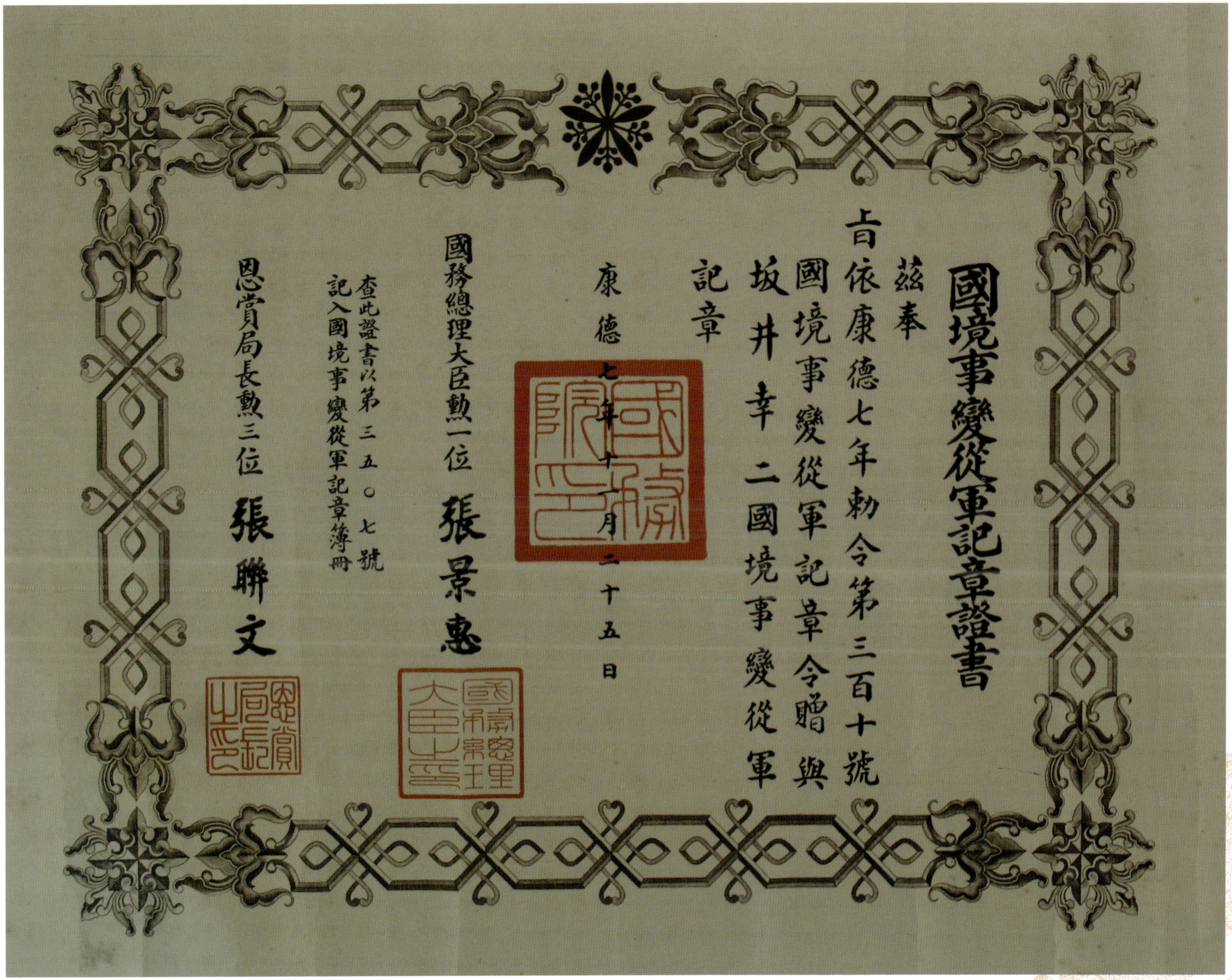

國境事變從軍記章證書

茲奉

旨依康德七年勅令第三百十號

國境事變從軍記章令贈與

坂井幸二國境事變從軍

記章

康德七年十一月二十五日

國務總理大臣勳一位 張景惠

查此證書以第三五〇七號

記入國境事變從軍記章簿冊

恩賞局長勳三位 張聯文

Opposite: This fifteen-yen war bond from 1943 features many interesting implements of war. *Author's Collection*

his rank because I have other award documents given to him (see Wound Badge pictured at the start of this chapter and Manchukuo Order of the Auspicious Clouds in previous chapter). This document is numbered rather low at 3507. The Border Incident Medal and Document are relatively common compared to other Manchukuo awards; yet, the award is popular with collectors. Private Sakai must have experienced bureaucratic entanglement when it came to his awards. He did not receive this award until two years after the battle. However, his permission to wear foreign awards document (which is in my collection) was not given until 1943. This slow bureaucratic speed was also seen in the bestowing of medals and orders during the initial phase of the Second Sino–Japanese War, which started in 1937 and the first large-scale awarding of honors was not till 1940.

The Battle at Nomonhan had far reaching effects for the Japanese and the course of World War II. Some realized the obvious, that they could not beat the Soviets without serious changes to their land doctrine. The politicians and diplomats in Japan signed a non-aggression pact with the Soviet Union in 1940. The pact was kept secret, but had far reaching consequences. Japan had to turn its attention south, towards the China and the Pacific Islands. The Soviets could now focus on their European border, which became invaluable during the German invasion of 1941. The defeat at Nomonhan brought to light numerous tactical doctrine issues with the Japanese army. First, there was a real lack of armor and anti-tank weapons. Second, the Japanese army had issues with their logistics and communications. Finally, the myth of the Japanese soldier's superiority had been debunked. The spiritual strength of the Japanese infantryman could not overcome the Soviet's superiority of armor and artillery on the battlefield. Not everyone in the Japanese general staff took these deficiencies seriously and these same issues would reappear in numerous battles in campaigns.[6]

Japan as a Military State

War bonds were a financial tool that governments used during WWII and other wars to fund the military and avoid inflation. Japan issued war bonds much like every other country. The economic state of Japan deteriorated after the start of the Sino–Japanese War. Inflation rose to double-digit levels annually. Taxes increased as Japan's economy became primarily focused on the military. Civilians were asked to make more and more sacrifices to the war effort, like the war bond picture above. The consumer economy was all but shut down in 1940. The buying power for the average Japanese fell and the black market became strong. In short, life in Japan became more difficult as the war in China continued. A woman who ran a bakery in Tokyo before the war described the decline of her business as follows. "We sold cakes until there were no more eggs and sugar; we sold sandwiches with whale ham until there was no whale ham or bread, and then we sold our machinery to the military before moving out of Tokyo."[7]

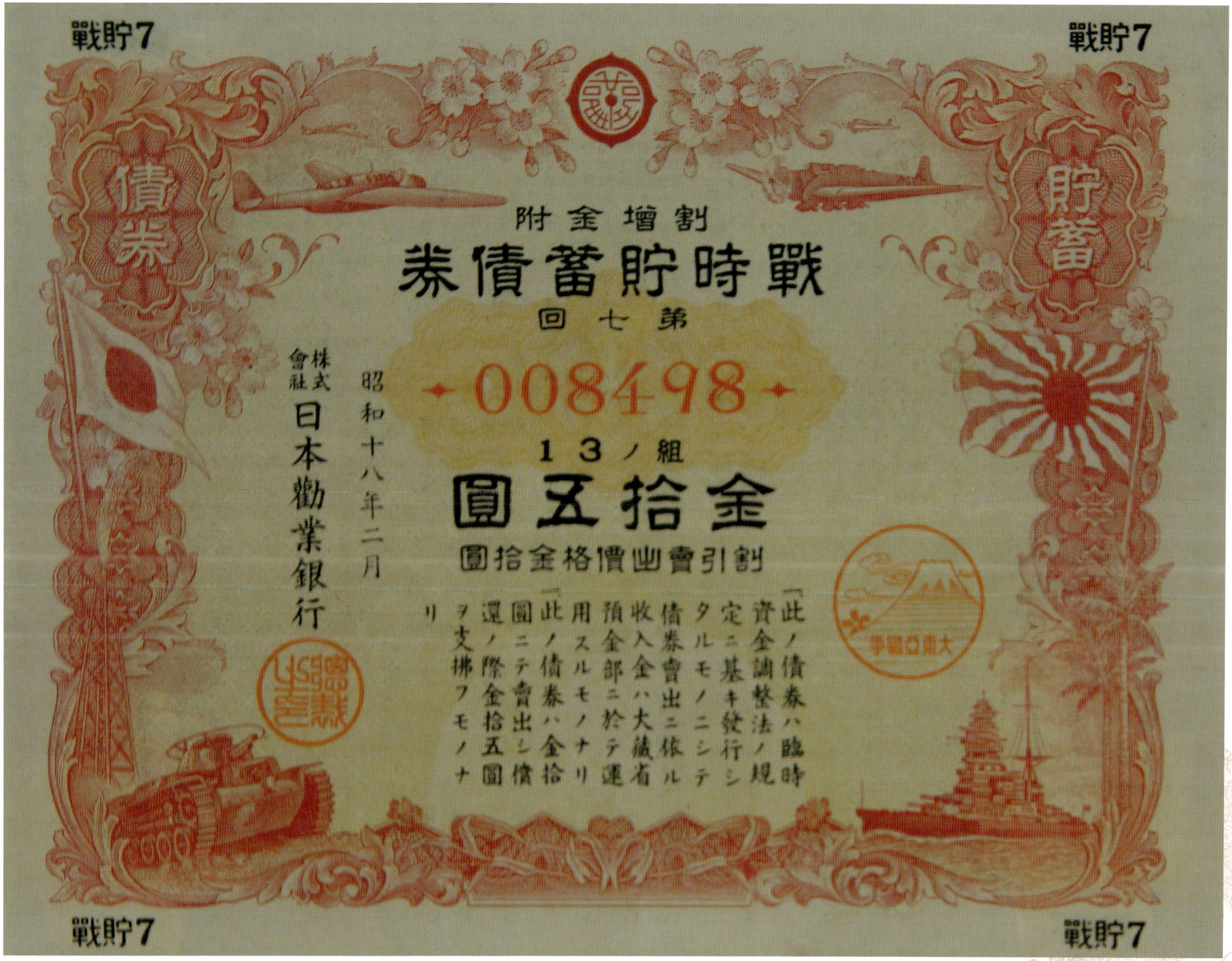
戰貯7
戰貯7
債券
貯蓄
割增金附
戰時貯蓄債券
第七回
008498
13ノ組
金拾五圓
割引賣出價格金拾圓
株式會社
日本勸業銀行
昭和十八年二月
一此ノ債券ハ臨時資金調整法ノ規定ニ基キ發行シタルモノニシテ債券賣出ニ依ル收入金ハ大藏省預金部ニ於テ運用スルモノナリ
一此ノ債券ハ金拾圓ニテ賣出シ償還ノ際金拾五圓ヲ支拂フモノナリ
大東亞戰爭
戰貯7
戰貯7

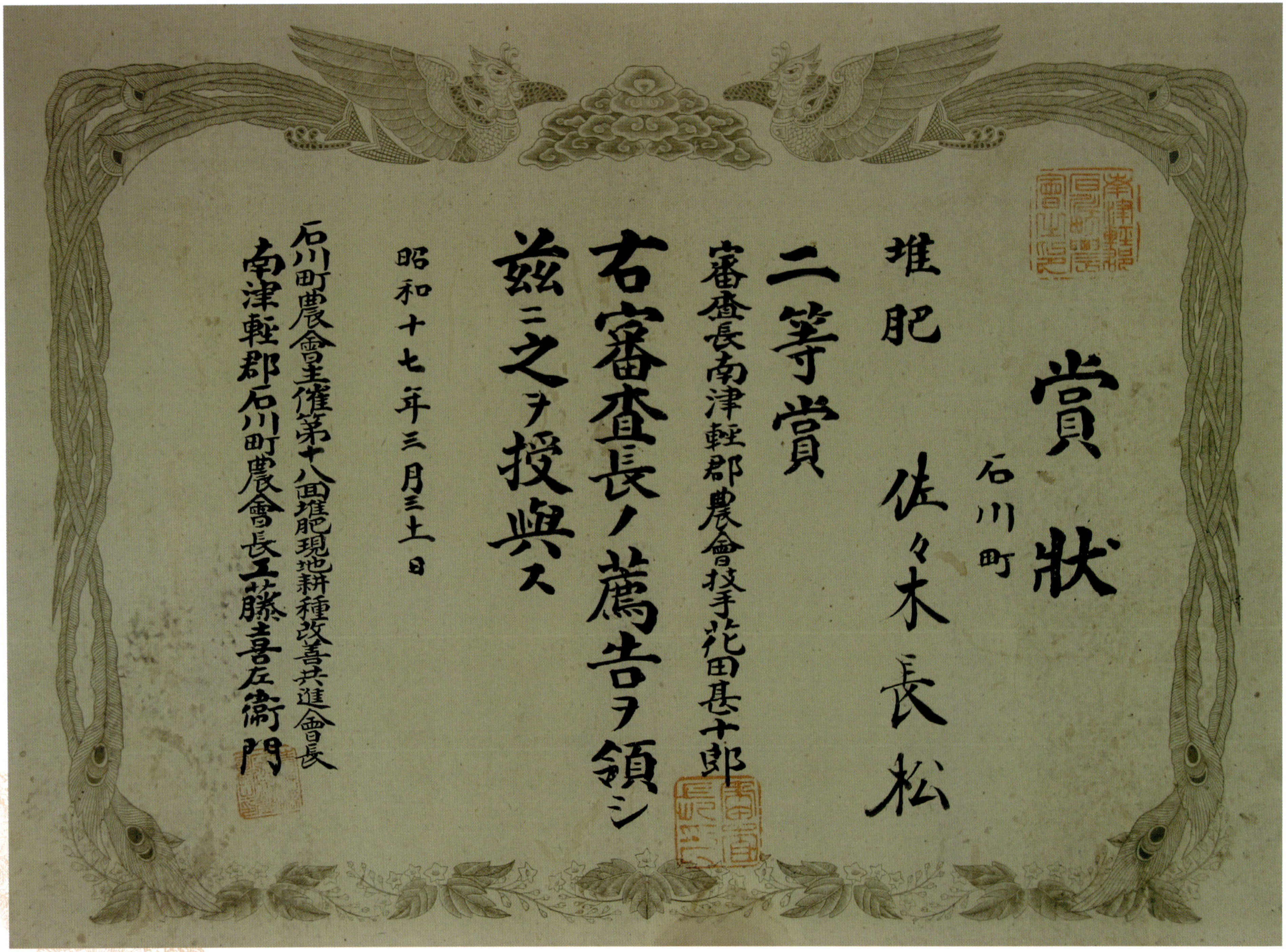
賞状

石川町
佐々木長松

堆肥

二等賞

審査長南津軽郡農會技手花田甚十郎

右審査長ノ薦告ヲ領シ
茲ニ之ヲ授與ス

昭和十七年三月三十日

石川町農會主催第十八回堆肥現地耕種改善共進會會長
南津軽郡石川町農會長工藤喜左衛門

Opposite: Translation of agricultural certificate of merit: "Certificate of Merit. Ishigawa city, Farm yard Sasaki Nagamatsu. Second prize. Examined by Hanada Kijuro, Assistant Agriculture Engineer of Minamitsugaru District. The prize is hereby awarded upon receiving the aforementioned examiner's recommendations. Showa 17 [1942], March 31st." *Author's Collection*

The lack of natural resources on the home islands became more acute as World War II escalated. Japan continued to encourage and reward innovation and efficiency in production and agriculture. The award document featured was given to Sasaki Nagamatsu for their excellent farm operation. Sasaki was from the Ishigawa City area. In this case, the award was for the 2nd class of a competition. The Japanese government put in place a variety of agriculture measures to ensure price control of agricultural products during the war. The government focused on increasing the living wage of the farm workers at the expense of the landlords. This situation caused conflict between agricultural workers and landlords, which countered the village harmony ideal in the agrarian rhetoric of totalitarian Japan.[8]

The industrial situation in wartime Japan became increasingly rigid. The government recognized in the late 1930s the need to develop complete mobilization and industrial laws. The initial moves that the Japanese government made to control the economic and social aspects of Japan were met with resistance. However, as the war progressed and millions of military-aged men were drafted into the armed forces, the government used the mobilization laws to conscript adult males and unmarried women into the work force. These numbers were eventually supplemented by forced labor and Japanese children. For instance, three million Japanese school children were drafted to work toward the war efforts.[9]

The 2600th Anniversary of Japan was a significant holiday in Japan. The 2600th Anniversary Commemorative Medal was given quite freely to people who participated in the festivities. This document was awarded to a sergeant of the Kempeitai Police named Yoshioka. The Kempeitai were a paramilitary organization that resembled the Gestapo of Nazi Germany. Founded in 1881, the Kempeitai was originally formed as a military police force. The organization became more brutal as the empire grew and annexed territory. The Kempeitai were responsible for the torture and deaths of tens of thousands of civilians. They were even feared in Japan as the organization was charged with maintaining loyalty among the Japanese.[10]

The rise of Tōjō Hideki from general in the army in 1938 to Japanese prime minister in 1941 illustrated the increasing militaristic nature of Japanese politics. While serving in the cabinet of Prime Minister Fumimaro Konoe, who did not come from the military, Tōjō advocated for widening the war in China and other imperial policies, which further deteriorated relations between the West and Japan. The principal antagonist became the United States as Europe erupted in war in September 1939. The Japanese political climate slowly crept further and further towards aggressive militaristic positions. War with the West quickly became the only inevitable course for many Japanese politicians. It should be pointed out that many leading Japanese officials were military men themselves, which only fed into Japan's ever-increasing belief in war. Tōjō slowly gained more power in the Konoe cabinet to the point when Prime Minister Konoe himself resigned in the middle of 1941. Some thought the prime minister position should be taken by a member of the imperial family. Emperor Hirohito went with Tōjō and preparations for war against the West went forward.[11]

紀元二千六百年祝典記念章之證

陸軍憲兵軍曹吉岡劉二

昭和十五年勅令第四百八十八號ノ旨ニ依リ
紀元二千六百年祝典記念章ヲ授與セラル

昭和十五年十二月三十一日

賞勲局總裁從四位勲三等瀬古保次

第二十七万七千三百九十一號ヲ以テ紀元二千六百年
祝典記念章簿冊ニ記入ス

賞勲局書記官從五位勲五等村田八千穗

Opposite: Translation of 2600th Anniversary Commemorative Medal document, right side only: "Record of Receiving the 2600th Anniversary Commemorative Medal. According to Imperial Rescript 488 of Showa 15 [1940]. The 2600th Anniversary Commemorative Medal is awarded to Kempeitai Sergeant Yoshioka. Showa 15 [1940]. December 31st." *Author's Collection*

The top of the 2600th Anniversary Commemorative Medal document features the imperial seal of the chrysanthemum with a floral wreath surrounding the seal. *Author's Collection*

The bottom center of the document displays the actual 2600th Anniversary Commemorative Medal above clouds. *Author's Collection*

Opposite: Translation of small award during Great East Asian War for Order of the Golden Kite 7th Class and Rising Sun 8th Class, right side only: "Army Lance Corporal Suzuki Seiichi. For Brave War Service during the Great East Asian War, the named person has received the 7th Class Golden Kite and 8th Class Rising Sun. Show 16 [1941] December 24." *Author's Collection*

Great East Asian War

The Great East Asian War opened the war to an enormous area in the Pacific. The conflict occurred from the Aleutian Islands of Alaska to Pearl Harbor of Hawaii, through Guadalcanal, Papa New Guinea, Australia, and the Indonesian islands, as well as Burma and the edge of India. The conflict also included the war in China that had been ongoing since 1937. It is difficult to pinpoint which theater the recipient earned the award from information on the award documents, if not impossible. The document featured was awarded to Suzuki Seiichi. The date on this document is remarkably early for the conflict, December 24, 1941. We do not know the rank or branch of service of this man. We do know that he was awarded the Order of the Golden Kite 7th Class and Order of the Rising Sun 8th Class. Thus, Seiichi was probably an enlisted man who participated in an early engagement of the Great East Asian War and performed his actions with valor.

Japan's surprise attack on the United States and allies differed from the previous engagements of the past decade. The war was not started by local military officials. The Great East Asian War was well planned and coordinated. War planners had been planning on two possible scenarios, either war with Soviet Russia or Allied powers in the Pacific. After the defeat at Nomonhan, Japan moved forward with a neutrality pact with the Soviet Union in early 1941. Even after the German attack on the Soviet Union in June 1941, Japan hesitated and then decided to ignore their tripartite pack with Germany and Italy, also known as the Berlin Pact, and not attack the Soviet Union. War planners now turned their full attention to the South Pacific. War with the Allies in 1941 seemed to fulfill Japan's immediate economic needs and long-term ideological plans. Japan had always been dependent on foreign trade for many of their natural resources. The recent oil and preexisting metal embargos by the United States over Japan's continued war in China and presence in Indochina endangered Japan's ability to continue the war and the economy as a whole. Japan viewed the rich natural resources of the Dutch East Indies and Malaysia as the key to becoming self-sufficient. The current course of the war in Europe indicated that Japan could move with relative ease in the area. Furthermore, the war in the South Pacific would follow their ideological argument of the Greater East Asian Co-Prosperity Sphere—Asia for Asians. This ideology would prove difficult to follow as Japan was more interested in securing resources than Asian independence movements. Nonetheless, the reasoning for the war made sense to the many leaders in Japan in late 1941. Even the surprise attack on the United States seemed logical because it was reasoned that an attack on the Allies would bring the United States into the war. Preparations for war were extensive and began early in the fall of 1941.[12]

The scale of Japan's six month offensive throughout the Pacific was unprecedented in joint naval, air, and land operations. The Japanese crippled the American fleet in Pearl Harbor on December 7, 1941. The British surrendered Hong Kong on December 26, after a short, intense battle. The strategic port and airbase at Rabaul was captured from Australia in late January 1942. Japan conquered Malaysia and captured Singapore by mid-February 1942. Many of the strategic locations in the Dutch East Indies were secured by late February. Rangoon in British Burma was

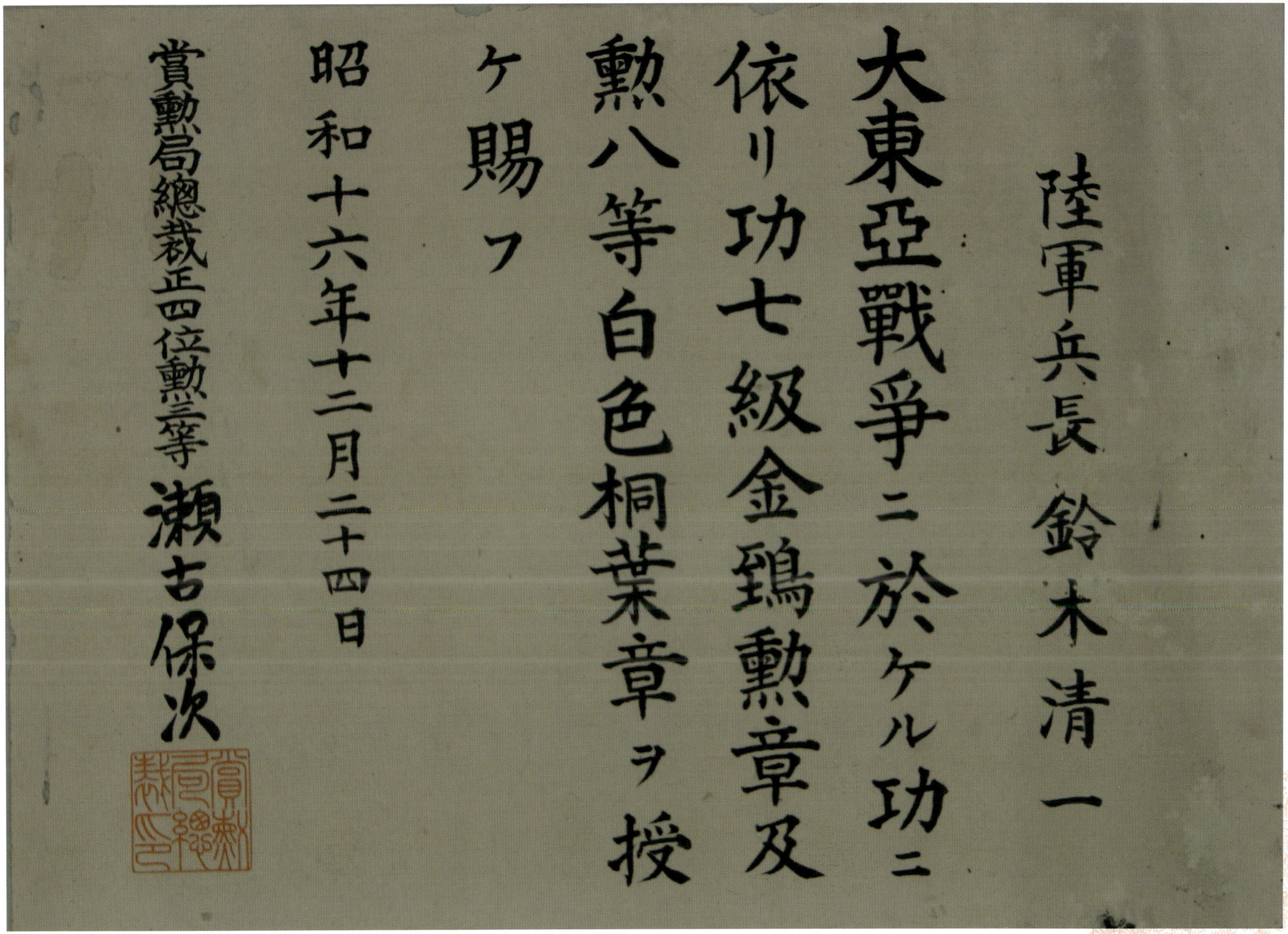
陸軍兵長 鈴木清一

大東亞戰爭ニ於ケル功ニ
依リ功七級金鵄勲章及
勲八等白色桐葉章ヲ授
ケ賜フ

昭和十六年十二月二十四日

賞勲局總裁正四位勲三等 瀬古保次

captured in early April, which set the stage for Japan's march towards the Indian border. Most of the Philippines Islands were secured by early May. The amazing speed of these conquests can be explained by a variety of factors. The Japanese had skillfully planned the multiple invasions and fought those battles with great skill. The Allies were also occupied with the war in Europe, and the United States was not ready for the war. Japan's success in the Pacific during these offensives meant that Japan was now in control of an empire that spanned almost 2.9 million square miles.[13]

The Japanese public learned about their successful attack on Pearl Harbor and subsequent new war on December 8. Almost immediately the Japanese government began its propaganda campaign for the Greater East Asian Co-Prosperity. The message of this propaganda was that Japan was going to restore and protect Eastern culture. From this time forward the war with the Allies and even China would be called the Great East Asian War. The goals of the Greater East Asian Co-Prosperity sphere were never actually fulfilled as Japan found itself unable to give full independence to other Asian nations for a variety of reasons. The most pressing issue was that Japan felt itself culturally superior to other Asian nations, and they had a need to acquire the vast resources of these areas for the war effort. While some of the Asians initially viewed the Japanese as liberators from Western colonists, most became disillusioned and resistant to the Japanese as the war progressed. The social and economic conditions for the average Japanese also decreased as the war continued, although most did not lose faith in the Japanese war effort.[14]

The land campaigns the Japanese fought from 1941 through most of 1942 highlighted their tenacity and skill as infantryman. The Japanese infantryman fought in grueling conditions with limited supplies and accomplished great feats. Furthermore, Japanese generals showed great brilliance and utilized the initiative of surprise in the early months. The quick campaign in Malaysia and Singapore highlight this fact. The Japanese were outnumbered in Malaysia at least two to one and still managed to outwit the Allied forces in the two month campaign. The Japanese high command expected the troops to advance south down the Malaysian Peninsula, around 620 miles, in just 100 days. Landing on December 8, the Japanese soldiers were relentless in their drive south, even using bicycles on the drive south. The Japanese also had an advantage with planes and other armaments as the Allies had their best equipment fighting Germany. This reality does not negate the ability and tenacity of the Japanese in the opening phase of their Great East Asian War. The Japanese seemed to have a knack for jungle fighting. Some British even labeled the Japanese as natural jungle fighters, even though most had never even been in a jungle before.[15]

Gen. Yamashita Tomoyuki, who commanded the Malaysian and Singapore invasion, utilized these advantages superbly. He capitalized on his troop's strengths as superior infantrymen and his opponent's tactile errors. The Japanese successfully fought their way south to the edge of Singapore, at the tip of the Malaysian Peninsula by January 28. Yamashita had only lost 2,000 killed and 3,000 wounded in the initial eight weeks. The siege and assault on Singapore would seemingly cost the Japanese dearly. Singapore was the major British fortress in Southeast Asia, dubbed the Gibraltar of the East. The Allies outnumbered the Japanese threefold in the siege. Yamashita launched his first assault on February 8, 1942. The Japanese focused on a weak section of the defense, which was caused by miscommunication by the British High Command. The assault succeeded within a day and the Japanese now had a bridgehead on Singapore Island. The British tried to reestablish a strong position against the bridgehead, but another miscommunication gave the Japanese the decisive edge. The Allied troops on the new defense line received a garbled order which they interpreted as meaning to continue the retreat towards Singapore. This action on February 9 opened the door to Singapore for the Japanese. The city would fall on February 15, after a week-long siege. This victory was a remarkable feat. The Japanese had similar successes across Southeast Asia during the first months of the war.[16]

The war brought enormous casualties and bogged down for the Japanese by the middle of 1942. Families like those of army corporal Mizoguchi Kajiurō were receiving notices and next-of-kin of pins in an ever-increasing number. The offensives in New Guinea and Guadalcanal were halted by Allied forces. They had lost two key naval battles, Battle of Coral Sea and Battle of Midway, which handed the naval initiative to the Americans. This initiative became apparent when the Japanese and Americans fought over Guadalcanal in the Solomon Islands. The Japanese had sizeable forces on Guadalcanal working on building airbases. These airbases would act to shield Rabaul in the north and provide forward bases towards Australia in the south. The Americans realized the significance of the Japanese bases and launched an assault on Guadalcanal in August 1942. The ensuing battle would become the source of legend for United States Marine Corps and a disaster for Japanese forces.

Opposite: Japanese soldiers in formation on a Pacific island near modern day Indonesia. The first six months of World War II were filled with great victories and conquests in the Pacific for the Japanese. *Author's Collection*

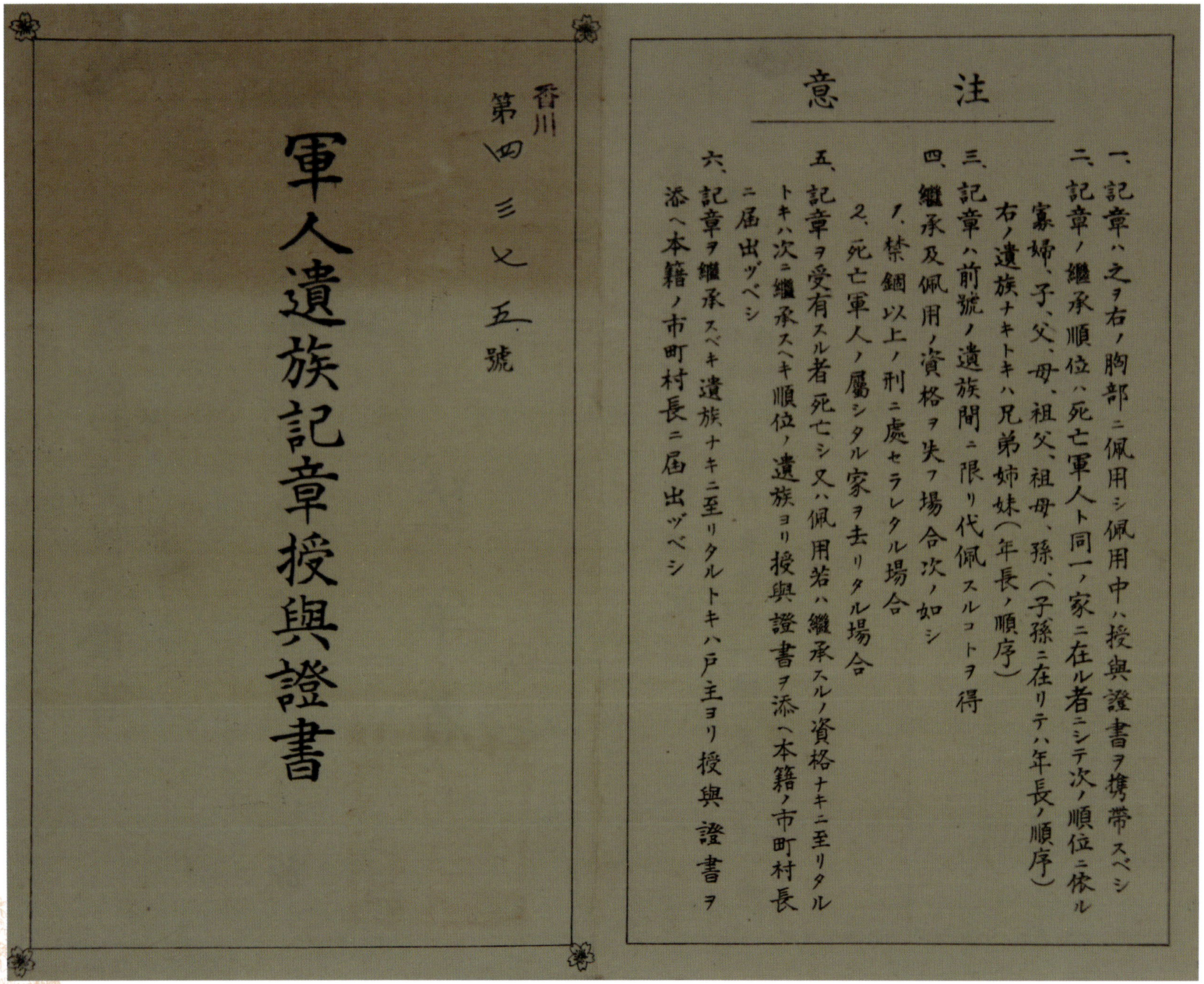

香川
第四三七五號

軍人遺族記章授與證書

注意

一、記章ハ之ヲ右ノ胸部ニ佩用シ佩用中ハ授與證書ヲ携帯スベシ
二、記章ノ繼承順位ハ死亡軍人ト同一ノ家ニ在ル者ニシテ次ノ順位ニ依ル
寡婦、子、父、母、祖父、祖母、孫、（子孫ニ在リテハ年長ノ順序）
右ノ遺族ナキトキハ兄弟姉妹（年長ノ順序）
三、記章ハ前號ノ遺族間ニ限リ代佩スルコトヲ得
四、繼承及佩用ノ資格ヲ失フ場合次ノ如シ
イ、禁錮以上ノ刑ニ處セラレタル場合
ロ、死亡軍人ノ屬シタル家ヲ去リタル場合
五、記章ヲ受有スル者死亡シ又ハ佩用若ハ繼承スルノ資格ナキニ至リタルトキハ次ニ繼承スヘキ順位ノ遺族ヨリ授與證書ヲ添ヘ本籍ノ市町村長ニ届出ヅベシ
六、記章ヲ繼承スベキ遺族ナキニ至リタルトキハ戸主ヨリ授與證書ヲ添ヘ本籍ノ市町村長ニ届出ヅベシ

Translation of observe side of killed in action document for next-of-kin, left half only: "Kagawa prefecture. Issuance number 4375 Certificate of Conferment of Soldiers' Bereaved Family Badge." *Author's Collection*

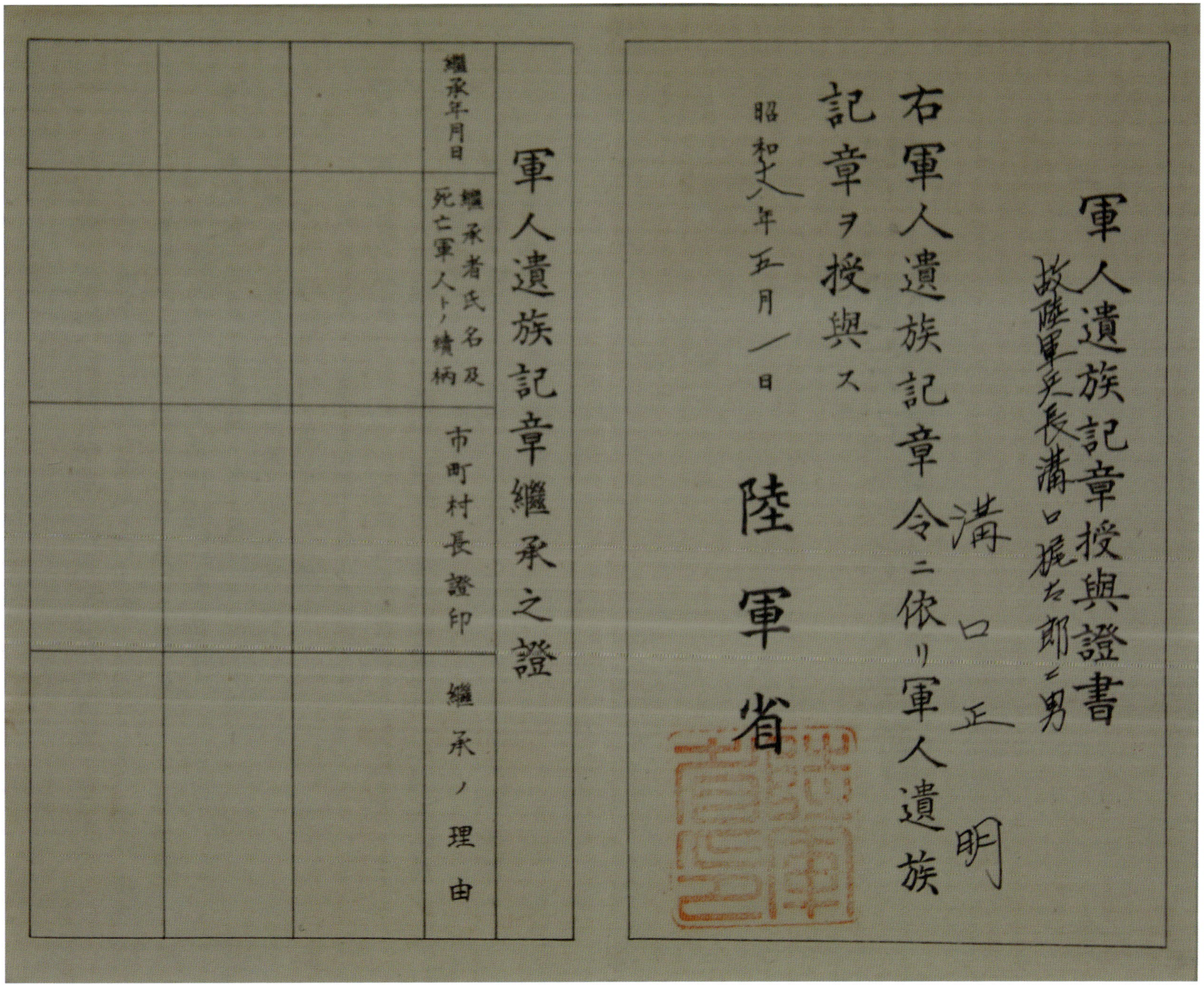

軍人遺族記章授與證書

故陸軍兵長溝口梶右郎ニ男

溝口正明

右軍人遺族記章令ニ依リ軍人遺族記章ヲ授與ス

昭和十八年五月一日

陸軍省

軍人遺族記章繼承之證

繼承年月日			
繼承者氏名及死亡軍人トノ續柄			
市町村長證印			
繼承ノ理由			

Translation of the reverse side of killed in action document for next-of-kin, right half only: "Certificate of Conferment of Soldiers' Bereaved Family Badge [to] the second son of the late Army corporal Mizoguchi Kajiurō, Mizoguchi Masaaki. A bereaved family badge is conferred to the person stated to the right in accordance with the Soldiers' Bereaved Family Badge Ordinance. Showa 18 [1943], May 1." *Author's Collection*

The Japanese launched numerous attacks to capture the American airfield, Henderson Field, which all ended in failure. Moreover, the Japanese suffered from acute shortages in supplies. The lack of supplies stemmed from the Japanese losing control of the sea and air in the Solomon Islands. While the Americans suffered from air and naval losses during the six-month Battle of Guadalcanal, they remained in control and were able to continually supply, defend, and destroy Japanese forces as they attempted to aid and reinforce the island. The resulting defeat for the Japanese was enormous. The Japanese fighting force was reduced to emaciated and starving men with only a small percentage being evacuated by February 1943. The Japanese lost around 25,000 experienced soldiers as well as desperately needed airplanes and warships. They had also lost the offensive momentum and would never regain it again in the Pacific theater.[17]

The greatest honor a Japanese soldier could have, besides victory, would be to be honored at the Yasukuni Shrine. The enshrined soldiers would be worshiped as divinities. This yearly event was a major event and would be attended by the emperor himself. This document was an invitation to the enshrinement even for the family members of Infantry Senior Private Nagai Toyoji. Pvt. Toyoji had earned Order of the Golden Kite 7th Class and Order of Merit 8th Class. The invitation includes the original envelope. The Japanese had particular rituals for their war dead and definitions of honor in battle. Fallen soldiers were to be taken from the battlefield and their ashes were sent back to Japan for ritual burial. When the battlefield did not allow for extraction of the body, then soldiers became practical. Lt. Tadahiro Ogawa found two of his comrades dead next to a British solider in Arakan Burma. He cut off the pinkies of both men and cremated the fingers in order to send at least some ashes back to Japan. The Japanese view of surrender and death on the battlefield has also been the subject of much discussion in the West. The Japanese treatment of prisoners of war was deplorable. We should not make excuses for such actions. However, the Japanese view of death in battle should at least be discussed. The Japanese placed a tremendous value on dying in battle. Surrendering to the enemy meant serving a master who was not the emperor and thus was the ultimate betrayal. A story of how the Japanese viewed dying Allied soldiers provides a glimpse of the pride they took in dying in battle. Maj. Misao Sato was fighting in Burma in 1942. He came across a mortally wounded British soldier. His wounds were in the abdomen and had to be painful. The solider was enduring the last moments of his life without showing pain, besides tears and a contorted face, and remained dignified. Sato described holding the British soldier's hand and crying. He described that soldier's strength as the origin of the strength of the British empire.[18]

The disastrous Japanese campaign in northern Burma in late 1944 highlighted the inability of Japan to mount significant offensives later in the war. The goal of the operation was to recapture some of the initiative from the allies by taking their strategic forward base at Imphal. The Japanese also wanted to threaten the Ledo Road, which was being built to connect China to Allied resources. The Japanese assault of 100,000 troops had to cover over sixty miles to capture the strategic towns of Imphal and Kohima. The assault was doomed from the start as the Japanese soldiers carried few provisions and were expected to live off cattle which were driven with troops. The terrain and inability of the cattle, to keep up with the troops meant that the Japanese were starving from malnutrition and were

Opposite: Translation of killed-in-action enshrinement document for next of kin with original envelope. The translation is for the card on the right with only the text on the right: "Deceased Army infantry senior private, order of merit 8th Class, Order of the Golden Kite 7th Class, Nagai Toyoji. The person stated to the right will be enshrined in the Yasukuni Shrine. This was instructed by the authority on October 14. This is to notify that a ceremony to invite the spirits [of the deceased] and an extraordinary grand festival will be held on the 15, 16, 17, 18, 19, and 20. Showa 17 [1942], October." *Author's Collection*

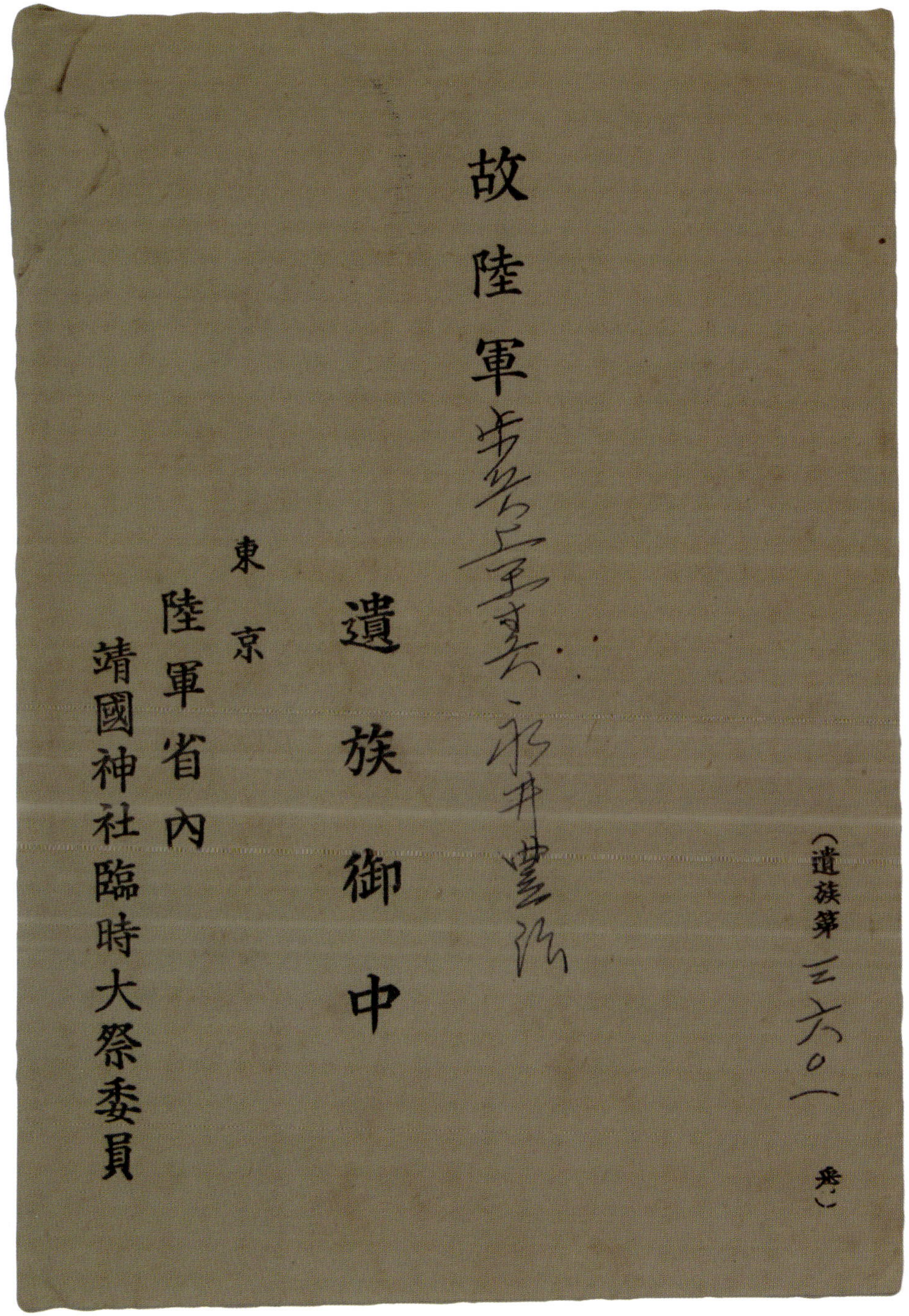

（遺族第 三六〇一 號）

故陸軍歩兵上等兵 永井豊治

遺族御中

東京 陸軍省内

靖國神社臨時大祭委員

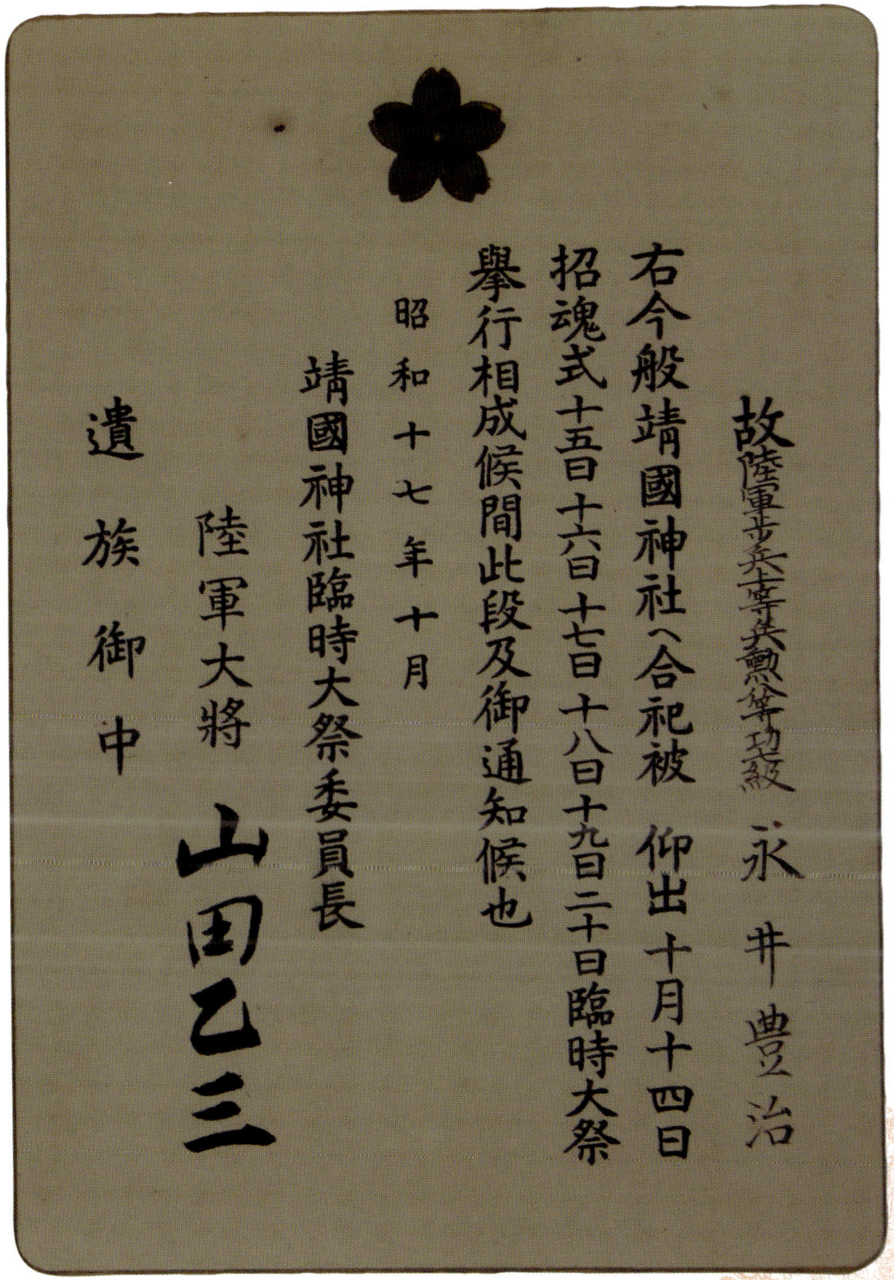

故陸軍歩兵上等兵勳八等功七級 永井豊治

右今般靖國神社ヘ合祀被 仰出十月十四日

招魂式十五日十六日十七日十八日十九日二十日臨時大祭

擧行相成候間此段及御通知候也

昭和十七年十月

靖國神社臨時大祭委員長

陸軍大將 山田乙三

遺族御中

undersupplied by the start of the battle in spring. Despite initial successes and even sieging Allied forces at both Imphal and Kohima, the Japanese were driven back by June and July 1944. The subsequent retreat south towards the Chindwin River in central Burma cost the Japanese dearly as soldiers died from exhaustion, disease, and starvation.[19]

The stories of retreat from Imphal and Kohima demonstrate the hardships and horrors that Japanese soldiers endured in the latter part of the war. A series of biographies from this front provided firsthand accounts of the events. Staff Sgt. Yasumasa Nishiji described the retreat as a vision of hell. He witnessed soldiers dying on the road. The weakened soldiers were unable to move out of the road due to complete exhaustion. Many soldiers chose suicide, even committing suicide in pairs by sharing a grenade. Even soldiers who were wounded during the actual battle and sent to the rear for medical treatment became victims of the retreat and logistical nightmare. The high command had planned on the Japanese soldiers feeding themselves on the move through scavenging. They had the utmost faith in the Japanese spirit and will. The battles and subsequent retreat was the worst defeat suffered by Japan up to that time. The Japanese soldiers' spirit and will had been exhausted by combat and high command blunders. The course of the war had turned against the Japanese and disasters like this were repeated across the Pacific.[20]

Here Emperor Hirohito is photographed leaving the Yasukuni Shrine during the annual commemoration of Japanese war dead. This Shinto shrine still exists today and has become a touchstone for controversy. The shrine contains the name of soldiers who were high level war criminals. *Author's Collection*

The Destruction of the Empire

The featured document was awarded to Tomiyasu Koutaro for his donations and long service in Fukuoka in May 1943. I have several documents given to Koutaro for helping with the war effort. The Great East Asian War became a total war for the Japanese people by 1943. Rationing was in full effect. Allied submarines began to sink increasing number of Japanese merchant ships. The loss of supplies and raw materials crippled the Japanese war economy and forced the Japanese to take drastic measures. For example, Tanaka Tetsuko experienced making balloon bombs on the grounds of her girl's high school in Yamaguchi Prefecture in 1944. The balloon construction focused on cheap and simple products such as paste. The manufacturing of the balloon bombs was rudimentary and not industrial. Their effect on the war was virtually none, though a few Americans were killed on the West Coast. Tanaka would later work in a munitions factory.[21]

The Japanese were being strangled by the Allied sea blockade of Japanese sea lanes. The Allied submarine campaign was so successful that by 1944 the Allies were running short of Japanese targets to sink. This campaign had a dramatic effect on the Japanese homeland. The strategic situation for Japan became worse in the air as well. The Americans were introducing the Boeing B-29 Superfortress. These planes could reach the Japanese homeland from Chinese bases. The Japanese were made aware of this new bomber and its great range. The Japanese high command decided to push back the front in China to capture advanced American airfields. Connecting French Indochina to Japanese controlled China would also help with the sea transport issue in 1944. The operation was named Ichi-Go and started in mid-April 1944. The first phase was launched from Chengchow (now called Zengzhou) in Central China towards Luoyang farther

This photograph shows Japanese soldiers in Burma looking into a dense jungle valley. The battlefields of Burma and the Indian border would become a hell on Earth for the many Japanese soldiers. *Author's Collection*

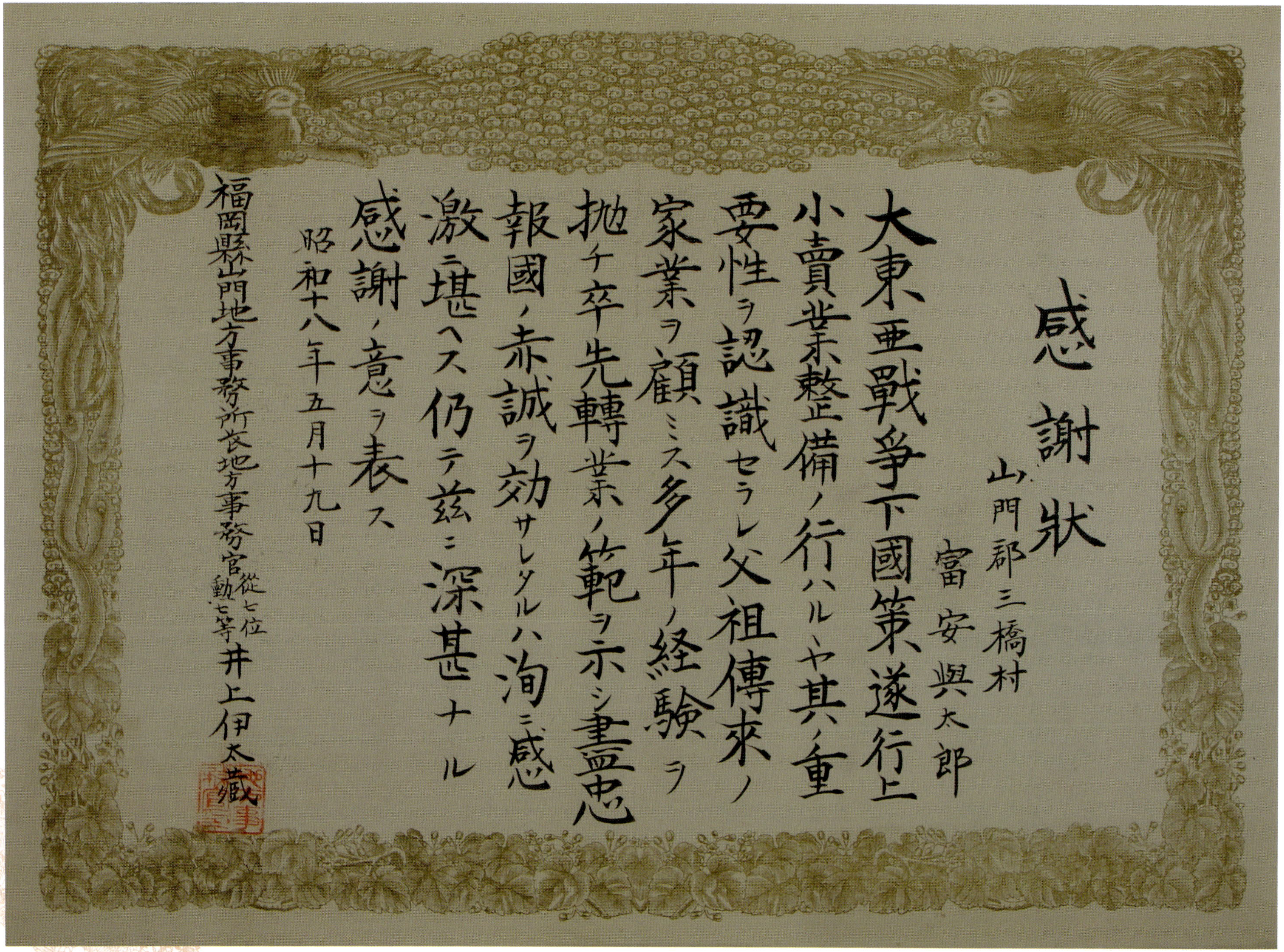
感謝狀

山門郡三橋村
富安與太郎

大東亜戰争下國策遂行上
小賣業整備ノ行ハルヽヤ其ノ重
要性ヲ認識セラレ父祖傳來ノ
家業ヲ顧ミス多年ノ経験ヲ
抛チ卒先轉業ノ範ヲ示シ盡忠
報國ノ赤誠ヲ効サレタルハ洵ニ感
激ニ堪ヘス仍テ茲ニ深甚ナル
感謝ノ意ヲ表ス

昭和十八年五月十九日

福岡縣山門地方事務所長地方事務官従七位勲七等井上伊太藏

Opposite: Translation of war effort appreciation document: "Certificate of Appreciation Yamato District, Mitsubashi-machi (town), Tomiyasu Yotarō. The retail industry has been streamlined in order to execute the national policies for the Greater East Asia War. You recognized the importance of the policies and became a role model in taking the initiative to switch trades by letting go of many years of experience [in your original trade], without reflecting on/being concerned about your family business that had been passed down for generations. It is truly impressive that you made your utmost to be loyal to the country and reciprocate its favors. Therefore, we hereby express our sincerest gratitude. Showa 18 [1943], May 19." *Author's Collection*

east. The main objective was secured in less than a month. The Japanese also pressed south from Chengchow and north from Hankow to take complete control of the railroad from Peking to Hankow. The Japanese force defeated a 300,000-man Chinese force by mid-June.[22]

The next phase of the Japanese operation was to move south towards Changsa and connect the railway from Japanese-controlled China to the border of French Indo-China. This phase of the operation involved 350,000 Japanese troops, which made it one of the largest for the Japanese during World War II. The assault on Changsa was the fourth attack on that city since 1939. The Japanese assault was bloody; however, they had initial success. They captured Changsa and Hengyang in south-central China by August. Nonetheless, the campaign had drained Japan of resources and initiative. They were still able to follow through with the last leg of the Ichi-Go Operation and secure the railroad through Guilin and Liuzhou in southern China. These last victories in late November 1944 enabled Japan to claim strategic success with the whole operation. However, the transportation line from French Indochina to Peking was never completely functional and guerillas still controlled the countryside in those areas. The Americans did pull their bomber force out of forward Chinese bases; yet, their victories in the Marianas allowed them to use the new B-29s against the Japanese homeland from these forward bases. These victories became the high point for Japan in China as they would be driven out of southern China by the summer of 1945.[23]

As the Americans advanced in their island hopping campaign through the Philippines, Mariana Islands, and Iwo Jima they were able to strike Japan with their powerful bomber fleet. The Americans changed their bombing tactics in March 1945 from high altitude strikes on pinpoint targets to low altitude firebombing of whole cities. The most devastating of these raids was on Tokyo on March 9–10, 1945. It is estimated that 100,000 people died and over fifteen square miles of the city was destroyed. Funato Kazuyo was a young girl in Tokyo during this air raid. She recalled the chaos that ensued that night. Everything was burning and the great winds which were created by the firestorm swept people off their feet. Funato lost track of her mother, father, and brother during the hell of that night. She was trapped, and the deadly dilemma of looking for shelter, which could erupt in flames at any moment, and facing the deadly fire and wind in the street which could suck people into the flames. The horrors of that night claimed her younger sister and

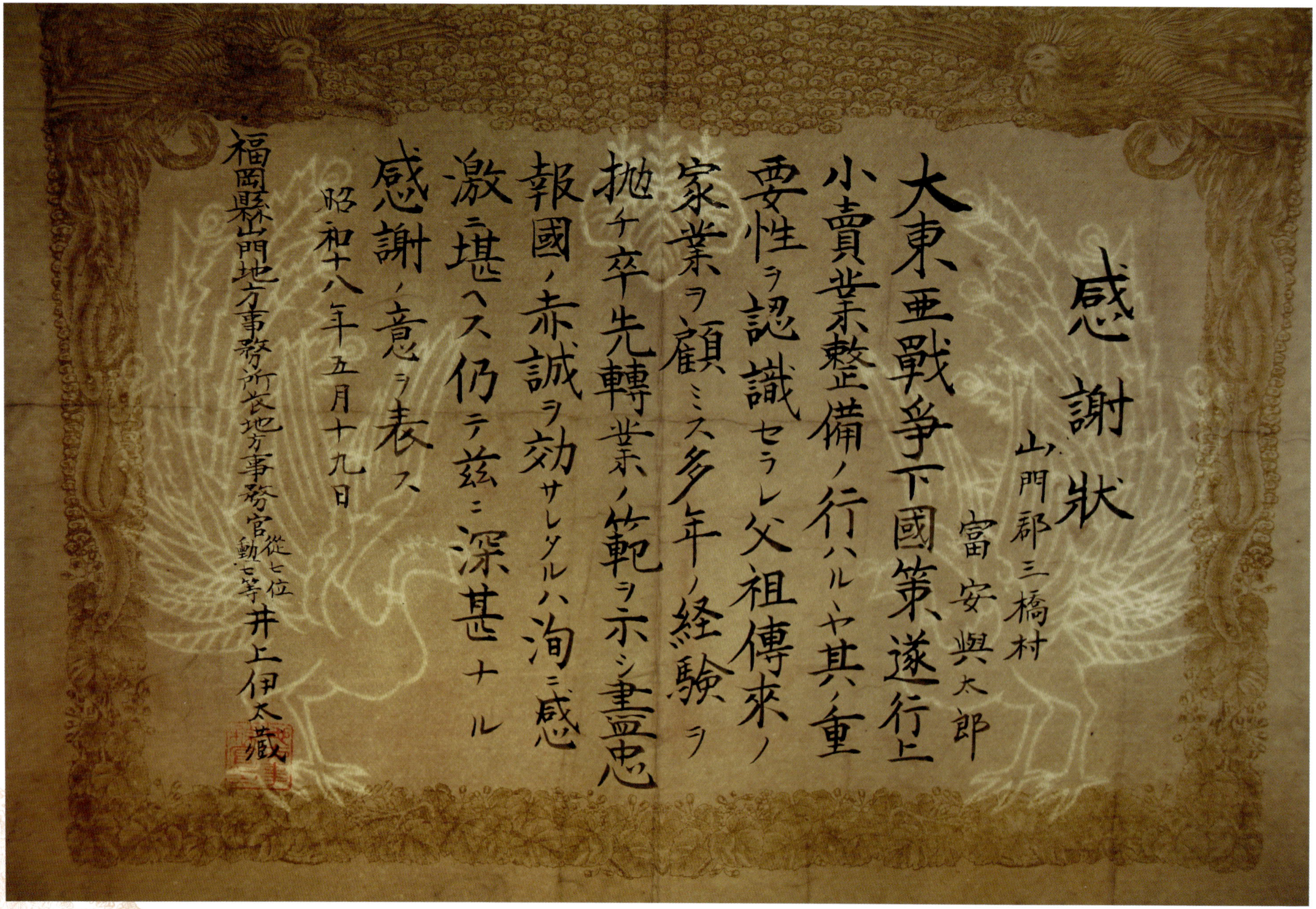

感謝狀

山門郡三橋村

富安與太郎

大東亜戰争下國策遂行上小賣業整備ノ行ハルヤ其ノ重要性ヲ認識セラレ父祖傳來ノ家業ヲ顧ミス多年ノ経驗ヲ抛チ卒先轉業ノ範ヲ示シ盡忠報國ノ赤誠ヲ効サレタルハ洵ニ感激ニ堪ヘス仍テ茲ニ深甚ナル感謝ノ意ヲ表ス

昭和十八年五月十九日

福岡縣山門地方事務所長地方事務官従七位勲七等井上伊太藏

Opposite: The watermark of the war effort appreciation document is one of the most beautiful of all watermarks in Japanese award documents. It features two *Ho-O* (also called Fenghuang) birds facing each other with the imperial seal in the center above the birds. *Author's Collection*

brother. These raids killed hundreds and thousands of Japanese and ground their industrial production down to almost nothing. Nonetheless, the Japanese seemed poised to continue the fight on their homeland in the summer 1945.[24]

The fall of Okinawa in spring of 1945 meant that the next island for the Americans to attack would be the actual home islands. The Japanese prepared for this final battle in earnest. If the Battle of Okinawa was any guide, the civilian population would be willing to sacrifice themselves in the face of an Allied invasion. Three things helped bring the Japanese government to peace terms. The first reason was the firebombing. The second reason was the two atomic bombs dropped by the Americans on Nagasaki and Hiroshima. The last reason, often overlooked in America, was the invasion of Manchukuo by the Soviets. The Soviet campaign started after the second bomb was dropped, continued after the announcement of surrender on August 15, and conquered much of Manchuria in just eleven days. Most of the Japanese government realized that any further resistance would be futile. Emperor Hirohito broadcasted the end of the war on August 15, though the fighting continued at different points in Asia for a few more weeks.[25]

The end of the war did not mean that the challenges for Japan and the rest of the combatants were over. The aforementioned document is an example of this situation. This quite damaged good conduct award was actually given after the war was over. It highlighted the utter disorder of Asia when the war was over. Hypothetically, the 157th Infantry Regiment had little power to issue such certificates; but, the chaos of the situation seemed to warrant this citation. Millions of Japanese soldiers and citizens were abroad. Some Japanese soldier refused to surrender right away and a few individual groups would continue to resist for another decade or more. The infrastructure of Japan was destroyed to a significant extent. However, the Allies realized that a weak Japan was not in their best interest as communism gained momentum in Asia. Reconstruction began in 1947 and a new Japan was born in the ashes of the previous Empire.

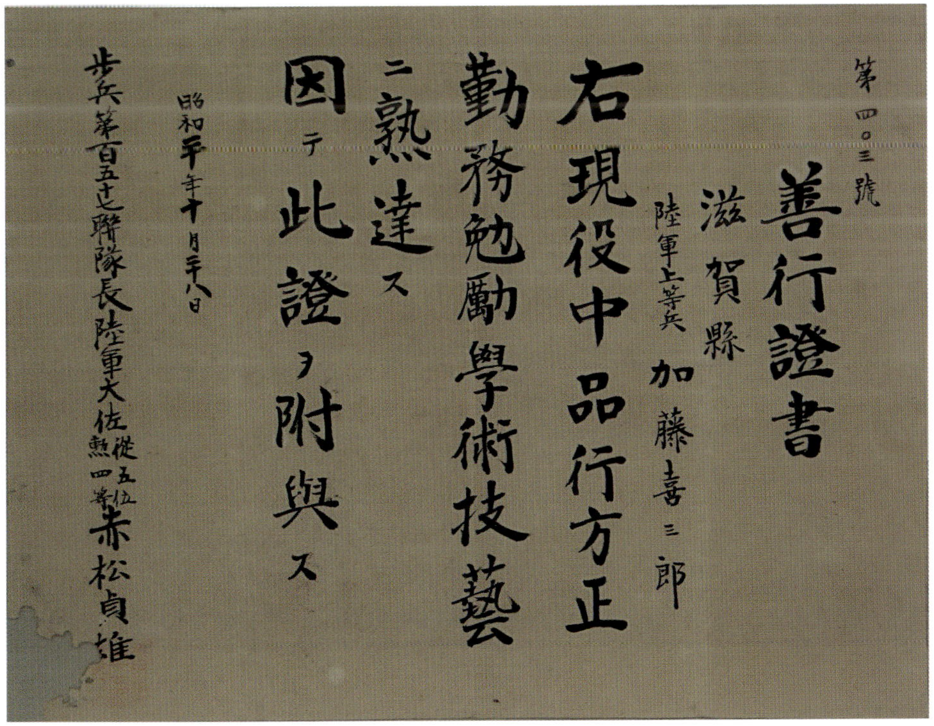
第四〇三號
善行證書
滋賀縣
陸軍上等兵 加藤喜三郎
右現役中品行方正
勤務勉勵學術技藝
ニ熟達ス
因テ此證ヲ附與ス
昭和廿年十月廿八日
歩兵第百五十七聯隊長陸軍大佐 従五位勲四等 赤松貞雄

Translation of post-war good conduct document: "#403. Good conduct certificate. Shiga Prefecture. Army private superior Katō Kisaburō. The person listed to the right, while in service, demonstrated high morals, worked diligently, and achieved a proficiency level in both academic knowledge and technical skills. Therefore, this proof is issued. Showa 20 [1945], October 28." *Author's Collection*

Chapter 5 Endnotes

1. H. Long-hsuen and C. Ming-kai, *History of the Sino-Japanese War (1937–1945)* (Taipei, Taiwan: Chung Wu Publishing, 1985), 175–212.

2. Reader's Digest, *The World at Arms: The Reader's Digest Illustrated History of World War II* (New York City, NY: Reader's Digest, 1989), 134.

3. H. Long-hsuen and C. Ming-kai, *History of the Sino-Japanese War (1937–1945)* (Taipei, Taiwan: Chung Wu Publishing, 1985), 222–248.

4. E. J. Drea, *In the Service of the Emperor: Essays on the Imperial Japanese Army* (Lincoln, NE: University of Nebraska Press, 1998), 1–2.

5. E. J. Drea, *In the Service of the Emperor: Essays on the Imperial Japanese Army* (Lincoln, NE: University of Nebraska Press, 1998), 2–3.

6. E. J. Drea, *In the Service of the Emperor: Essays on the Imperial Japanese Army* (Lincoln, NE: University of Nebraska Press, 1998), 5–13.

7. A. Gordon, *A Modern History of Japan: From Tokugawa Times to the Present* (New York: Oxford Press, 2009), 215.

8. A. Gordon, *A Modern History of Japan: From Tokugawa Times to the Present* (New York: Oxford Press, 2009), 212.

9. A. Gordon, *A Modern History of Japan: From Tokugawa Times to the Present* (New York: Oxford Press, 2009), 209–211.

10. M. Felton, *Japan's Gestapo: Murder, Mayhem, and Torture in wartime Asia* (Barnsley, UK: Pen & Sword Books, 2009), 9–24.

11. D. Bergamini, *Japan's Imperial Conspiracy* (New York: William Morrow and Company, 1971), 793–795.

12. E. Hotta, *Pan-Asianism and Japan's War 1931–1945* (New York City, NY: Palgrave Macmillan, 2007), 181–184.

13. Reader's Digest, *The World at Arms: The Reader's Digest Illustrated History of World War II* (New York City, NY: Reader's Digest, 1989), 136–155.

14. E. Hotta, *Pan-Asianism and Japan's War 1931–1945* (New York City, NY: Palgrave Macmillan, 2007), 185–186.

15. Reader's Digest, *The World at Arms: The Reader's Digest Illustrated History of World War II* (New York City, NY: Reader's Digest, 1989), 141–144.

16. R. B. Edgerton, *Warriors of the Rising Sun: A History of the Japanese Military* (New York: W. W. Norton company, 1997), 266–268.

17. Reader's Digest, *The World at Arms: The Reader's Digest Illustrated History of World War II* (New York City, NY: Reader's Digest, 1989), 346–350.

18. K. Tamayama and J. Nunneley, *Tales by Japanese Soldiers of the Burma Campaign 1942–1945* (London: Cassell Company, 2000), 63–64, 139–142.

19. Reader's Digest, *The World at Arms: The Reader's Digest Illustrated History of World War II* (New York City, NY: Reader's Digest, 1989), 396–398.

20. K. Tamayama and J. Nunneley, *Tales by Japanese Soldiers of the Burma Campaign 1942–1945* (London: Cassell Company, 2000), 196–212.

21. H. T. Cook and T. F. Cook, *Japan at War: An Oral History* (New York: the New Press, 1992), 187–191.

22. H. Long-hsuen and C. Ming-kai, *History of the Sino-Japanese War (1937–1945)* (Taipei, Taiwan: Chung Wu Publishing, 1985), 416–421.

23. H. Long-hsuen and C. Ming-kai, *History of the Sino-Japanese War (1937–1945)* (Taipei, Taiwan: Chung Wu Publishing, 1985), 421–433.

24. H. T. Cook and T. F. Cook, *Japan at War: An Oral History* (New York: the New Press, 1992), 343–349.

25. Reader's Digest, *The World at Arms: The Reader's Digest Illustrated History of World War II* (New York City, NY: Reader's Digest, 1989), 443–444.

6 COLLECTING JAPANESE AWARD DOCUMENTS

Translation Guide

The following is a short list of translation to help collectors quickly identify some of the more common characters found on Japanese award documents. A complete listing of characters is beyond the scope of this section and my expertise. Some characters used during the imperial age in Japan are now extinct, so this can be a challenge. I apologize to the reader for any omissions and slight differences in translations. Remember, translating is an art and not a science.

Dates and Numbers

明治 – Meiji Era [Japan during the reign of Emperor Meiji]
大正 – Taishō Era [Japan during the reign of Emperor Taishō]
昭和 – Showa Era [Japan during the reign of Emperor Hirohito]
大同 – Daidou [Manchukuo before the reign Emperor Pu Yi]
康徳 – Kōtoku [Manchukuo during the reign of Emperor Pu Yi]
零 / 〇 – Zero
一 / 元 – 1
二 – 2
三 – 3
四 – 4
五 – 5
六 – 6
七 – 7
八 – 8
九 – 9
十 – 10
二十 – 20
百 – 100
千 – 1000
万 – 10,000
明治一 – 1868
明治二 – 1869
明治三 – 1870
明治四 – 1871
明治五 – 1872
明治六 – 1873
明治七 – 1874
明治八 – 1875
明治九 – 1876
明治十 – 1877
明治十一 – 1878
明治十二 – 1879
明治十三 – 1880
明治十四 – 1881
明治十五 – 1882
明治十六 – 1883
明治十七 – 1884
明治十八 – 1885
明治十九 – 1886
明治二十 – 1887
明治二十一 – 1888
明治二十二 – 1889
明治二十三 – 1890
明治二十四 – 1891
明治二十五 –1892
明治二十六 – 1893
明治二十七 – 1894
明治二十八 – 1895
明治二十九 – 1896
明治三十 – 1897
明治三十一 – 1898
明治三十二 – 1899
明治三十三 – 1900
明治三十四 – 1901
明治三十五 – 1902
明治三十六 – 1903
明治三十七 – 1904
明治三十八 – 1905
明治三十九 – 1906
明治四十 – 1907
明治四十一 – 1908
明治四十二 – 1909
明治四十三 – 1910
明治四十四 – 1911
明治四十五 – 1912
大正一 –1912
大正二 – 1913
大正三– 1914
大正四 – 1915
大正五 – 1916
大正六 – 1917
大正七 – 1918
大正八 – 1919

大正九 – 1920
大正十 – 1921
大正十一 – 1922
大正十二 – 1923
大正十三 – 1924
大正十四 – 1925
大正十五 – 1926
昭和一 – 1926
昭和二 – 1927
昭和三 – 1928
昭和四 – 1929
昭和五 – 1930
昭和六 – 1931
昭和七 – 1932
昭和八 – 1933
昭和九 – 1934
昭和十 – 1935
昭和十一 – 1936
昭和十二 – 1937
昭和十三 – 1938
昭和十四 – 1939
昭和十五 – 1940
昭和十六 – 1941
昭和十七 – 1942
昭和十八 – 1943
昭和十九 – 1944
昭和二十 – 1945
隆熙一 – 1907
隆熙二 – 1908
隆熙三 – 1909
隆熙四 – 1910
大同一 – 1932
大同二 – 1933
大同三 – 1934
康徳一 – 1934
康徳二 – 1935
康徳三 – 1936
康徳四 – 1937
康徳五 – 1938
康徳六 – 1939
康徳七 – 1940
康徳八– 1941
康徳九 – 1942
康徳十 – 1943
康徳十一 – 1944
康徳十二 – 1945

Army Ranks

元帥 – Marshall General
陸軍大将 – General
陸軍中将 – Lieutenant General
陸軍少将 – Major General
陸軍大佐 – Colonel
陸軍中佐 – Lieutenant Colonel
陸軍少佐 – Major
陸軍大尉 – Captain
陸軍中尉 – First Lieutenant
陸軍少尉 – Second Lieutenant
陸軍准尉 – Warrant Officer
陸軍曹長 – Sergeant Major
陸軍軍曹 – Sergeant
陸軍伍長 – Corporal
伍長勤務上等兵 – Junior Corporal [special rank]
陸軍兵長 – Lance-Corporal
陸軍上等兵 – Superior Private
陸軍一等兵 – Private 1st Class
陸軍二等兵 – Private 2nd Class

Army Specializations

This list is not a complete list of army specializations.

歩兵 – Infantry
工兵 – Engineer
騎兵 – Cavalry
砲兵 – Artillery
憲兵 – Military Police (Kempeitai)
航空兵 – Air Force

Full Army Rank and Specializations Titles

This list illustrates how an infantryman's full ranks and specialists would appear on a document. The trick to translating these phrases is to know where the rank and specialty is placed in the phrase.

陸軍歩兵大佐 – Army Infantry Colonel
陸軍歩兵中佐 – Army Infantry Lieutenant Colonel
陸軍歩兵少佐 – Army Infantry Major
陸軍歩兵大尉 – Army Infantry Captain
陸軍歩兵中尉 – Army Infantry First Lieutenant
陸軍歩兵少尉 – Army Infantry Second Lieutenant
陸軍歩兵曹長 – Army Infantry Sergeant Major
陸軍歩兵軍曹 – Army Infantry Sergeant
陸軍歩兵伍長 – Army Infantry Corporal
陸軍歩兵上等兵 – Army Infantry Superior Private
陸軍歩兵一等兵 – Army Infantry Private 1st Class
陸軍歩兵二等兵 – Army Infantry Private 2nd Class

Navy Ranks

Generally speaking, navy personal do not have specializations. The sailors rank is usually the only military title preceding their name.

大元帥 – Grand Marshal
海軍大将 – Marshal Admiral
海軍大将 – Admiral
海軍中将 – Vice-Admiral
海軍少将 – Rear-Admiral
海軍大佐 – Captain
海軍中佐 – Commander
海軍少佐 – Lieutenant Commander
海軍大尉 – Lieutenant
海軍中尉 – Sub-Lieutenant/ Lieutenant Commander
海軍少尉 – Ensign
海軍兵曹長 – Warrant Officer
海軍少尉候補生 – Midshipman
海軍一等兵曹 – Petty Officer 1st Class [before 1942] or 海軍上等兵曹 – Chief Petty Officer [after 1942]
海軍二等兵曹 – Petty Officer 2nd Class [before 1942] or 海軍一等兵曹 – Petty Officer 1st Class [after 1942]
海軍三等兵曹 – Petty Officer 3rd Class [before 1942] or 海軍二等兵曹 – Petty Officer 2nd Class [after 1942]
海軍一等水兵 – Seaman 1st Class [before 1942] or 海軍水兵長 – Leading Seaman [after 1942]
海軍二等水兵 – Seaman 2nd Class [before 1942] or 海軍上等水兵 – Able Seaman [after 1942]
海軍三等水兵 – Seaman 3rd Class [before 1942] or 海軍一等水兵 – Seaman [after 1942]
海軍四等水兵 – Seaman 4th Class [before 1942] or 海軍二等水兵 – Seaman Recruit [after 1942]

Orders

This list is for Japanese orders only. Korean and Manchurian orders were not included.

大勲位菊花章 – Supreme Order of the Chrysanthemum

勲一等旭日大綬章 – 1st Class Order of the Rising Sun, Large Ribbon
勲二等旭日重光章 – 2nd Class Order of the Rising Sun, Heavy Rays
勲三等旭日中綬章 – 3rd Class Order of the Rising Sun, Medium Ribbon
勲四等旭日小綬章 – 4th Class Order of the Rising Sun, Small Ribbon
勲五等双光旭日章 – 5th Class Twin Rays Order of the Rising Sun
勲六等単光旭日章 – 6th Class Single Rays Order of the Rising Sun
勲七等青色桐葉章 – 7th Class Green Paulownia Leaves Order of the Rising Sun
勲八等白色桐葉章 – 8th Class White Paulownia Leaves Order of the Rising Sun

勲一等瑞宝章 – 1st Class Order of the Sacred Treasure
勲二等瑞宝章 – 2nd Class Order of the Sacred Treasure
勲三等瑞宝章 – 3rd Class Order of the Sacred Treasure
勲四等瑞宝章 – 4th Class Order of the Sacred Treasure
勲五等瑞宝章 – 5th Class Order of the Sacred Treasure
勲六等瑞宝章 – 6th Class Order of the Sacred Treasure
勲七等瑞宝章 – 7th Class Order of the Sacred Treasure
勲八等瑞宝章 – 8th Class Order of the Sacred Treasure

功一級金鵄勲章 – 1st Class Order of the Golden Kite
功二級金鵄勲章 – 2nd Class Order of the Golden Kite
功三級金鵄勲章 – 3rd Class Order of the Golden Kite
功四級金鵄勲章 – 4th Class Order of the Golden Kite
功五級金鵄勲章 – 5th Class Order of the Golden Kite
功六級金鵄勲章 – 6th Class Order of the Golden Kite
功七級金鵄勲章 – 7th Class Order of the Golden Kite

勲一等宝冠章 – 1st Class Order of the Precious Crown
勲二等宝冠章 – 2nd Class Order of the Precious Crown
勲三等宝冠章 – 3rd Class Order of the Precious Crown
勲四等宝冠章 – 4th Class Order of the Precious Crown
勲五等宝冠章 – 5th Class Order of the Precious Crown
勲六等宝冠章 – 6th Class Order of the Precious Crown
勲七等宝冠章 – 7th Class Order of the Precious Crown
勲八等宝冠章 – 8th Class Order of the Precious Crown

Medals

明治七年従軍記章 – 1874 War Medal
明治二十七八年従軍記章 – 1894–1895 War Medal
明治三十三年従軍記章 – 1900 War Medal
明治三十七八年従軍記章 – 1904–1905 War Medal
大正三四年従軍記章 – 1914–1915 War Medal
大正三年乃至九年戦役従軍記章 – 1914–1920 War Medal
昭和六年乃至九年事変従軍記章 – 1931–1934 War Medal
支那事変従軍記章 – 1937–1945 War Medal
大東亜戦争従軍記章 – Great East Asia War Medal
帝国憲法発布記念章 – Imperial Constitution Promulgation Commemorative Medal
大婚二十五年祝典之章 – 25th Wedding Anniversary Celebration Medal
皇太子渡韓記念章 – Crown Prince's Voyage to Korea Commemorative Medal
韓国併合記念章 – Korea Annexation Commemorative Medal
大禮記念章 – Taishō Emperor Enthronement Commemorative Medal
戦捷記章 – War Victory Medal
第一回国勢調査記念章 – First National Census Medal
昭和大禮記念章 – Showa Emperor Enthronement Commemorative Medal
帝都復興記念章 – Imperial Capital Rehabilitation Commemorative Medal
朝鮮昭和五年国勢調査記念章 – Korea National Census Medal
紀元二千六百年祝典記念章 – 2600th National Foundation Commemorative Medal
支那事変記念章– China Incident Commemorative Medal
建国功労章– National Foundation Merit Medal [Manchukuo Medal]
大典記念章 – Enthronement Commemorative Medal [Manchukuo Medal]
皇帝訪日記念章 – Imperial Visit to Japan Commemorative Medal [Manchukuo Medal]
建國神廟創建記念章 – National Shrine Foundation Commemorative Medal [Manchukuo Medal]
国境事変従軍 – Border Incident War Medal [Manchukuo Medal]
国勢調査記念章 – National Census Medal [Manchukuo Medal]

Army and Navy Badges

This is just a few of the many badges from the Japanese Army and Navy.

剣道徴章 – Swordsmanship [Kendo] Badge
射撃徴章 – Marksmanship Badge
小銃徴章 – Small Arms Shooting Badge
艦砲射撃優等徽章 – Gunnery Proficiency Badge
工作優等徽章– Carpentry Proficiency Badge
通信優等徽章 – Correspondence Proficiency Badge
魚形水雷準手優等章 – Torpedo Firing Proficiency Badge
操舵優等章 – Seamanship Proficiency Badge
見張優等章 – Navy Lookout Badge

Military Terms

歿 – Posthumously
徽章 – Badge
善行 – Good Conduct
勲等 – Medal or Order
下士 – Non-Commissioned Officer [NCO]
軍人 – Soldier
分隊 – Squad
小隊 – Platoon
中隊 – Company
剣 – Sword
小銃 – Rifle
拳銃 – Handgun
弾薬 – Ammunition
戦車 – Tank
牽引車 – Tractor
自動車 – Truck
鉄道 – Railroad
瓦斯 – Gas [poison]
軍 – Army
空軍 – Air Force
航空機 – Aircraft
戦闘機 – Fighter
海軍 – Navy
航空母艦 – Aircraft Carrier

Other Words and Phrases

日本 – Japan
中国 – China
韓国 – Korea
満州 国 – Manchukuo
競争 – Competition
賞 – Award
勲記 – Diploma
会員 – Membership
叙 – Class Promotion
赤十字 – Red Cross
海員掖済会 – Seafarer Relief Association
戦死者 – Killed in Action

Name Guide

Once you have located the recipient's name on the award document, you may want to know how to pronounce it or maybe even do a little online research to see if any extra information about the person is available. If one can read Japanese even at a basic level, there are so many tools to use. However, many collectors do not read Japanese. What should they do? Here are some hints that may help you identify the kanji. A list of the 100 most common family names in Japanese is used at the end of this section.

There are a few ways to try and identify kanji. One is of course to start studying, and using a printed kanji guide to begin with will make the name ID easier. One guide I have been using for twenty years is *Kodansha's Compact Kanji Guide* (1991). You can begin by learning radicals (usually the left part of the kanji) and these can assist you in pegging down meanings of other kanji. Since the above-mentioned guide contains the most commonly used kanji, many of these appear in names.

Another way is to use online kanji guides. Some are similar to the printed guides and they begin with finding the radicals. A good online guide is something like jisho.org, that shows all the radicals in one easy chart. Select the radical that matches and a list of appropriate kanji appear. Find the one that appears in the name on the document, cut and paste it, and then proceed to look for the other kanji until all have been found. Then cut and paste that combination into a search engine (preferably a Japanese one like yahoo.co.jp) and you can often find the pronunciations in the links.

Finally, there is a way to handwrite the kanji into the computer. Just search for "kanji drawing pad" or similar terms. A good website is http://kanji.sljfaq.org/draw.html because of the extensive lists of kanji. Again, draw the kanji in and cut and paste as described above.

Of course, in the last resort, one could always post a picture of the document to any number of military forums and ask for help. However, it is quite satisfying to do it alone and, with practice, the search gets easier.

This list is the 100 most popular Japanese family names. This is a recent nationwide ranking. Local rankings and rankings from a different era would differ. However, these are names that appear quite frequently on documents.

佐藤 Sato
鈴木 Suzuki
高橋 Takahashi
田中 Tanaka
伊藤 Itoh
山本 Yamamoto
渡辺 Watanabe
中村 Nakamura
小林 Kobayashi
加藤Kato
吉田 Yoshida
山田 Yamada
佐々木 Sasaki
山口 Yamaguchi
松本 Matsumoto
井上 Inoue
木村 Kimura
林 Hayashi
斎藤 Saito
清水 Shimizu
山崎 Yamasaki
阿部 Abe
森 Mori
池田 Ikeda
橋本 Hashimoto
山下Yamashita
石川 Ishikawa
中島 Nakashima
前田 Maeda
藤田 Fujita
後藤 Goto
小川 Ogawa
岡田Okada
村上 Murakami

長谷川 Hasegawa
近藤 Kondo
石井 Ishii
坂本 Sakamoto
遠藤 Endo
藤井 Fujii
青木 Aoki
福田 Fukuda
三浦 Miura*
西村 Nishimura
藤原 Fujiwara
太田 Ohta
松田 Matsuda
原田 Harada
岡本 Okamoto
中野 Nakano
中川 Nakagawa
小野 Ono
田村 Tamura
竹内 Takeuchi
金子 Kaneko
中山 Nakayama
和田 Wada
石田 Ishida
工藤 Kudo
上田 Ueda
原 Hara
森田 Morita
酒井 Sakai
横山 Yokoyama
柴田 Shibata
宮崎 Miyazaki
宮本 Miyamoto
内田 Uchida

高木 Takaki
谷口 Taniguchi
安藤 Ando
丸山 Maruyama
今井 Imai
大野 Ohno
高田 Takata
菅原 Kushiwara
河野 Kawano
武田 Takeda
藤本 Fujimoto
上野 Ueno
杉山 Sugiyama
千葉 Chiba
村田 Murata
増田 Masuda
小島 Kojima
小山 Oyama
大塚 Ohtsuka
平野 Hirano
久保 Kubo
渡部 Watabe
松井 Matsui
菊池 Kikuchi
岩崎 Iwasaki
松尾 Matsuo
佐野 Sano
木下 Kinoshita
野口 Noguchi
野村 Nomura
新井 Arai*
斉藤 Saito

Useful books:

P. G. O'Neill. *Japanese Names: A Comprehensive Index by Characters and Readings*. Weatherhill, Inc., 1989.

Kodansha International. *Kodansha's Essential Kanji* Dictionary. Kodansha USA, 2002.

Seitosha editors.ワープロ・パソコン　漢字辞典 *JIS*第*1*・2水準 *[Word Processor・PC Kanji Dictionary JIS 1st and 2nd Levels]*. (Seitosha, 1996).

H. T. Creswell, J. Hiraoka, and R. Namba. *A Dictionary of Military Terms: English–Japanese, Japanese–English*. Chicago, University of Chicago Press, 1946.

Useful websites:

Online Dictionary – http://dictionary.goo.ne.jp/je/
Find Kanji by Radicals – http://jisho.org/#radical
Write Kanji with Mouse – http://kanji.sljfaq.org/

Storing and Displaying Documents

Storing and displaying Japanese award documents is a critical component of collecting. The first fundamental question is to decide whether to store the documents rolled up or flattened. Some collectors store their documents rolled up, often in the same wooden boxes that the recipient received during that era. This system works fine if this is the direction you want to go.

The system I use now maximizes the viewability of the document while protecting them. I have refined this system of storage through trial and error. Frist, I store all of my documents flattened. The larger documents (i.e., orders, war medals, and commemorative medals) are stored in 24" by 18" sheet protectors. For smaller documents I use sheet protectors that are 11" by 17". I utilize sheet protectors with holes on the side and secure the edge with fasteners. I also label the documents by using slips of paper attached to the sheet protector using contact paper. The label has been the most difficult component of my storage process and has taken many years to refine. I try to use the best materials to preserve the documents, such as acid-free paper. This system allows me to easily flip through, admire, and study the documents at my leisure. I will continue to tweak this system as my collection grows and morphs. I encourage collectors to experiment with different storage and display methods that meet their needs. The number one key is preserving the document.

This is a closed and tied wooden document box. The characters on the box indicate that the document is an Order of the Sacred Treasure 3rd Class.
Author's Collection

This is a view of an open box. These boxes can be quite fragile and need to be handled with care.
Author's Collection

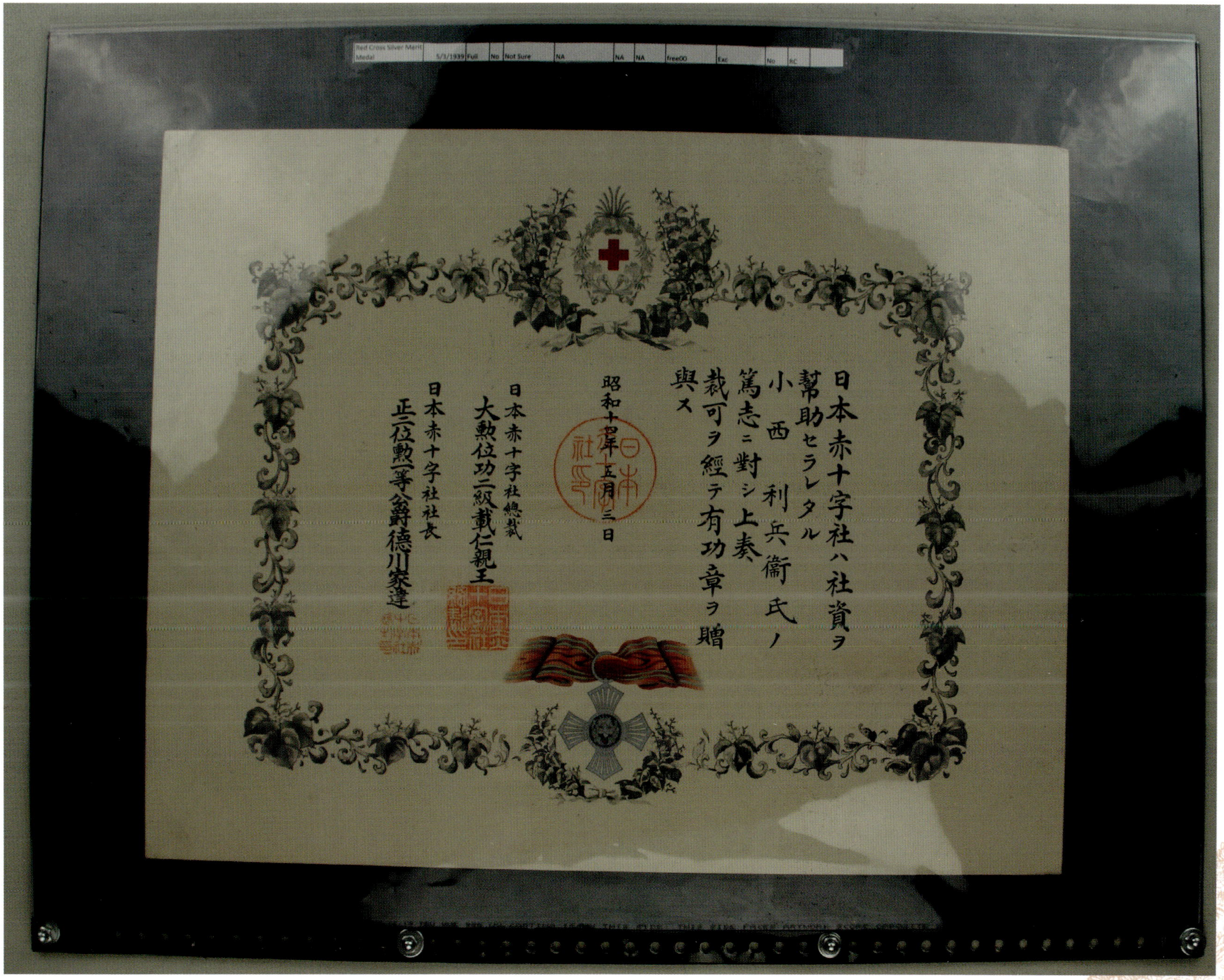
日本赤十字社ハ社資ヲ
幇助セラレタル
小西　利兵衛　氏ノ
篤志ニ對シ上奏
裁可ヲ經テ有功章ヲ贈
與ス

昭和十四年五月三日

日本赤十字社總裁
大勲位功二級載仁親王

日本赤十字社社長
正二位勲一等公爵徳川家達

A larger Red Cross Medal document highlighting my storage and labeling system of my larger documents. *Author's Collection*

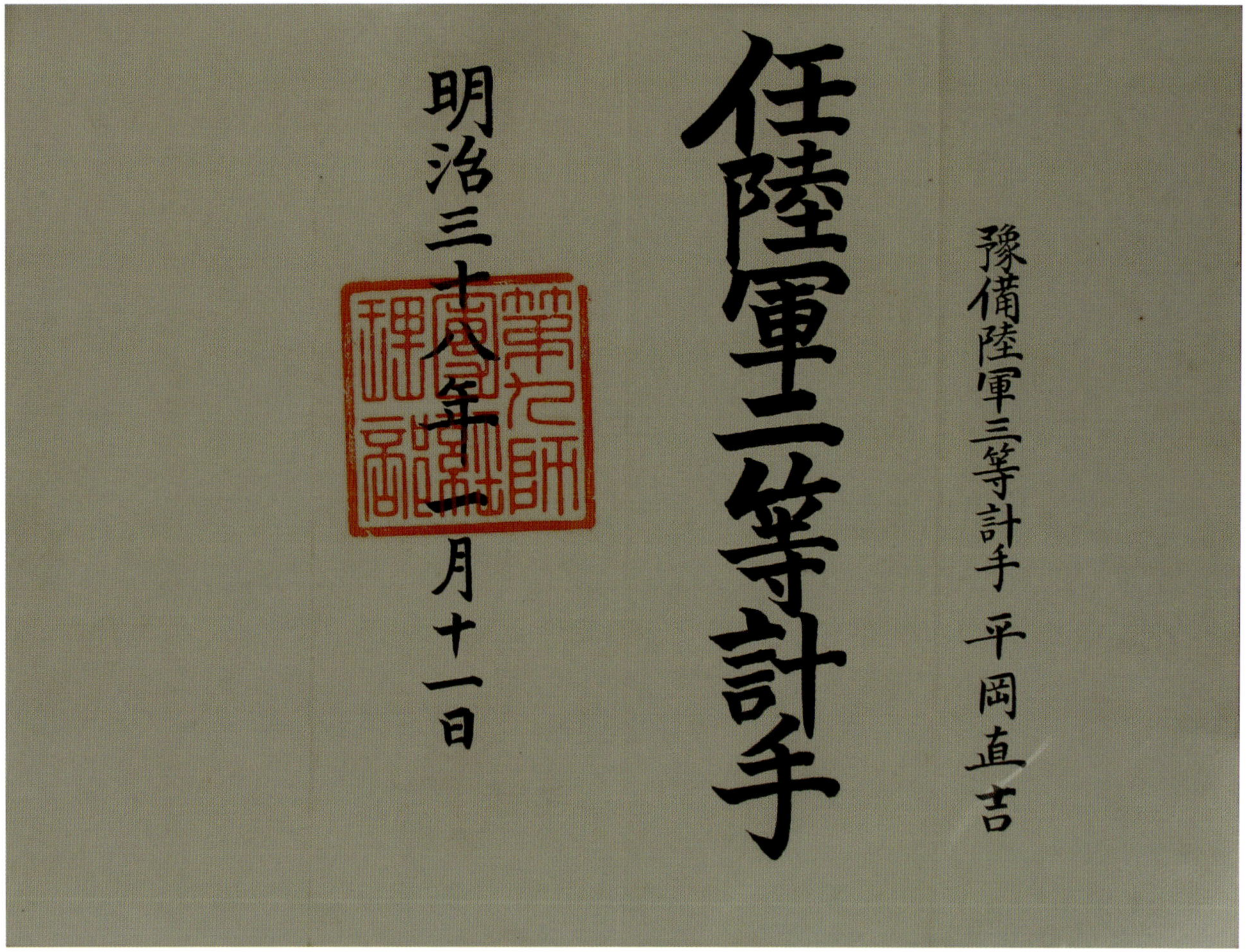

豫備陸軍三等計手 平岡直吉

任陸軍三等計手

明治三十八年一月十一日

I have framed a few documents from my collection and hung them on my office wall. This is an expensive process and should be done in moderation. My wife wisely tells me that my wall space is limited! I prefer to highlight my collection by displaying only a few of what I consider to be the most impressive or particularly beautiful. They look gorgeous and provide interesting talking points for visitors. My framing system utilizes the same style and color of frame and matting for consistency. This is a decision which is up to the collector. Once again, preservation of the document is the key. I would not shortcut the framing process for the sake of money. Documents hanging on a wall are often subjected to more elements, including the sun, which can endanger documents through fading or drying out.

This photograph is a commission document showing my storage and labeling system of my smaller documents. *Author's Collection*

Opposite: A document from my collection framed and matted. All of my framed documents follow the same frame design and matting color and design. *Author's Collection*

戰貯7
割増金附
戰時貯蓄債券
第七回
008498
13ノ組
金拾五圓
株式會社日本勧業銀行

BIBLIOGRAPHY

Beasley, W. G. *The Modern History of Japan*. New York: Praeger, 1974.

Benson, John, and Takao Matsumura. *Japan, 1868–1945: From isolation to Occupation*. Essex, UK: Pearson Education, 2001.

Bergamini, David. *Japan's Imperial Conspiracy*. New York: William Morrow and Company, 1971.

Cook, Haruko, and Theodore F. Cook. *Japan at War: An Oral History*. New York: the New Press, 1992.

Drea, Edward J. *In the Service of the Emperor: Essays on the Imperial Japanese Army*. Lincoln, NE: University of Nebraska Press, 1998.

Duara, Prasenjit. *Sovereignty and Authenticity: Manchurian and the East Asian Modern*. Lanham, MD: Rowman & Littlefield, 2003.

Edgerton, Robert B. *Warriors of the Rising Sun: A History of the Japanese Military*. New York: W. W. Norton company, 1997.

Felton, Mark. *Japan's Gestapo: Murder, Mayhem, and Torture in Wartime Asia*. Barnsley, UK: Pen & Sword Books, 2009.

Gordon, Andrew. *A Modern History of Japan: From Tokugawa Times to the Present*. New York: Oxford Press, 2009.

Hotta, Eri. *Pan-Asianism and Japan's War 1931–1945*. New York City, NY: Palgrave Macmillan, 2007.

Imperial Solider Relief Association. *History of the Imperial Soldier Relief Association.* Imperial Solider Relief Association: Japan, 1940.

Keene, Donald. *Emperor of Japan: Meiji and His World, 1852–1912*. New York: Columbia University Press, 2002.

Jowett, Phillip S. *Rays of the Rising Sun: Armed Forces of Japan's Asian Allies, 1931*. Solihull, England: Helion & Company, 2004.

Kim, C. I. E., and Han-Kyo Kim. *Korea and the Politics of Imperialism, 1876–1910*. Berkley, CA: University of California Press, 1967.

Long-hsuen, Hsu, and Chang Ming-kai. *History of the Sino–Japanese War (1937–1945)*. Taipei, Taiwan: Chung Wu Publishing, 1985.

Makito, Saya. *The Sino–Japanese War and the Birth of Japanese Nationalism*. Tokyo: International House of Japan, 2009.

Martin, Christopher. *The Boxer Rebellion.* New York: Abelard-Schuman, 1968.

Reader's Digest. *The World at Arms: The Reader's Digest Illustrated History of World War II*. New York City, NY: Reader's Digest, 1989.

Paine, S. C. M. *The Sino–Japanese War.* Cambridge, MA: Cambridge University Press, 2003.

Tamayama, Kazou, and John Nunneley. *Tales by Japanese Soldiers of the Burma Campaign 1942–1945*. (London: Cassell Company, 2000).

The Times. *History of the War, Vol. 2*. London: The Times, 1915.

Young, Louise. *Japan's Total Empire: Manchuria and the Culture of Wartime Imperialism*. Berkeley, CA: University of California Press, 1998.